*More Praise for*

# THE PINE TAR GAME

"In his smart, whimsical *New York Daily News* columns, Filip Bondy has long projected a big-city voice along with a healthy appreciation and sympathy for small-market challengers. He does it again in *The Pine Tar Game*, with a richly reported and written account of the Yankees-Royals rivalry that gave us memorable characters and zany circumstances. Bondy was there. With his book, you will be, too."

—Harvey Araton, *New York Times* bestselling
author of *Driving Mr. Yogi*

"The teenage Yankee fan inside of me is still angry at Lee MacPhail for upholding Kansas City's protest and wiping out perhaps the most bizarre ruling in baseball history. None of us who watched live will ever forget the sight of George Brett making like Jack Nicholson in *The Shining* as he charged from the dugout, and none of you who read this book will ever forget how the great Filip Bondy, the perfect chronicler of this imperfect moment, brought a wild and crazy Yankee Stadium day back to life."

—Ian O'Connor, *New York Times* bestselling
author of *The Captain: The Journey of Derek Jeter*

"Masterfully offers context and a history of the Yankees-Royals complicated sports rivalry . . . [the book] is worthy for devoted professional baseball fans and for its artfulness in creating a narrative focused primarily on just one pitch."

—*Kirkus Reviews*

ALSO BY FILIP BONDY

*Who's on Worst?*
*The Lousiest Players, Biggest Cheaters, Saddest Goats*
*and Other Antiheroes in Baseball History*

*Tip-Off:*
*How the 1984 NBA Draft*
*Changed Basketball Forever*

*Chasing the Game:*
*America and the Quest for the World Cup*

# THE PINE TAR GAME

THE KANSAS CITY ROYALS, THE NEW YORK YANKEES,
AND BASEBALL'S MOST ABSURD AND ENTERTAINING
CONTROVERSY

## FILIP BONDY

SCRIBNER

New York   London   Toronto   Sydney   New Delhi

Scribner
An Imprint of Simon & Schuster, Inc.
1230 Avenue of the Americas
New York, NY 10020

Copyright © 2015 by Filip Bondy

All rights reserved, including the right to reproduce this book or portions thereof
in any form whatsoever. For information, address Scribner Subsidiary Rights
Department, 1230 Avenue of the Americas, New York, NY 10020.

First Scribner paperback edition August 2016

SCRIBNER and design are registered trademarks of The Gale Group, Inc.,
used under license by Simon & Schuster, Inc., the publisher of this work.

For information about special discounts for bulk purchases,
please contact Simon & Schuster Special Sales at 1-866-506-1949
or business@simonandschuster.com.

The Simon & Schuster Speakers Bureau can bring authors to your live event.
For more information or to book an event, contact the Simon & Schuster Speakers
Bureau at 1-866-248-3049 or visit our website at www.simonspeakers.com.

Manufactured in the United States of America

1  3  5  7  9  10  8  6  4  2

The Library of Congress has cataloged the hardcover edition as follows:

Bondy, Filip.
The Pine Tar Game : the Kansas City Royals, the New York Yankees,
and baseball's most absurd and entertaining controversy / Filip Bondy.—First Scribner
hardcover edition.
pages cm
1. Pine Tar Game, New York, N.Y., 1983. 2. Kansas City Royals (Baseball team)—
History—20th century. 3. New York Yankees (Baseball team)—History—20th century.
4. Baseball—New York (State)—New York—History—20th century. 5. Baseball rules—
History. I. Title.
GV863.N72N48 2015
796.35709747'1—dc23      2014049797

ISBN 978-1-4767-7717-7
ISBN 978-1-4767-7718-4 (pbk)
ISBN 978-1-4767-7719-1 (ebook)

To the late, great
Eugene Hancock,
father-in-law and baseball fan

# Contents

# CONTENTS

# Introduction

The story begins, as all the best ones do, with a bat and a ball. The tale is layered with rules, with politics, with tantrums, with a David and Goliath rivalry, with judicial procedures, with Roy Cohn working for one side and Rush Limbaugh for the other, with deep, lasting friendships and with strong, quirky ballpark personalities. But the saga of the Pine Tar Game centers on a Hillerich & Bradsby model T (for Marv Throneberry)–85 Louisville Slugger, 34½ inches long, 32 ounces in weight. Some players, as Pete Rose once did, constantly fiddle with bats during their careers, changing models, lengths, and weights as often as they do their socks. They create hybrid models, mutants. Others, like Derek Jeter, retain the same design and weight for every game they play. Jeter swung the P-72 Louisville Slugger for 20 years with the Yankees. The T-85 was George Brett's model and the pine tar bat was his favorite T-85, ever. The bat now rests inside a glass display case in Cooperstown. Some of the pine tar has been scraped off, or worn off. Look closely and you'll see a red line where that nasty stuff once rose to a level deemed sinful by the umpires, until it wasn't.

The bat was a small botanical miracle, just seven grains of ash. "You look at these grains now, maybe, a good bat might be a 10-, 11-, 12-grainer, a normal bat would be 13, 14, 15 grains going through it," George Brett says. "But this one had seven, which meant it was really, really hard." Brett had a contact at Hillerich & Bradsby, a fellow he knew only as Tiny. Tiny would look out

1

for the Kansas City Royals' third baseman, search the lumber for the very best stock. He manufactured this bat for Brett, and then Tiny marked red stars on top of the knots, which highlighted the hardest parts of the wood. This Louisville Slugger would not snap or splinter easily, not like those maple toothpicks that shatter today at the first sight of a cut fastball.

In 1983, almost all the bats were still Louisville Sluggers, made from ash trees. Since then, an epidemic of emerald ash borers—an Asian beetle invasion—has hurt the stock. Besides, a lot of ball-players simply decided they preferred maple, which is a heavier, harder, smoother wood with thinner grains; or even birch wood, a compromise material. Nathan Stalvey, curator at the Louisville Slugger factory and museum, estimates that the percent of ash bats used in the major leagues has dipped in the past few decades from about 95 percent to 40 percent. Hillerich & Bradsby's share of the market has also slipped substantially, because of global-ization and player endorsements. The Louisville company that once held a monopoly on bats must now share the market with 32 other manufacturers, including Rawlings, Mizuno, Old Hick-ory, Trinity, and Chandler. Only about 30 percent of the bats in major league games are now produced by Hillerich & Bradsby. Brett kept his own precious bat unvarnished, raw. "I just liked the way it felt, liked the way it looked," he says. "Plain, tempered, raw ash, that came out real white." But plain only went so far. He kept applying more of a sticky hydrocarbon substance, made from the stumps of pine trees, for a better grip. He was one of the few players then or now who never wore batting gloves, prefer-ring bare hands on raw bat. Brett was also one of only a few hit-ters to use so much pine tar. Great batters like Pete Rose and Ted Williams preferred their bats much tidier. Both would douse their bats daily in wood alcohol. Brett was a bat slob, and is the first to admit it. "What happens in my case is the pine tar gets in the grain and starts growing inside," Brett says. "It's not just caked on the bat, it's kind of growing inside the grain. As a result of using a bat for three or four weeks and putting pine tar on three, four times a day, it's gonna get pretty ugly. And the bat was pretty ugly. But it was still working."

It was working very well on Sunday, July 24, 1983, the finale of a tight, four-game series in the Bronx. The Yanks had taken two of the first three games and were within spitting distance of winning the fourth when Brett knocked a ripping fastball from Goose Gossage over the right-field wall at Yankee Stadium. The home run arrived with two outs and one runner on base in the ninth inning, the Yanks up, 4–3, and with the best reliever in baseball about to close out a save against the pesky, small-market rivals. Suddenly, the Royals were ahead, 5–4. And then, just as suddenly, they weren't, which is when the story of the baseball itself comes into play.

This was a different time, and the economics of Major League Baseball were considerably more modest. While George Steinbrenner was relatively extravagant in all eras, he was still spending only $13 million total on his player payroll in 1983, about $40 million in 2015 dollars. The Yankees are now forever flirting with a $200–$225 million payroll, more than five times as great, not always with wonderful results. Brett, a veteran superstar, was earning $1 million with the Royals. At this juncture, it was still possible for a merely wealthy man to own a baseball team. He didn't have to be a billionaire or a conglomerate. One such owner, a famous miser, was Calvin Griffith, who took over the Washington Senators in 1955, moved them to Minnesota in 1961 as the Twins, and held on to the reins until 1984. Griffith was a cantankerous man, who unfortunately remains best known for explaining in 1978 why he relocated his team to Minneapolis: "I'll tell you why we came to Minnesota," the Canadian-born owner told a local Lions Club. "It was when we found out you only had 15,000 blacks here. Black people don't go to ballgames, but they'll fill up a rassling ring and put up such a chant it'll scare you to death. We came here because you've got good, hardworking white people here." The poor Lions at the meeting left the place understandably disturbed. One businessman told a *Minneapolis Star Tribune* reporter, "I can see why he has trouble with some of his players after listening to him talk."

Again, this was a different time, and such ignorant speech did not disqualify Griffith from owning the Twins, or even earn him a suspension. Over the years, Griffith became thoroughly annoyed at the costs of running a franchise and began to micromanage his team's budget in much the same way as Charlie Finley with the A's. Among his pet peeves was that the Twins were exhausting more than their designated allotment of baseballs in games, replacing dirty ones with fresh ones too often. By today's standards, the baseballs then were being mightily overused, because now they are directly tossed into the dugout at a pitcher's discretion, or whenever they so much as touch the dirt. Not so long ago, a pitcher dissatisfied with a seam or the slickness of a baseball would have to relay it for inspection to the umpire, who might reject the plea and throw the old ball right back into play. Griffith began to look into the causes of soiled baseballs and discovered that many were stained by contact with dirt on bats. In particular, contact with that sticky, contagious black pine tar. As Lee MacPhail, president of the American League, confirmed in 2003, "The clubs were losing a lot of balls because the pine tar was getting on them, and they'd have to be thrown out in batting practice and everything else." If only pine tar were white, like the accessible rosin bags that pitchers use before gripping the baseball, this would never have become an issue. Rosin was just fine for pitchers, even encouraged. Pine tar was a different story—as starter Michael Pineda of the Yankees discovered in April 2014, when he was caught with a strip of the dark substance on his neck and tossed from a game against the Red Sox in Boston.

Back in 1976, Griffith retained considerable influence with the rules committee and, aided by other skinflint owners, was able to push through Rule 1.10 (c), which stated, in passive-aggressive fashion, "The bat handle, for not more than 18 inches from its end, may be covered or treated with any material or substance to improve the grip. Any such material, including pine tar, which extends past the 18-inch limitation, in the umpire's judgment, shall cause the bat to be removed from the game. No such material shall improve the reaction or distance factor of the bat."

The issue was complicated, however, and interpretations murky. There were two related rules that possibly could render a ball struck by an illegal bat an illegal hit. Or not. There were gray areas, and contradictory precedents. The pine tar rule actually had some organic roots in the Big Bang beginnings of baseball. The origins of the decree, and that 18-inch mark, can be traced all the way back to 1885. According to baseball historian John Thorn, a rule was then put into place stating, "The handle of the bat may be wound with twine not to exceed 18 inches from the end." The next year, 1886, another statute was added to deal with such gritty stuff as rosin and dirt: "A granulated substance may be applied to the bat handle not to exceed 18 inches from the end." In 1893, this same rule was modified a bit, into, "The bat must be made wholly of hard wood except that the handle may be wound with twine, or a granulated substance applied, not to exceed 18 inches from the end."

This was then refined, yet again: "The bat shall be round, not over 2¾ inches in diameter at the thickest part, not more than 42 inches in length, and entirely of hard, solid wood in one piece. Twine may be wound around it or a granulated substance applied to it, for a distance of 18 inches from the end of the handle, but not elsewhere."

For decades, that sufficed. The 18-inch margin never changed. There was no denying, however, that baseballs were getting dirtier faster, and concern had grown in the sport about discolored, hard-to-spot baseballs ever since Ray Chapman was killed by a soil-camouflaged fastball from Carl Mays in 1920. Some batters used a combination of rosin and pine tar for a better grip. Others, most famously Stan Musial, would apply beeswax to the handle. When it became fashionable during the 1950s to wrap the handle of bats with adhesive tape (every kid's sandlot bat in that era was swathed in black tape), the Playing Rules Committee enacted more specific modifications in 1954: "The bat shall be a smooth, rounded stick not more than 2¾ inches in diameter at the thickest part and not more than 42 inches in length. The bat shall be one piece of solid wood or formed from a block of wood consisting of two or more pieces of wood bonded together with an adhesive in such a way that the grain direction of all pieces is essentially parallel to the length of the bat. Any such laminated bat shall contain only wood or adhesive, except for a clear finish. For a distance of 18 inches from the end by which the bat is gripped, it may be roughened or wrapped with tape or twine."

Ergo, the origin of it all, the primordial ooze that begat one of the most absurd, most entertaining baseball games in major league history. Or maybe it was two games, depending on how you look at it.

No sporting event is played exclusively outside some degree of social context. The year 1983 was a particularly apprehensive time in New York City, fraught with fears over the spread of a relatively new plague, AIDS. By the end of the year, more than 850 New Yorkers were known to have died from the disease, which was still not understood at all. Could it be spread by close contact in large crowds? By public toilet seats at ballparks? Mayor Ed Koch, serving the sixth year of his 12-year term, seemed curiously uninterested in the growing epidemic. The administration had spent a grand total of $24,500 on the subject. Two New York gays, Michael Callen and Richard Berkowitz, published a book, *How to Have Sex in an Epidemic*, considered somewhat reckless at this stage by many doctors.

In Kansas City, the impact of this disease was yet to be felt in full. Instead, the city was immersed in a fiscal battle with its Missouri neighbors over school busing and desegregation, hoping to end a pattern of white flight to the suburbs by creating an attractive magnet system within its borders. The battle was eventually lost and cost a small fortune. Kansas City was also fighting a more stereotypical, outsider's view of the place that it was good for ribs, barbecue sauce, and little else. There was a lot of bad news to deal with in the early eighties, the worst of which was the walkway collapse at the Hyatt Regency on July 17, 1981, which killed 114 people and injured 200 more. That tragedy became something of a symbol for the crumbling infrastructure of the inner city. So these were not easy times for either metropolis, but the cities' baseball teams could always supply some small relief. This game on July 24, 1983, would provide the sort of escapist fun and debate badly required by all. It would also sell newspapers, never a bad thing at any time.

• • •

I was there in the press box at Yankee Stadium when it happened, when Brett went nuts. Honest. I got one of those "I Covered the Pine Tar Game" T-shirts handed out to the Yankee beat writers by the team's playful public relations director, Ken Nigro—though I don't for the life of me know what happened to that precious relic. My wife probably threw it out, as she does many other things, which is her only bad habit. At the time, I was the beat writer for the *Bergen Record* in Hackensack, New Jersey, and about to accept a job with the *New York Daily News* sports department for more money to support a young family. This was a big career transition for me, and when researching this book it became a bit of an inconvenience. To read my coverage of the game, and my take on Lee MacPhail's surprising decision to replay the final inning, I went through a reel of microfiche in Hackensack's Johnson Library for old *Record* articles. But to retrieve my stories on the court proceedings and the actual replay that followed, I needed to pester helpful *Daily News* library researchers for copies of the yellowed clippings.

Those articles told of a very different era, of course. The relationship between the media and the baseball teams in New York was just beginning to turn adversarial. I recall being on the road with the Yankees in 1983, having a beer with Mike McAlary of the *New York Post* and Bill "Killer" Kane, traveling secretary for the club. Kane was lamenting how we all used to be partners in this business, and how the reporters had changed that with their intrusive, negative coverage. There was no going back, however. The Yankee Stadium press box then was the center of the sports universe—the communications nexus between George Steinbrenner and the public that he so desperately wished to convince about one ridiculous matter or another. Reporters like Murray Chass and Joe Durso of the *New York Times*, McAlary and Henry Hecht of the *New York Post*, Bill Madden and Phil Pepe of the *Daily News*, and Moss Klein of the *Newark Star-Ledger* would spend great lengths of time in the locker room named after longtime equipment manager Pete Sheehy. They would chat with players and listen to Billy Martin rant in his office about some slight perpetrated upon him by an umpire or imagined enemy. On his better days, Martin would share some of his tactical insight, his genius, and make us remember why anybody bothered to put up with him. Having completed this pregame ritual, we would carry our clunky, primitive computers from the basement press room to the elevator in the Bronx, then walk along the concourse to the press box for a perfect view of a renovated, yet somehow ageless, ballpark.

Telephones were everywhere, and dictated our lives. Martin had a telephone on his desk that was a hot line from the owner. When it rang, he often smirked and ignored the call. We didn't have that option. Each media outlet had one or two phones in the press box. If these devices rang, the call was either from an editor demanding to know what was happening or it was from a Steinbrenner operative, hand-delivering a scoop to the favored journalist du jour, who was summoned to the big man's office. The Boss was a manipulative son of a gun. If he planted a story, he expected favorable press in return. Negative stories about the owner were punished quickly enough by a news blackout, or a leak to a rival reporter. When it was time to file our stories, we needed those phones again. Our computers—our machines, as we called them—could only relay copy back to the office through couplers that needed to fit snugly over receivers.

Deadlines for the three or four editions of each newspaper were tight, chaotic for night games. We got a break with the Pine Tar Game, though. It was played on a Sunday afternoon, which meant that we had plenty of time to figure out what was going on out there, to interview all the players and reread the rule book before filing. We didn't need to post on the internet. We didn't blog. We didn't tweet. We just went back down to the clubhouses and talked with Brett, with Gossage, with Martin—who was looking very much like the cat who had swallowed the canary.

Reading about the Pine Tar Game once more in these clips, it became clear all over again: When umpire Tim McClelland laid Brett's bat down on the ground to measure it against the width of the plate, this was a special moment, the sweet collision of chaos and structure in sport. Nothing could ever again be as much fun.

# 1

## Aristocrats and Vandals

Before entering the Royals' clubhouse these days at Kauffman Stadium, a visitor must pass by a glass case featuring the old, woolen uniforms of the Kansas City Monarchs. It is a nice touch by the club, a reminder that the elemental history of baseball in Kansas City was at different times exemplary and humbling, divided quite literally into black and white chapters.

For more than three decades, from 1920 as charter members of the Negro National League until the arrival from Philadelphia of the sad-sack Athletics in 1955, the Kansas City Monarchs were the single most dominant franchise in the Negro Leagues, prideful pioneers and a pure civic treasure. Their legacy is retold these days inside the Negro Leagues Baseball Museum, founded in 1990 within the 18th and Vine District by former team stars and sharing space with another fine Kansas City institution, the American Jazz Museum. Baseball and jazz are an inseparable part of Kansas City's past and present. In fact, the redbrick building that houses the two museums is located next to the Blue Room jazz club, and across the street from the Gem Theater, both old-style performance spaces. The baseball museum became a place of considerable pride to those who worked so hard to establish it. Buck O'Neil, a former Monarch first baseman and manager, once walked up to a youthful Derek Jeter and said, "Young man, I really enjoy watching you play." Then he invited Jeter to visit the museum with him. Jeter is just a bit embarrassed to admit he procrastinated and waited to see the museum until after O'Neil had died in October 2006, but the Yankee shortstop went nonetheless and left both impressed and better educated on the subject.

There is much to learn here. The Monarchs were a big deal in Kansas City, filling a baseball vacuum while providing a real entertainment option for locals of all colors. Monarch players were considered guests of honor at neighborhood barbershops. They had their own set of booster clubs, too. The 12th Street Roosters and the 18th Street Roosters organized an annual parade for Opening Day, with men dressed up in suits and hats. The games were well-attended, occasionally sold out, and celebrities such as heavyweight champ Joe Louis would go well out of their way to appear and throw out the first pitch.

Jesse Williams, a shortstop on the Monarchs, once said, "It was the ambition of every black boy to be a Monarch, just as it was for every white boy to become a Yankee." A Monarch was a highly respected member of the community, and might be the featured speaker at the Young Men's Progressive Club or at other integrated functions. Most restaurants in Kansas City celebrated the Monarchs, gave them the best service. The players were invited to dinner at some of the highest-society functions. The veterans on the team enforced a strict dress code on the road to maintain their image. They purchased their own baseball gloves and shoes, but were equipped by the team with three sets of white-with-maroon-trim uniforms.

Such high status was not necessarily afforded to Negro League players in other towns. The second-tier Black Yankees, for example, played in relative obscurity in New York and New Jersey. But the Monarchs competed at an extremely high level and their talents were comparable to those of their contemporary major league peers, and even to modern-day rosters. "I guarantee you the team I was playing on in 1954 would win the division and probably go on to win the World Series," O'Neil bragged, not long before he died.

Some of the Monarchs' greatest stars—Jackie Robinson, Satchel Paige, Ernie Banks, and Elston Howard—were fortunate enough to gain entry into the major leagues for at least some parts of their careers. When Paige was at his peak, though, he played on the Monarchs and his teammates swore he was the best pitcher who ever lived. In testimony at the museum, O'Neil claims that Paige wouldn't warm up in the bullpen using a plate. Instead, he'd lay down a chewing gum wrapper and then throw pitches aimed at the corners of his three-inch target. Other players who came earlier never played in the major leagues, yet left indelible marks of their own and were eventually inducted into the Cooperstown Hall of Fame for their work.

Bullet Rogan, a Ruthian figure, joined the Monarchs in their inaugural 1920 season and immediately became their greatest attraction both on the mound and at the plate. In 1923, he hit .364 while leading the league with 16 wins and 146 strikeouts. The next season, he was even better, batting .392 with an 18-6 pitching mark. In the 1924 Black World Series, Rogan collected 13 hits and was the winning pitcher in two games. He kept dominating like this until a knee injury slowed him down a bit, but his career stats remained otherworldly: a 119-50 win-loss record and a batting average of .338.

Jose Mendez, the Black Diamond, a Cuban superstar and right-handed power pitcher, once outdueled Christy Mathewson in an exhibition, briefly tempting Giants manager John McGraw to break the color line. Mendez became player-manager of the Monarchs, winning three successive pennants in the Negro Leagues from 1923 to 1925. He won two games for the Monarchs when they defeated the Hilldale Daisies, five games to four (with one tie) in the first Black World Series in 1924. Mendez finished with a 1.42 ERA in four appearances, one of them a shutout.

Andy Cooper, a tall, left-handed pitcher with outstanding breaking stuff, helped lead the Monarchs to the pennant in 1929. He once threw 17 innings during a 2–2 playoff tie against the Chicago American Giants and managed the Monarchs to three Negro American League titles in 1937, 1939, and 1940. Willard Brown, a Louisiana outfielder, knocked a slew of homers for the Monarchs with his giant 40-ounce bat. He eventually became the first black player to homer in the American League, but played only 21 games for the St. Louis Browns.

The Monarchs won ten league championships, appearing in

four Negro League World Series. They suffered only one sub-.500 season in 45 total years of existence and sent more players to the majors than any other Negro Leagues club. They were such a well-organized institution in Kansas City during their prime years that they actually established their own farm club, the Monroe Monarchs. The team's white, visionary owner and founder, J. L. Wilkinson, was a flamboyant showman by nature. Born in Algona, Iowa, in 1878, Wilkinson flamed out as a pitcher but never gave up on the game. He started a women's baseball team in 1909, which toured the Midwest by train with its own mobile grandstand. That club featured a male catcher who would wrestle volunteers from the crowd, as an added attraction. Wilkinson then founded the All Nations team in Des Moines, composed of racial groups banned or ignored by the major leagues—Native Americans, blacks, Polynesians, Asians, and, for good measure, one woman. After he created the Monarchs from this group in 1920, "Wilkie" would send black staff members out into the Kansas City community to strengthen ties with local officials. On the road, Wilkinson often lodged with his players as a demonstration of solidarity, and, no doubt, for budgetary reasons as well. Sometimes, the Monarchs were treated well on these tours. Other times they were banished from hotels and restaurants. Pitcher Chet Brewer remembered that the Monarchs were promoted in Montana as world champions, yet a local restaurant wouldn't serve them. The establishment relented when the Monarchs threatened to pull out of the scheduled game, and then the players were mobbed by autograph seekers while they dined. "Prejudice was a mean thing, but we overcame a lot of things," O'Neil said. Wilkinson also became a pioneer in night baseball during the Depression. Whenever the Monarchs went on one of their barnstorming tours, they would bring with them portable light systems—five years before any major league team attempted to play at night. The owner eventually sold the team to Tom Baird in 1948 and was finally, correctly, inducted into Cooperstown in 2006.

By the late 1940s and 1950s, after Jackie Robinson made his debut with the Dodgers, the Monarchs' roster was often raided by major league teams. The Negro League club was never quite the same. The Monarchs had played their games in substantial Muehlebach Field beginning in 1923, successfully competing for fans with a Yankees farm club in Kansas City, the Blues. But the Athletics' arrival changed things, hiking the rent at Muehlebach to an exorbitant, unaffordable sum. The club then became nomads, essentially without a home base. Baird sold his players and fired his manager, O'Neil, in order to meet the bills. The Monarchs hung on in one form or another until 1965, but their era was done, and the Athletics became the dominant baseball club in the city—a woeful franchise with considerably less courage or purpose.

Long before Brett's bat sent a baseball soaring in the Bronx, the loyal baseball citizenry of Kansas City had good reason to resent the New York Yankees, who strip-mined the A's back in the 1950s for their own utilitarian purposes. This was an incestuous, parasitic relationship from the start, smelling badly of fish oil and tobacco juice. When Connie Mack's family decided to dump the Philadelphia Athletics in 1954, the Yanks' principal owner, Dan Topping, navigated the sale so that his business associate, Arnold Johnson, would buy the A's and move them to Kansas City— where the Yanks operated a farm team for 18 seasons, and accurately assumed that this feeder system would continue. The town of Kansas City seemed like the bush leagues to the Yankees and to their players in every way. When Mickey Mantle was a struggling 19-year-old rookie in 1951, he very nearly walked away from the sport, demoralized, after he was demoted in midseason for 40 games to the Triple-A Kansas City Blues of the American Association. His father, Mutt, traveled to the Muehlebach Hotel in that city, called him a gutless quitter, and basically embarrassed Mantle back onto the field.

Arnold Johnson had at one point purchased Yankee Stadium as a tax strategy, then leased it back to Topping and partner Del Webb. This triumvirate of Johnson, Topping, and Webb proceeded to do a great deal of bartering, almost always to the Yankees' great advantage. At different times, the Washington Senators, Detroit Tigers, and Chicago White Sox all protested this relationship to commissioner Ford Frick, who turned the other clean-shaven cheek to such shenanigans.

During the late fifties into 1960, over the course of six years, the Yanks and A's completed sixteen trades. Altogether, the Yankees received some cash and thirty-five players. These acquisitions included several stars and valuable assets, such as Roger Maris, Clete Boyer, Ralph Terry, Bob Cerv, and Bud Daley. In return, Kansas City received considerably more cash, plus 27 players who were either washed up, like Hank Bauer, or a disciplinary problem for Yankee manager Casey Stengel, like Billy Martin. The 1961 Yankees, one of the greatest teams in baseball history, featured ten former Athletics. And during every one of those six years, Kansas City finished near the bottom of the eight-team American League. The Athletics, it seemed, had never outgrown their status as farm team of the Yankees.

Kansas City fans burned at the club's subservient role. When Charlie Finley bought a controlling interest of the team from Johnson's widow in 1960 for $1.975 million, he soon vowed never to make another trade with the Yanks, a team he despised. He ordered his ballpark announcer to declare over the public address system that balls hit past a certain point in right field would have been cheap homers into the porch at Yankee Stadium. That was good fun, fine with the local populace. The gaudy yellow and green uniforms were also acceptable novelties. Ultimately, however, Finley presented major problems for the city, most of them having to do with money. Finley was a glorified insurance agent from Indiana, always on the make, and the A's in Kansas City weren't making him enough profit. He played nasty politics with the city, threatening to relocate the club to Louisville shortly after signing a four-year lease with Municipal Stadium. The other owners vetoed that migration, but American League president Joe Cronin negotiated a compromise that allowed Finley to move the A's to Oakland in 1968.

Kansas City was suddenly baseball-less, though not for long. There was a savior in the pipeline named Ewing M. Kauffman, the man who would respectfully be called Mr. K by everyone associated with the team. Like George Steinbrenner, Kauffman was an entrepreneur. But all other parallels were, in fact, perpendiculars.

# 2

## The Renaissance

In 1968, Ewing Kauffman was a man in search of a hobby. He also was very much the right man in the right place at the opportune time. Stuart Symington, a Missouri senator, lobbied Major League Baseball for a replacement team in Kansas City. He didn't just lobby, actually. Symington threatened to revoke baseball's sacred antitrust exemption, which might have opened the door to competition, free agency, and other unwanted concepts. Quickly, one of four expansion franchises was awarded to the city, which would again become the westernmost outpost for the game, other than the Pacific Coast teams. Kauffman, with the encouragement of his wife, Muriel, purchased the rights to the team, which began play in 1969, two years ahead of the original schedule—again, thanks to Symington's not-so-veiled threats. The franchise was named Royals for a couple of reasons: There was, and remains, an American Royal livestock show and rodeo that is extremely popular in Kansas City. There was also an odd, presumptuous tradition of tagging the local professional sports teams with dynastic nicknames, such as the Monarchs, Chiefs (football), and Kings (basketball).

The inaugural Opening Day in Kansas City for the Royals arrived on April 8, 1969, against the Minnesota Twins. Among the 17,688 in attendance were Symington, American League president Joe Cronin, and the Kansas City mayor, Ilus Davis. There was no great rush for tickets. It had been only one season since the Athletics deserted the place, and the local populace was to some degree confused and guarded about its own loyalties. That first season, the Royals would draw only 902,414 fans, seventh best in the 12-member American League. They would finish 69-93 with a low-paid roster that featured nobody earning a salary of more than $44,000 (veteran second baseman Jerry Adair was the top wage earner), and only six players receiving more than $20,000. After Opening Day at Municipal Stadium, however, the *Kansas City Star* reported, "By the end of the first inning there was no doubt—they were 'our Royals' and 'our home team.'" Many expansion franchises during this era fielded older, washed-up players whose names were familiar to fans and might attract more ticket buyers. The 1962 Mets were perhaps most famous for this policy, finishing their debut season at 40-120, but with considerable panache. Kauffman had a different notion. General manager Cedric Tallis, with the help of farm director Lou Gorman and Charlie Metro, started a relatively young starting lineup, largely acquired through the expansion draft on October 15, 1968. Adair was the only over-thirty fellow. Manager Joe Gordon called the Royals his "dead end kids," and on that first day in Royals history, Kansas City defeated Minnesota, 4–3. The Twins started two future Hall of Famers, Rod Carew and Harmon Killebrew, plus a perennial All-Star, Tony Oliva. A 25-year-old castoff from the Cleveland Indians named Lou Piniella was the first Royals' batter and rocketed a double beyond the reach of third baseman Killebrew. Piniella, acquired in a late-spring training deal from the Seattle Pilots, another expansion team, would go four for five in this opening game and finish the season batting .282, highest on the team, all for a $10,000 salary. More than 14 years later, a considerably older Piniella would be playing in the Pine Tar Game, in pinstripes. Meanwhile, Graig Nettles, another key participant in the Pine Tar Game, played left field for the Twins and knocked the first homer ever in a Royals' game.

Other players in that inaugural Opening Day lineup for Kansas City included the journeyman Adair, 32 years old, batting second and playing second base; Ed Kirkpatrick, 24, a part-timer for several years with the Angels; Joe Foy, 26, a pickup from the

Red Sox, who played third base and batted cleanup; first baseman Chuck Harrison, 28, who had spent 1968 batting .251 in Richmond of the Triple-A International League; right-fielder Bob Oliver, 26, promoted after a strong season with Denver, a Twins' affiliate of the Pacific Coast League; catcher Ellie Rodriguez, 23, whose major league experience amounted to nine games with the Yankees; and shortstop Jackie Hernandez, 28, another former Minnesota property. The starting pitcher was Wally Bunker, 24, a promising right-hander drafted from the Orioles' roster as the 25th pick in the expansion draft who would become the team's first ace. Moe Drabowsky, 33, made his first appearance as the Royals' closer. Jim Campanis, son of Dodgers general manager Al Campanis, pinch-hit in the game and finished the season batting .157.

Kauffman's Royals quickly evolved into everyone's idea of a model expansion franchise, in large part because of the owner's enterprising methods and his ability to delegate key duties to competent men. "We became the new Kansas City professional franchise," said John Schuerholz, who spent 22 years in and around the Royals' front office. "We built quickly and we became division champs more quickly than any expansion team in history to that point. We had a good program in place immediately and were developing good teams."

The Royals would soon have a stadium to match their ambitions. Even while Finley was still in the process of planning his escape from Kansas City, Jackson County voters had agreed to fund the construction of a new baseball-only park. Kauffman was then given considerable rein to invent the place. Royals Stadium opened on April 10, 1973, near Arrowhead Stadium, home of the Chiefs. It was an architectural wonder for its time, built to endure—which it still does, as Kauffman Stadium, thanks in part to a $250 million infrastructure upgrade before the 2009 season. Back in 1973, the new stadium was already a great step up for the Royals from Municipal Stadium. The large clubhouse featured a massage room, whirlpool room, training room, interview room, and lockers with shelves for the players' personal items, unusual at the time. There was also a private players' lounge, which is now standard in every ballpark clubhouse. Two days before the opener, the *Kansas City Star* waxed enthusiastically about the place:

> There will be something for everyone including the, oh, yes, players! They will play, for the first time in the American League, on a diamond covered completely by synthetic turf. Only the mound, sliding areas around the bags and home plate will be dirt. Also, the architects have made things equal for both hitters and pitchers as the foul lines are 330 feet from home plate, the power alleys 385 and the center field fence 410. But the player's view from inside Kansas City's multimillion-dollar baseball bailiwick will also be quite different from that of the old and staid Municipal Stadium. The clubhouse, where the game's participants perform such common chores as dressing for the game, is considered one of the best and most modern in the major leagues.

The stadium opener was a great aesthetic and athletic success, a 12–1 victory over the Texas Rangers behind a five-hit complete game from Paul Splittorff. Freddie Patek was the first Royals' batter in the new park, while John Mayberry drilled the first hit and the first homer in front of 39,464 fans.

Because of the city's relatively isolated geography, Kauffman figured his team would attract crowds from all over the Great Plains, and possibly from the Southwest. If fans were going to come from that far away, they needed to believe a short downpour wouldn't cancel the game. So Kauffman installed an Astro-Turf field with the sort of drainage that put a halt to flooding. The ballpark wasn't merely practical, though. The stadium featured an enormous fountain, or "water spectacular," beyond the center-field outfield fence. The cascading falls were more than a hundred yards wide (322 feet, to be exact), the largest fountain of its kind in the world. The feature made the ballpark immediately identifiable in any television broadcast. The stadium also fit Kauffman's vision for what his go-go team would become. It was a pitcher's park and the perfect place for a hustling, base-to-base lineup. The fences were deep, making it hard to hit homers, yet easier to line doubles and triples. The artificial turf favored base stealers, not lumbering, power-hitting teams. Behind the scenes, in the clubhouses and corridors, Royals Stadium also provided the sort of modern, spatial features that older ballparks didn't offer. When the *New York Times* surveyed major leaguers in 1983, asking them to rank their favorite stadiums, Royals Stadium was number one. Hallowed Yankee Stadium finished number four, though its newer counterpart across the street in the Bronx likely would fare better today.

The Royals installed other innovations and introduced public relations coups, many of them truly radical. As Kauffman wrote in 1983, part of a remarkable piece in the *New York Times*, "I do not put a special premium on conformity. Experience teaches us that in baseball a tremendous magic is at work." Kauffman, eager to develop young talent, invented in September 1969 something called the Kansas City Royals Baseball Academy, created to identify golden prospects and then develop high schoolers into major league players. This was truly the forerunner for academy models employed later in tennis and golf. Student athletes, recommended by high school coaches anywhere in America, would live, study, and play baseball near Sarasota, Florida. The place featured a dormitory, classrooms, a swimming pool, recreation halls, a cafeteria, and four perfectly groomed baseball fields. Kauffman poured $1.5 million of his own money into this concept and by the summer of 1969 there were nearly 8,000 teenagers at tryout camps in 41 states hoping to qualify. Forty-two kids were accepted into the program, attending mandatory morning classes at Manatee Junior College before practicing baseball with a staff of top coaches. Syd Thrift, a Royals' scout, was the academy director. The Royals always made certain that the families of their youngest prospects felt they were part of a baseball family as well. Kansas City general manager Lou Gorman would send out reports to mothers and fathers, on Royals letterhead, describing the progress of these players in largely glowing terms. The end result of all this was a mixed one.

"The Academy did succeed in a way, because Frank White and

U. L. Washington both came out of the program," Schuerholz said. "That's two important middle infielders, and I rank Frank White right up there with Bill Mazeroski or Nellie Fox at second base. So it worked, but it didn't have enough economic sense to it. It wasn't getting value for the dollars of investment."

Eventually, the program was ditched, the facilities used for a while as a training site. Even if it hadn't really paid off from a fiscal standpoint, Kauffman already was being hailed as something of an innovative genius. He had other ideas, too, when it came to marketing and enjoying the game. Some of them were hokey. The team went to powder blue uniforms on the road and Kauffman was one of the first owners to hire a woman to sweep the bases between innings—not exactly an enlightened policy. Most of his notions weren't crass or silly, however, not like those from Finley or Marge Schott. They were more cerebral. Long before computers became a part of mainstream life, and before Rotisserie Leagues flourished, Kauffman wanted to set up a special section in the stands with a system for the fans that would allow the crowd to manage the game. The spectators could choose player moves, get involved in the play-by-play. That was his vision, anyway, though the technology wasn't quite available to install such a system. Back in the seventies, before sabermetrics became the rage, Kauffman had workers at Marion Labs compile detailed statistics about players that were never really used, because baseball managers and general managers weren't ready for them yet. The Royals were pacesetters, too, among major league teams when it came to community outreach programs. Every winter, several players would travel on a publicity junket, called the Goodwill Caravan, to drum up support in neighboring and sometimes far-reaching areas in Kansas, Missouri, and Nebraska.

"Mr. K was ahead of his time in terms of his thought process," said Dean Vogelaar, the longtime public relations director. "It was maybe a little bit of *Moneyball*, things that are now fairly common. Mr. K saw it all early on, even if they weren't utilized."

Kauffman was not a dictator. He didn't impose these far-reaching ideas on those in charge of baseball matters. He was more the delegator. He allowed Tallis, the team's first general manager,

Joe Burke, its second, and then Schuerholz to build an uncommonly strong farm system and to nurture homegrown stars.

"He was not only a great boss, he was a great mentor for hard work and success," Schuerholz said about his boss, Kauffman. "He was a successful, self-made millionaire, and he was more than that. He had vision and determination. He was about never giving up."

As might be expected, the Yankees tried to plunder the Royals' well-oiled developmental machine. In September 1975, they went right after Schuerholz, who was then assistant director of player development for Kansas City under Gorman. George Steinbrenner offered Schuerholz the position of farm director, with a substantial raise, and he actually accepted—for twenty-four hours. This was a move that might have changed baseball history considerably, except it never happened. When Schuerholz returned to Kansas City from his meeting with the Yanks in Chicago, Burke promoted him to director of player development and gave him a bump in salary, and Schuerholz quickly reneged on his deal with the Yankees. The Yanks were furious. "I didn't give the Yankees a chance to sweeten their offer, and that was the hardest part about it," Schuerholz would write in his memoir, *Built to Win*. "I felt worm-high, but I had made the right decision."

Kauffman, to his great credit, demonstrated a healthy respect and loyalty toward the local fans in Kansas City. While other owners would do anything to sell a seat in their ballpark, Kauffman actually cut back sales of season tickets after the Royals lost the 1980 World Series to the Phillies. He ordered his staff to cap early ticket orders at 15,000, so that fans who could not afford season packages would still be able to purchase seats in the postseason. In that 1983 *New York Times* essay, Kauffman wrote about his belief that baseball is something precious, belonging to the world, not to any player or owner. The sport was a national resource that must be taken seriously:

> There is a considerable body of evidence that tells us how deeply Americans in general and baseball fans in particular feel about the game.

21

Very little of it is apt to be viewed as playful sentiment.

Almost daily, I receive letters couched in terms that leave little room for rebuttal. . . . Some are cold and relentless accountings. And they may state, as in one instance, that it is a breach of managerial duty "no less than a misdemeanor" to fail to signal for a bunt in certain circumstances. . . .

There is ample proof of baseball's tendency to make slaves, or fools, of us all.

Kauffman would have done anything to improve his Royals, short of moving them to a bigger market. It was long thought, incorrectly, by outsiders that the owner had some deep philosophical beef against the signing of free agents, that it somehow went against his puritan grain and that he deeply resented Steinbrenner for such financial forays. In truth, he badly wanted to recruit a star and bring him to Kansas City. It just wasn't easy convincing these celebrity-athletes to park their futures in a remote, small market. "There was a time when Mr. K's heart told him to sign free agents," Vogelaar said. On several occasions, Kauffman personally became involved in the chase. The Royals in their early years considered the traitorous, nomadic Oakland A's to be their chief rivals, not the Yankees. When Catfish Hunter won his freedom from Finley's A's in 1974 due to a contract violation, the Royals actually drew up a contract offer that was uncannily close to the five-year, $3.35 million deal Hunter would later sign with the Yanks. "Mr. K and Joe Burke really designed the contract that the Yankees matched to sign him," Vogelaar said. Kauffman wanted Vida Blue and Reggie Jackson to migrate east to Kansas City from the A's. When Pete Rose was available after the 1978 season, Kauffman met with the star attraction in an effort to convince him that Kansas City was not that much unlike Cincinnati. Kauffman's efforts, again, were to no avail, as Rose signed with the Phils for similar dollars, four years and $3.225 million. "Same thing as Catfish," Vogelaar said. "We were trying to sign him and he signed with the Phillies in the last minute. Rose said he wanted to stay in the National League so that he could break Stan Musial's record (3,630 hits). Mr. K said, 'Why are you thinking about the National League record? You should be thinking about the major league record.'"

Rose, of course, went on to break Ty Cobb's mark of 4,189 hits. He might have done it for the Royals, instead of beating them in the World Series two years after he snubbed Kauffman.

# 3

## The Entrepreneur
## and the Lady

Julia Irene Kauffman arrived for lunch at the upscale Café Provence in Prairie Village, Kansas, wearing a flowing, fuchsia dress and a sense of purpose. She had many things to do on this day, no different from any other. Julia Kauffman successfully used her late father's money to build and launch her late mother's dream, the Kauffman Center for the Performing Arts in Kansas City. It opened on Broadway, a different Broadway, in September 2011, a pretty conch shell of a building constructed without a penny of taxpayer funds, other than the cost of a parking lot across the street. It was something she was rightfully proud about, and it also wasn't easy. Those all-nighters she pulled with her father—"Ewing" . . . "Mr. K" . . . "Daddy"—learning about the ways of business, they really paid off. "People say to me, 'Isn't the music great at the Center?' I love music, but I never heard any of it for years," Julia Kauffman said. "It's got to do with bottom lines, construction materials. It has nothing to do with the music. Music?!"

Her father, Ewing, was actually her second father. Her first one, Lorne Dennie, died when she was just 14. For a while, Dennie had a radio gig—a show in which he sang, in which future *Bonanza* star Lorne Greene announced, and in which Percy Faith played the piano. Dennie's two coworkers went on to more illustrious show business careers. The Dennie family lived in Toronto, where

Julia grew up on food and weather very different from the common fare in Kansas City. A year after Lorne Dennie's death, her 44-year-old widowed mother, Muriel, suffered a broken foot and was recovering with her own mom, Eileen, at the Deauville Hotel in Miami. Eileen was a trustee on the Toronto Board of Education, which was having a meeting down in Florida. She insisted Muriel come along.

Muriel was no wallflower. She'd actually just won a dance contest with a cast on her foot. But she was hobbling a bit, had to complete her therapy at the Deauville, and made it down to the pool at around five o'clock, after the heat of the day had expired. Eileen arrived there fully dressed, with her diamond brooch and hat, her pool outfit. "The queen mother," Julia said. As it turned out, a man named Ewing Kauffman was at the same hotel for an American Medical Association meeting, on behalf of his Marion Laboratories company.

Kauffman was a calm, thoughtful man by nature, an inventive fellow who soothed and smoothed. If this had been 1776, Kauffman would be Thomas Jefferson to George Steinbrenner's Samuel Adams. Kauffman was a disciplined, self-driven fellow from the start, born on a farm near Garden City, Missouri. When he became ill as a youth with a heart problem, Ewing reportedly devoured forty books a month, educating himself on a variety of topics. A disciplined Eagle Scout, Kauffman then attended junior college and served in the navy during World War II. He sailed around the world, then swore he'd seen enough of it and never wanted to travel much again. He also earned a nickname, "Lucky," for good reason. Whenever he gambled, Ewing Kauffman almost always won, whether it was at craps or a high-stakes card game. He didn't appear to cheat, either, or his nickname might have been something else entirely. Kauffman stowed away his winnings, which were considerable by the standards of the day.

After he was done with the service, and after a stint as salesman for a local drug company, Kauffman decided to start his own firm—which he began in the basement of his family home. He used the money he saved from his job, and also that nest egg from gambling. He founded a pharmaceutical company, Marion Laboratories, Inc., and proceeded to make a great midwestern fortune. In naming the corporation, he used his middle name so that customers wouldn't assume this was simply a one-man, Kauffman operation. The firm was not immediately profitable, though it surely would become a classic American Dream success story. In its first year, the pharmaceutical company reported total sales of $36,000 and a net profit of $1,000. By the time Kauffman sold the business to Merrell Dow in 1989, Marion Labs reported nearly $1 billion in sales and boasted 3,400 employees.

So this was the accomplished, entrepreneurial Ewing Kauffman who happened to walk down to the pool at the Deauville Hotel in 1960. He swam some laps, performed some dives, because that was part of his daily ritual. A few of those dives were difficult, gainers and flips, but Muriel Dennie was not particularly impressed. The way Julia heard it later, her mother was thinking, "Look at this old, bald-headed coot, he's going to kill himself!" When he got out of the pool, Eileen, the grandmother, was calling for a drink from a steward. The steward didn't come. So Ewing suddenly strode over and said, "I'm Ewing Kauffman from Kansas City, and I would love to buy you a drink." Muriel stuck her nose in the air and said no thanks. Eileen, however, introduced herself. "I'm Eileen from Toronto, Canada, and I would love a drink."

Off they went to the hotel bar and Muriel followed them. That very first night, Ewing was smitten. He was also a complete klutz on the courting front. Ewing told Muriel her hair looked out of place. He asked Muriel her age. He did everything the pursuing male should not do. "She wanted to get rid of him," Julia said. Ewing wouldn't give up, though. That was one of his most endearing, or annoying, traits. When Muriel returned from Florida to Canada, Julia took one look at her and said, "Mother, you met a man." She had. There were phone calls between Ewing and Muriel. In the pre-internet age, Julia was always driving to the post office to mail letters. "They were in love," Julia said.

The night before the wedding, Julia and Muriel had some sort of argument, "teenage stuff," and Ewing interfered. Muriel turned to the groom and said, "Damn it, Ewing, do you really want to get into this? You can have her." Ewing responded, "I'll take her, but you don't get her back." When Muriel and Ewing married, Julia moved with her mother into his Mission Hills mansion outside Kansas City and called him Uncle Ewing. Before long, he was just Daddy. He already had two adopted children. Years later, after she'd gone through three marriages and three divorces, Julia would officially become his third adopted daughter, after she promised him there would be no more husbands. He nicknamed her Doo, short for Doodle.

"When I met him at sixteen, we clicked," she said. "There were days I went to school and I hadn't been to bed, because I stayed up all night with Daddy talking Marion. So I was getting an MBA and didn't realize it. We were always very close business-wise. I was honored to be his gofer. At the ballpark, he'd say, 'Doo, go get Joe Burke. Doo, get Dean Vogelaar.' And I'd travel with them. I'd be the stewardess on the plane, the secretary in the hotel, but I was thrilled. We met exciting people." Ewing was nothing like her first father, nothing like her mother. "Daddy knew nothing about music," she said. "He only knew three songs: 'Take Me Out to the Ballgame,' 'The Star-Spangled Banner,' and 'Onward Christian Soldiers.'" He only became involved with baseball, at first, because of his wife and because of a health crisis, a circulation problem with that troublesome heart. The doctor advised him to reduce his stress, get a hobby. Muriel had been a big fan of the minor league Toronto Maple Leafs of the International League. Lorne Dennie had bought season tickets for the family back in Canada. She suggested to Ewing he think about baseball, which he did. He bought himself an expansion franchise and ran it the only way he knew how, as a real business. Unlike the other owners, he didn't hire former baseball players to manage the whole operation, the commercial end of things. He hired finance people. He thought of every angle.

Ewing allowed his attractive daughter to be a part of the team, but ordered her not to fraternize with the players, cutting off any possibly nasty rumors. She especially was to stay away from George Brett. "My parents had nicknames for all the players, and his was 'Baby Brother,' supposedly my baby brother," Julia said.

"George kind of knew his nickname and he didn't like it. I didn't like it, either. We didn't develop a relationship until much later. He was always Crazy George back then, who drank too much. I steered clear of him in those days." By keeping her distance, Julia was able in later years to maintain a closer friendship with Brett and the others. It all worked out.

Ewing Kauffman had a similar rule for himself. "You can't expect to go drinking with people and have them take orders from you the next morning," he'd say. He never did. He almost always went to bed early, too, though Ewing was no puritan. He had a habit of drinking German wine when he first met Muriel, then switched to scotch when his new wife disapproved of his selection. "He'd get tired, have a drink, have a second drink, go home with a driver," Julia said. "He drank Cutty Sark and water, a tall glass. Watered-down scotch." He also kept up his gambling habits, lucky as ever. At a baseball meeting in New York, his mother-in-law, Eileen, complained that she heard mice in the walls of their fancy suite, in a luxury hotel. Everyone thought the elderly woman was hearing things. As it turned out, the noise was coming from the adjacent room, where Ewing Kauffman was involved in a game of craps with Charlie Finley. "Lucky" prevailed, of course. Years later, Julia was comfortable enough saying that Finley eventually paid off his debt from that night with some sort of baseball-related transaction between the A's and Royals, unbeknownst to the commissioner.

That's how Kauffman dealt with Oakland. The Yankees were another, stickier matter. The Royals' owner wasn't a big fan of huge salaries, the kind that George Steinbrenner paid, though he would do what he had to do. Kauffman also wasn't a fan of unions. He always said if you treated your employees well, they wouldn't want a union. Kauffman never had to deal with one at Marion Labs, a situation he claimed was testimony to his workers' satisfaction. He was a staunch Republican who on occasion hosted and mentored Texas Rangers' owner George W. Bush on the nuances of baseball management. When Bush became president and involved in the sticky Iraq War, Julia would remind herself that the chief executive of the United States had studied under her father and would surely find a way out of this mess. Unfortunately, Iraq was even more complicated than the collective bargaining agreement.

Steinbrenner was a very different sort of owner than Bush, and the Royals didn't always know how to handle interactions with the blustery fellow. When Cedric Tallis, Joe Burke, or John Schuerholz were forced to deal directly with Steinbrenner, they often had Kauffman on the line as well. "Ewing was the only one who could reason with him," Julia said. "His feelings about the Yankees, about George, he was always business. Mr. K never made emotional decisions, he was very good about that." Ewing Kauffman didn't particularly enjoy his necessary trips to New York, or anywhere else. In middle age, he had no further use for big cities. Whenever he attended one of those Yankees-Royals playoff games, it became tiresome and frustrating for him. He'd fight the traffic, arrive at the big Bronx stadium, only to discover there were no tickets left for him. He was irritated, didn't like that kind of treatment. Kauffman would skip a lot of the Royals games in New York, never sitting in the owner's box with Steinbrenner. He and his family instead would be assigned seats in a long row behind the visitors' clubhouse. If things weren't going well, and even if they were, he'd often want to leave before the ninth inning. "I was on notice," Julia said. "He'd suddenly turn to me and say, 'Doo, let's go.'"

Ewing Kauffman was by no means an urban animal, and Steinbrenner held the home-field advantage whenever negotiations took place in and around New York. The Royals had another weapon, though. Muriel Kauffman was very different from her husband when it came to lifestyle preferences. She was a cosmopolitan woman and maintained an apartment on the Upper East Side of Manhattan, one that the Kauffman family still uses. There was space for Ewing in there, even a room for him to work, but he rarely stayed there when he was in the city. He'd lodge downtown in a hotel and exit quickly for the airport. Ewing made Muriel an official co-owner, at least while he was fully in control of the team. Her name was on the deed to the club. She was one month older than Ewing, yet a considerably freer spirit. Muriel loved New York, loved the parties, and made a lot of friends there in baseball. She came to know Steinbrenner very well. "My mother adored him for party reasons," Julia said. "She'd bump into him in after-hour clubs in New York. He'd send her a bottle of champagne. George lived big and Muriel did, too. Ewing was back home going to bed early. Muriel was in New York going around the town." Steinbrenner adored Muriel, and when Ewing Kauffman finally died at age 76 in 1993, the largest bouquet of flowers delivered to the family's Mission Hills mansion was from the Yankees. It was a nice touch, greatly appreciated.

At Ewing Kauffman's funeral, three songs were played: "Take Me Out to the Ballgame," "The Star-Spangled Banner," and "Onward Christian Soldiers."

# 4

## The Magnificent
## Robber Barons

At present, in the past, and maybe forever into the future, the Yankees have an image problem. Not in New York, where their prosperous, predatory, pinstriped nature and 27 world championships are greatly appreciated by all classes of fans, from the Bleacher Creatures to the Legends Suite holders. But in other parts of the baseball nation, their reputation is one of insatiable procurers in search of the next best mercenary. It has been this way, really, since the Babe Ruth trade in 1919, and was enhanced greatly in December 1975, by way of the Seitz decision that ushered in the free agency era.

This characterization is understandable enough, though not altogether true, historically speaking. While the franchise has gone shopping on many occasions, the Yankees also at odd times have produced and nurtured their own share of homemade superheroes. Of the 16 players represented by the first 15 retired uniforms on the Yankees, only Ruth, Roger Maris, and Reggie Jackson played for another major league team before they competed for the Bombers. That is not an entirely fair statistical assessment, because the Yankees are more likely to enshrine players who put in the most seasons with them, and less likely to celebrate free agent visitors. But there have been some obvious instances in which money played only a peripheral role in acquiring great talent.

Nobody, after all, could have been more of a New Yorker than

Lou Gehrig, who was born the son of German immigrants in East Harlem in 1903, grew up in Washington Heights, and played for both the New York School of Commerce and Columbia University. A star pitcher and slugger for that Ivy League college, Gehrig was signed to a Yankee contract in 1923 by scout Paul Krichell. Within the next two decades, the Bombers inked Phil Rizzuto in 1937 and then Yogi Berra in 1942 for paltry bonuses.

Mickey Mantle, a native Oklahoman, was spotted in 1948 by Yankee scout Tom Greenwade at a game he was playing with the Whiz Kids club team in Baxter Springs, Kansas. Greenwade was there to scout Mickey's teammate. Then Mantle knocked three homers. Greenwade was hooked and returned to sign Mantle out of Commerce High School at age eighteen for $140 per month and a $1,500 signing bonus.

Thurman Munson was picked fourth overall by the Yanks in the 1968 draft, while Ron Guidry was drafted by them in 1975. Derek Jeter, also, never played a professional game for a team that wasn't in the Yankees' organization. Jeter was selected sixth by the Yanks in the 1992 amateur draft, out of Kalamazoo Central High School in Michigan. Scouts from at least two teams picking earlier, Houston and Cincinnati, recommended drafting Jeter, but were ignored by club officials who feared Jeter might ask for a large signing bonus in lieu of heading to the University of Michigan on a scholarship. The Yankees weren't worried about the money, as per usual, and scout Dick Groch assured his higher-ups that Jeter would skip college. "The only place Derek Jeter's going is to Cooperstown," Groch told club officials. George Steinbrenner doled out a signing bonus of $800,000, only to watch Jeter bat .202 in 47 games with Class A Tampa. Things improved quickly enough, however, when he was sent to another farm team, Greensboro, to join teammates Andy Pettitte and Jorge Posada. They, in turn, later joined up with another prospect, Mariano Rivera. The Core Four.

So no, the Yankees don't always purchase their biggest stars. It just seems that way. The Seitz ruling that nullified baseball's reserve clause, turning Andy Messersmith and Dave McNally into free agents, essentially gave Steinbrenner free license to sign stars as he pleased. Joe DiMaggio's reverential words, "I want to thank the good Lord for making me a Yankee," were no longer entirely accurate. George Steinbrenner could now play the role of God, picking and choosing which stars he would adorn with pinstripes and transform into multimillionaires. He did just that, plundering smaller-market franchises while acquiring the corner-stones of seven world championships.

Steinbrenner threw outrageous sums of money at the likes of Catfish Hunter, Reggie Jackson, Dave Winfield, David Cone, David Wells, Randy Johnson, Roger Clemens, and Hideki Matsui. His general managers over the years committed some terrible financial errors, importing and overpaying players such as Kei Igawa ($46,000,194 for two victories), Carl Pavano, Ed Whitson, Javy Vazquez (twice), Kevin Brown, Hideki Irabu, Jaret Wright, and Jason Giambi. Even though mistakes were committed on a regular basis, Steinbrenner had enough money and clout to absorb the losses and place down his next bet. In New York, this was what separated the Yankees from the money-strapped Mets, who grew insular and cautious after any of their gambles failed. It also separated the Yanks from virtually every other franchise in Major League Baseball, both in total payroll and in the standings.

Steinbrenner was pilloried by other owners and executives for such extravagant behavior, yet he put on a brave front in the face of infuriated peers. "The only thing I care about is the Yankee fans," he said. "I couldn't care less what the other people or detractors say. It really doesn't bother me." In fact, the snipes did bother Steinbrenner, who always felt he deserved more credit as a franchise builder. He fumed in 2002 when Red Sox president Larry Lucchino termed the Yankees "The Evil Empire," after they signed pitcher José Contreras to a $32 million contract. In 1983, during the season of the Pine Tar Game, Steinbrenner contacted Schuerholz, the Royals' general manager, to complain about public criticisms. Schuerholz, frustrated by yet another Yankees spending spree, had told a Jacksonville sportswriter that life in the majors was no longer very fair due to Steinbrenner's splurges. Schuerholz likened it to a shootout on Main Street in an old western town. The smaller-market teams were just freckle-faced kids with no real weaponry. "At the far end, dressed in black with a big hat and two six-shooters, were the Yankees, more than ready to duel," Schuerholz said. Steinbrenner sent a personal letter to the Kansas City general manager with the article attached. He understood Schuerholz's resentment, Steinbrenner wrote judiciously, but thought it was unfair to single out the Yankees as the only big-market villain. Schuerholz responded in kind, and a truce of sorts was declared. "My efforts to characterize the problems we face in our business, especially those of us in smaller markets, should have been more broad-based and not as personal," Schuerholz wrote to Steinbrenner. "You have my word that when the frustrations of a small-market general manager bubble over in the future, they will deal in generalities and not personalities."

There had been Yankees executives long before Steinbrenner who dabbled in these same procuring ways. While Steinbrenner now gets most of the credit—or discredit—for the franchise's avaricious image, the club had established its credentials in that department far earlier. Steinbrenner merely made it official policy. The Yanks of old didn't plunder opponents through free agency, yet they managed to build or supplement many of their championship rosters through some form of legalized banditry. In baseball, there are fair trades, and then there is outright thievery. The Yankees traditionally have been involved in both kinds of dealings. They have rarely lacked for money, because they played in the country's largest baseball city and held a virtual monopoly in the American League. Money begat winning, which begat more money, which begat even more winning and the whole pinstriped mythology.

Give them credit for profiting on their own success. Ever since the Highlanders morphed into the Yankees, this club had been able to prey on franchises from smaller markets with great efficacy. Everybody knows about the Red Sox mugging in 1919, which netted Babe Ruth for $125,000 and a $300,000 loan. But it can be argued effectively that nearly every one of their 27 World Series titles was to some extent the result of the team's resourcefulness in dealing with less fortunate opponents.

From 1923 to 1928, the Yanks won three titles while led by Ruth (and, yes, a "natural" Yankee, Gehrig). On May 6, 1930, when they required a serious pitching boost, the Yanks sent $50,000 and 33-year-old outfielder Cedric Durst to the Red Sox for an in-prime, 26-year-old Red Ruffing. Durst lasted only the one season in Boston, batting .245. Ruffing went 15-5 for the Yankees the remainder of 1930 and spent 15 more years in New York, where he anchored the starting rotation, won 20 games in four straight seasons, and was a six-time All-Star. Ruffing pitched in seven World Series, with a record of 7-2 and an earned run average of 2.63. Like Ruth, Ruffing was a magnificent athlete who could also swing a bat. He hit over .300 eight times. Combined, Ruth and Ruffing were part of nine Yankee championships.

There was another highly significant contributor to these titles around this time. Joe DiMaggio was acquired by the Yankees on November 21, 1934, from the Class AA San Francisco Seals of the Pacific Coast League in a direct deal between an independent minor league team and a major league club. DiMaggio had hit safely in 61 straight games for the Seals, who would briefly become a farm team for the Brooklyn Dodgers in 1936. If DiMaggio, just 20 years old at the time, had played two more seasons with his hometown Seals, he would likely have become a Dodger. Instead, the Yanks sent another $50,000 in cash to San Francisco and the promise of four players, who later would be identified as Floyd Newkirk, Jim Densmore, Ted Norbert, and Doc Farrell (a shortstop who declined to move west to this minor league team and played out his career in Newark). The Yanks were among only a few teams that could muster such resources. The *New York Times* largely missed the importance of the deal at the time, folding the DiMaggio news into a longer Associated Press story about a transaction between the Cubs and Cardinals involving three pitchers—none of whom had won more than 16 games. The headline read, simply, "Yankees Obtain DiMaggio, Coast League Batting Star, in Player Transaction." The Yanks were more patient than rapacious in this case. The Seals had hoped to bank $100,000 for DiMaggio's contract, but he suffered torn ligaments in his left knee and the injury scared off most bidders. The Yankees' scout Bill Essick, however, persisted. Part of the deal was that DiMaggio would play one more season with the Seals in 1935, and he did that while batting .398 with 34 homers and 154 runs batted in.

By 1946, again, the Yanks' rotation required refurbishing. This was accomplished at first with a relatively fair exchange—on paper, at least—in which the Bombers sent second baseman Joe Gordon and Eddie Bockman to Cleveland for 30-year-old Allie Reynolds. Reynolds was already something of a star, having led the American League in strikeouts in 1943. He proceeded to go 131-60 during the next eight seasons in New York, evolving from a starter to a reliable reliever. In 1951, he threw two no-hitters. The next season, he was the league leader in earned run average (2.06) and strikeouts (160). From 1947 through 1953, he went 7-2 with a 2.79 ERA in six World Series—all of them Yankee championships. Gordon, 31 years old at the time of the deal, had been the American League MVP in 1942 and would continue to produce during three productive seasons with Cleveland, leading the Indians to a championship in 1948. He tailed off in 1950, however, and then retired. Bockman, a utility infielder, played only one season with the Indians.

Reynolds was joined at the start of the 1948 season by starter Ed Lopat, who had been acquired in an outright heist from the White Sox for Fred Bradley, Aaron Robinson, and the main attraction, Bill Wight. Lopat, 29 years old, was already established as a solid workhorse starter who had gone 16-13 with a 2.81 ERA in 1947, while throwing 252⅔ innings. He went on to post a 113-59 record during eight seasons with the Yanks, throwing more than 200 innings in his first four years. During five World Series, Lopat went 4-1 in seven starts with a 2.60 ERA. In 1953, he was 16-4 with a league-leading 2.42 ERA. Wight, meanwhile, was something of a bust. He was 25 years old and had pitched a total of only 49⅓ innings in the majors at the time of the trade. The White Sox saw him as a potential star mainly because of his performances with the Yanks' farm team in Kansas City, where in 1947 Wight had been 16-9 with a 2.85 ERA. Once transplanted to Chicago, he quickly lost 20 games with a 4.80 ERA for the White Sox in 1948.

Together, DiMaggio, Reynolds, and Lopat were the anchors of six world championships, bringing the total of acquisition-based, pinstriped titles to 15. As they aged out, manager Casey Stengel was looking again to reinvent his pitching staff with younger arms. Whitey Ford filled the role and was a homegrown, in-system star. But the next Yankee dynasty really began with one of the largest trades in major league history on November 17, 1954. By the time the dust and agate type settled two weeks later, 17 players had been exchanged between the Yanks and Baltimore Orioles. Most important, the Yankees received "Bullet Bob" Turley, a future Cy Young winner in 1958, when he threw 19 complete games with a 2.97 ERA. Turley was part of four championship teams from 1955 to 1962. The titles were also greatly aided by the Kansas City refugees Ralph Terry and Roger Maris.

After a lengthy drought, Steinbrenner and a group of investors purchased the team in 1973 from ham-handed CBS in perhaps the greatest steal of them all. Depending on the account and the accounting, the group paid anywhere from $8.7 to $10 million for a franchise now estimated to be worth more than $2 billion. The Seitz decision then allowed Steinbrenner to spend to his heart's content. Luxury taxes and revenue sharing that were built into later collective bargaining agreements eventually punished the Yanks for their methods, yet did not halt the outflow of cash. At the start of the 2014 season, the Yankees' payroll stood at $197 million—and was only that low because Alex Rodriguez's salary had dipped from $28 million in 2013 to $3.8 million in 2014 after his suspension for the use of performance-enhancing drugs. This development rescued the Yankees from considerable financial responsibility, but did nothing for their image. They were still the league's magnificent robber barons. In this case, one of their own simply had been caught red-handed.

# 5

## All the Boss's Men

It is very easy to draw some obvious, unflattering contrasts when comparing George Steinbrenner with Ewing Kauffman. Kauffman was a homegrown, self-made entrepreneur who built a pharmaceutical empire from the basement of his parents' home, founded his own baseball team, and never really left Kansas City. Steinbrenner, quickly dubbed "the Boss" by New York's playful tabloids, was a wealthy Ohioan who took over the family's shipping company, purchased the dynastic Yankees on the cheap, and ran the club from his American Shipbuilding office in Tampa, Florida. Employing a well-worn baseball metaphor, some might say Steinbrenner was born on third base and firmly believed he'd hit a triple.

Kauffman was squeaky clean, a chronic nonoffender. Steinbrenner was suspended twice from the sport—once for illegal contributions to Richard Nixon, later for his shady investigation into a star ballplayer, Dave Winfield. He might have been suspended a third or fourth time, for some of his antics. Kauffman was steady, cerebral, and self-controlled. Steinbrenner was short-tempered, emotional, and manipulative with the media, demanding beyond reason with employees. As Yogi Berra once said, the Yankees' owner could wake up mad about something and stay mad all day. Steinbrenner might fire a secretary during such an extended duration of huffiness for failing to bring him his tuna fish sandwich—a true story—then quietly donate thousands of dollars to unemployed workers the following day. He

41

never quite grasped the contradiction in this sort of behavior. The differences between Steinbrenner and Kauffman came down to a matter of balance and priorities. Kauffman had other interests, besides the Royals. The baseball team was his beloved hobby, but it had a place in his life somewhere beside, or below, family and Marion Labs. Steinbrenner, for much of his existence, cared first and foremost about winning championships, winning games, winning innings. The rest of life was his hobby.

Steinbrenner's ownership of the fabled Yankees in 1973 was actually something of a fateful accident. He first tried to buy his hometown team, the Indians, but they weren't for sale at the time. Gabe Paul, in charge of running the Indians' baseball operations, set him up with CBS officials, who were eager to dump the New York franchise at a loss after a period of lousy athletic and financial performances. The team at this time was producing less than $10 million in annual revenues. WPIX, Channel 11 in New York, had a monopoly on broadcast rights and decided to show fewer games because of low ratings. Steinbrenner joined with Yankees president Michael Burke, who had run the team for CBS, to purchase the team for less than a year's worth of revenues. Steinbrenner himself put up about $2 million, correctly pronouncing this "the best buy in sports today . . . a bargain." When asked about operating the team, he said, famously, "I'll leave that to Mike and Lee MacPhail. I'll stick to building ships." Soon, Steinbrenner essentially replaced Burke with Paul, leading Burke to tell people, "I'll be fine when I get this knife out of my back."

Soon thereafter, such pretense was abandoned and Steinbrenner became all Yankees, all the time. He was the man in charge, full of both good and bad suggestions. He could be incredibly insightful—as when he suggested the Yankees break with tradition and finally name a new captain, Thurman Munson, after decades of leaving that post empty in honor of Lou Gehrig. He could be absurd, insisting on football-style, walkie-talkie communications between the manager and "eye-in-the-sky" coaches to set the defense. When the Yankees played the Reds in the 1976 World Series, Cincinnati manager Sparky Anderson stopped the game to protest the existence of three such spies, and commissioner Bowie Kuhn ordered two of them to cease and desist. Steinbrenner was so infuriated by this Kuhn fiat, and by the Reds' sweep, he ordered his staff to boycott the traditional post–World Series party. "Parties are for winners," Steinbrenner told all Yankee officials, top to bottom. "You guys are a bunch of losers. You're all confined to your rooms." Soon after, he wooed and signed Reggie Jackson, another stroke of genius.

Steinbrenner had a few other interests in addition to the Yankees, foremost among them his Kinsman Stud Farm for thoroughbreds in Ocala, Florida. He would later develop another sporting obsession, too: the Olympics. Steinbrenner decided to fix the United States Olympic team, wanted his country to win many gold medals. He curried considerable favor within the United States Olympic Committee with checkbook diplomacy, donations of $5,000 at a time to various sports federations and individual athletes. In the 1990s, he eventually served as vice chairman and head of the Steinbrenner Commission that called on the USOC to set up a more definitive reward system for medal winners and potential medal winners. The Yankees always came first and foremost, however. He was shattered by a two-year suspension from Commissioner Bowie Kuhn—the first of two banishments—on November 27, 1974, for his felony conviction on a charge of obstruction of justice regarding illegal campaign contributions to Richard Nixon. "It's certainly a wonderful Thanksgiving present," he dictated to Marty Appel, his public relations man. "Let me be perfectly frank. I don't agree with the commissioner's decision."

Appel witnessed a lot of this sort of drama. The people who understood Steinbrenner best, really, were not necessarily the friends who dined with him at Elaine's or partied with him at the Carlyle Hotel—his occasional East Side Manhattan haunts. The ones who truly knew Steinbrenner, in all his glory and monstrosity, were the many Yankees' public relations directors, a virtual parade of victims. They were his lifeline, his link to the one thing he cared about most, his ballclub. Steinbrenner's own immediate family was wary of becoming too involved in his baseball enterprise. His wife, Elizabeth Joan, was rarely seen around the team. His oldest son, Hank, might come down to Florida for spring training, but he headed for the horse farm once the regular season began, and when he saw how his dad treated employees. Steinbrenner would have welcomed the greater participation of his family, albeit on his own paternalistic terms. In 1998, his son-in-law Steve Swindal became a general partner and something of an heir apparent by default, since sons Hank and Hal wanted little to do then with their father's obsession. But Steinbrenner's daughter Jennifer filed for divorce and that essentially was the end of Swindal's potential reign. The other sons, daughters, and even shirttail relatives kept their distance, for good reason, until Steinbrenner's mental powers diminished and he could be shunted aside. As John McMullen, the former Yankee investor, once famously said of working relationships with the Boss, "There is nothing in life quite so limited as being a limited partner of George Steinbrenner."

Since family members would not be lured into his web, Steinbrenner relied on the next best thing: public relations directors, loyal by nature to the bone, who were there to perform his bidding at the drop of a Yankee cap. These men were expected to be forever on the scene, Steinbrenner's eyes and ears, reporting back to him at all hours of the day and night the way military scouts report to generals. They needed to share his obsession, the way everybody needed to share his obsession. "There was no cell phone yet, but you had to be available," said Harvey Greene, who was the Yankees' public relations director in the late 1980s. "The easiest way to be on George's good side, or bad side, was availability."

Greene made the mistake of staying out too late during one night of spring training, dining at 15th Street Fisheries in Fort Lauderdale. He returned to his hotel room to see the dreaded red light flashing on his phone. There was a message from Steinbrenner, who wasn't happy about his absence. Greene immediately was prescribed a strict curfew of 9:00 p.m. when he had to be back in his hotel room, answerable to the Boss. This went on every day, all year. When Greene went to a Knicks game in mid-February, he would leave a courtside number with Steinbrenner's office, in case there was reason for a phone call. And sure enough, Greene was summoned from his seat at Madison Square Garden to deal with some issue involving the Yankees.

"On February 14, Valentine's Day, I'm not thinking about the Yankees," Greene said. "But George is. To his credit, he was always thinking about them, always thinking about winning. He was fine as long as you had the same priority. The day something else becomes important to you—hobbies, family, whatever—then you have problems."

Yankee games weren't always available on television in Tampa. So Appel, one of Steinbrenner's early PR guys, would do play-by-play and analysis over the phone, from the ballpark, for the Boss whenever he was in Florida. Jeff Idelson, another Yankees public relations man and later president of the Baseball Hall of Fame in Cooperstown, took a call from the Boss while stepping out of the shower and knew better than to ask Steinbrenner to wait a few moments. Instead, Idelson jotted down notes from his employer with an index finger on a foggy bathroom mirror. Larry Wahl once was forced to recall all 12,000 copies of the team's yearbook because the cover photo of Steinbrenner didn't do the owner justice. A very similar thing happened to Appel. During the owner's first suspension, Yankee players were permitted to wear their hair longer. When he returned, they were immediately ordered to the barbershop by Steinbrenner to be shorn. But the 1976 yearbook showed photos of the players from 1975, with their longer hair, and Steinbrenner literally threw the book at Appel. Then he pointed out the offending pictures, commenting, "Hair's too long . . . hair's too long . . . hair's too long . . ."

Steinbrenner was involved in the minutest detail at the ballpark, from the scoreboard presentation to the assignment of limited parking passes at Yankee Stadium for reporters driving to the games. He often didn't announce these decisions until the last minute. Because of his maddening, spontaneous behavior, Steinbrenner's public relations directors made a habit of fleeing for the hills before very long. He went through them with great alacrity, in almost cartoon fashion. Bob Fishel . . . Appel . . . Mickey Morabito . . . Wahl . . . Dave Szen . . . Irv Kaze . . . Ken Nigro . . . Joe

Safety . . . Greene . . . Idelson . . . Rob Butcher . . . eventually, even, the fictional George Costanza, on *Seinfeld*. Butcher was fired for having the nerve to travel home to Ohio for Christmas in 1995, after receiving specific permission from Steinbrenner to do so. It turned out David Cone signed with the Yankees as a free agent on December 21, which was very bad timing by Butcher as far as the Boss was concerned. Like many of these tormented souls, Butcher later landed a far more normal job, in his case with the Cincinnati Reds. Of all these men, however, Ken Nigro probably was the very worst suited for the job, and he happened to come around just in time for the pine tar season in 1983.

Nigro didn't really have a public relations background. He was a newspaper guy, a sportswriter who covered the Orioles for a dozen years with the *Baltimore Sun* until 1982. While there, he mentored younger sportswriters, such as future *Boston Globe* columnist Dan Shaughnessy, about journalistic professionalism: Protect sources. Respect the players' space. Maintain a healthy, objective distance. Nigro joined the Orioles' front office for a year before taking the job as public relations director for Steinbrenner, a terrible mismatch. He was detested by Steinbrenner, perhaps because the cynical ex-sportswriter was not enough the flack. Nigro related far better to the New York reporters than to his bosses, so there was an ongoing question of where his true loyalty resided. And Nigro didn't always answer the hot line from his boss quickly enough. "I'd pick it up and he'd already be talking," Nigro said. "You couldn't pick it up fast enough." After a while, Steinbrenner didn't even bother with Nigro and went through other channels. Early in the 1983 season, Miller Lite contacted Steinbrenner to propose a lighthearted commercial alongside his tortured public relations directors. Perhaps Steinbrenner would tell them the beer "tastes good," and the PR guys would have to abandon their "less filling" press release. Normally, Steinbrenner leaped at these opportunities at public self-parody. He appeared on *Saturday Night Live* and made a prominent Visa commercial with Derek Jeter, in which a stern lecture to his young short-stop eventually turns into a bar-hopping experience for both of them. He adored being portrayed as General Von Steingrabber by *New York Daily News* cartoonist Bill Gallo. But when Steinbrenner heard that Nigro would be part of the Miller Lite ad, the owner declined the offer. He wanted no part of a commercial that would pair him with Nigro and provide his public relations director with added income.

Despite this sort of miserly behavior, Steinbrenner could be quite generous at times—though more often toward people and causes outside his ballclub than with his own employees. He would donate considerable amounts of money to various charities, including the Silver Shield Foundation for widows and children of firefighters and police officers killed in the line of duty. Whenever he did this, Steinbrenner wanted nobody to know about it—a very different philosophy from the Yankees today, who combine their annual charitable Hope Week with an accompanying nonstop publicity campaign.

Back in 1983, Nigro lasted only the one year with the Yankees before hightailing it back to Baltimore. It just so happened his one season included some of the craziest stuff ever seen around a ballpark. That year, there wasn't a public relations man alive who could spin things the way George Steinbrenner wanted them spun.

# 6

## A Different Kind
## of Rivalry

*"Despite the disparity in our ability to have the*
*weapons, if you will, to do battle with the mighty*
*Yankees, we found the wherewithal to do it, even*
*with our pop guns."*
—John Schuerholz

During the late seventies and early eighties, the Yankees and Royals produced one of the three greatest postseason rivalries in the history of the sport. They not only faced each other four out of five years in the American League Championship Series, they generated some of the most tortuous plot twists imaginable. The two franchises may have followed very different paths over recent decades, but the upstart Royals were at the time a very real threat to the haughty supremacy of the pinstriped empire.

Before 1969 and baseball's expansion to four divisions, when there were no playoff tiers, postseason enmity could only exist between an American and a National League team in the World Series. Such rivalries were few and far between. From 1921 to 1923, the Yanks and New York Giants faced each other three straight times in the World Series, then met again in 1936 and 1937. The Yankees were considered the upstarts back then, evicted from Manhattan by the Giants and relocated to the Bronx. From

1952 to 1956, the Yanks and Brooklyn Dodgers played four out of five times in the World Series, the Bombers against the Bums. These were series between interborough teams from the same city, creating a level of passion in New York City that will never be matched again in a single metropolis. Yet baseball's fan base west of the Delaware River was often a dispassionate observer of this incestuous theater. Whether or not New Yorkers wanted to admit such sacrilege, the sport also was being played west of the Hudson River. Kansas City versus New York was something completely different, a war between two worlds.

The Yankees, of course, have long experienced a different rivalry with the Red Sox in the American League, steeped in history and tradition. That venomous feud started with the very first meeting between Boston and the New York Highlanders on May 7, 1903. The game, played in the Washington Heights section of Manhattan, featured a dugout-emptying brawl after Boston pitcher George Winter was knocked down with a high, inside pitch. The Red Sox earned the upper hand in these games for many years, until their fortunes were famously reversed on the day after Christmas in 1919, when Harry Frazee, Red Sox owner, sold Ruth to the Yankees so he could finance his Broadway musical, *No, No, Nanette.*

This changed everything, leading directly and then indirectly to 22 world championships for the Yankees by 1983. The sting was particularly harsh for Bostonians in 1978, when the Red Sox lost a 14-game lead over the charging Yankees, finishing in a first-place tie in the American League East and forcing a one-game playoff at Fenway Park. Bucky Dent looped a decisive homer over the Green Monster in left field and Goose Gossage got the save. The Yanks won, 5–4, and were off to another World Series title.

Until the Red Sox exacted their revenge with a miracle comeback of their own in the 2004 American League Championship Series, this remained a bitter, one-sided rivalry, something akin to whale versus plankton. "We were not greeted very well in Boston, and that's always been the way," said Ron Guidry, the great Yankees starter. "In 1975, it was my first trip into Fenway. The people didn't even know who I was, I was a no-name, but the fans already were pelting me in the bullpen with stuff, throwing garbage at me and calling me names." While resentments still bubbled in the early 1980s, this rivalry had fallen into something of a dormant state, at least in the standings. From 1979 through 1983, the Yanks and Red Sox didn't compete in a single tight pennant race—other than the first-half standings in 1981, a season disrupted by a lengthy players' strike. In 1983, the year of the Pine Tar Game, the Sox were stuck in a down cycle and would finish the season 78-84, in sixth place out of seven teams in the American League East and 20 games behind the Baltimore Orioles.

What the Yankees were to the Red Sox, the Oakland A's were to the Royals, only in a condensed historical form. This matchup offered its own special bite. Psychological wounds were still unhealed in Kansas City from Charlie Finley's act of civic betrayal. It hurt considerably to watch the struggles of the new home team, the Royals, while the A's were winning five straight American League West division titles, from 1971 to 1975, along with three World Series championships. In 1973, Kansas City finished second, six games behind Oakland. In 1975, they were second again, seven games back.

Eventually, in 1976, the Royals overcame their chief obstacle in Oakland, only to discover a new one in New York. The A's slipped a notch and the Royals' 90-win season was good enough to win the division by two and a half games. George Brett captured his first batting title, hitting .333, to finish second behind Thurman Munson in the Most Valuable Player voting. Seven-plus years after their birth, the Royals at last found themselves in the postseason. Kansas City would face the Yankees, the same franchise that had strip-mined the city's Athletics franchise for years.

"It was made more intense, because of the David and Goliath element that didn't exist with the Red Sox–Yankees," Schuerholz said. "And there were natural rivalry items in place. Kansas City, when Charlie Finley owned the A's, was just a feeder system for the Yankees. When we started winning our division, we had to beat the East. We suddenly had to beat the Yankees."

Both teams in this best-of-five, 1976 American League Championship Series were extremely hungry, practically starved for success. The Yanks hadn't been to a World Series in a dozen years, since they lost in seven games to St. Louis, and hadn't captured a championship since 1962. This represented the longest franchise drought in the post-Ruthian era, and Steinbrenner promised to end it. The team had just moved back to a renovated Yankee Stadium from an uncomfortable time-share with the Mets at Shea Stadium and wanted very badly to christen the place with a title. Meanwhile, Kansas City had never experienced a single playoff game at the major league level, thanks to the persistent ineptitude of the Athletics while they were playing there.

Surprisingly, there was already some bad blood between the Royals and Yankees. Unsurprisingly, it was mostly due to Billy Martin, the volatile New York manager. Larry Gura, the Royals' ace, ripped Martin in print before the series because of his treatment by the Yankees earlier in the season, before Gura was dealt in mid-May to the Royals for backup catcher Fran Healy. Martin didn't like Gura at all, didn't pitch him in a single game during the early season. Before this series against Kansas City, Martin said he'd dump Gura again if he had the chance. Brett also had a beef with the Yankee manager, because Martin had used his brother, Ken, a left-handed pitcher, for a grand total of only two and one-third innings during the same season before dealing him to the Chicago White Sox on May 18.

The 1976 series itself proved something of a precursor to the Pine Tar Game some seven years later, a warm-up of sorts, because it ended in a controversy that also tested the rules of the day. The Yankees didn't necessarily accept the Royals as a serious threat. After all, their top starter, Gura, was a Yankee castoff. On the bus to the hotel from the Kansas City airport, Lou Piniella cracked, "How are we going to lose if we're going against a pitcher who was traded for Fran Healy?" While Healy took this ribbing in the spirit it was intended, he did not appreciate that the quotation was dutifully reported by *New York Daily News* reporter Phil Pepe, who was on the bus with the team (yet another example of why this courtesy to sportswriters was soon eliminated by baseball clubs). The first two games of the series were played at Royals Stadium and proved uncharacteristically sloppy. Brett, young and nervous, made two throwing errors in the very first inning of the opener, leading to two runs. That was all Catfish Hunter required as the Yanks won, 4–1. This also marked the first time that Brett really experienced a good dose of unfiltered, rampaging Billy Martin, the shameless bench jockey.

Martin was bred from a different era, when hostilities among opposing players and managers were the rule, not the exception. He was a great proponent and practitioner of taunts and heckles. By 1976, this sort of behavior was just beginning to fade. Players were changing teams on the fly through free agency, forging friendships outside the ballpark with endorsements and at special events. This became even truer as the decades passed. By 2010, Derek Jeter might knock a single, then chat at length with the first baseman, a teammate at the World Baseball Classic. When he reached second base, he'd converse with a shortstop who shared his management agency. The third baseman might be Jeter's former teammate on the Yankees. In Martin's day, however, it was different. Players nurtured their grudges against opponents, and he brought that with him to the dugout, forever stirring the embers. He imparted that view to Willie Randolph, a second baseman who was every bit as competitive as Martin. When Randolph became manager of the Mets for the 2005 season, he still refused to abide amicable behavior from his players. It rubbed him the wrong way, flew in the face of his Brooklyn sandlot days, when every game ended in a fight. Randolph often had a tough time convincing the Mets to play the same way as Martin had taught him. "One time, David Wright made a great slide at second base, got tangled up with the shortstop, and before he walked off the field he wanted to know if the guy was okay," Randolph said. "It fried my ass when he did that. So David walks back to the dugout, and I say to him, 'Why don't you just kiss him?' He kind of gave me a funny look, said, 'Come on, Willie.' Like I was a hard-ass. I wasn't trying to be a dick about it, but that's not the way we did it."

For just such reasons, Randolph quickly became one of Martin's favorites. He was a tough guy from Brooklyn who always knew he wanted to play for the Yankees and did not easily accept the softer traditions of the sport. When he first was acquired for the 1976 season, Randolph asked to wear uniform number 30, the number he'd worn with the Pirates. He was told that had been Mel Stottlemyre's number, and the Yankees were reluctant to give it away so quickly. "I don't give a shit about Mel Stottlemyre," Randolph said. That was that. Whenever he played against the Royals or Red Sox, Randolph fully expected hostile chatter and harsh slides, the way Martin had played and taught the game. "You look at the field now, they're all mum, they don't say anything," Randolph said. "You don't hear a guy say a peep. Weird. You grow up in Little League, it's part of your upbringing."

Martin fed those brushfires. He wouldn't behave himself or obey conventional customs. When Brett came to bat in the fourth inning of that first game, the Yankee manager suddenly started screaming at him, "Your brother's a shit!" Brett was stunned for a moment, but composed himself and laced a single to right. It happened again in the seventh, then again in the ninth inning. "Every time I came to bat," Brett said. "That's really high class, really a tribute to baseball." Brett, though, wouldn't give Martin the satisfaction of believing he had been rattled. "If I had a grudge against every team that traded my brother, I'd have a grudge against every team in baseball," he said.

The Yankees usually didn't know what Martin was screaming at other teams, because he would direct his venom toward the field. They just understood he was screaming on their behalf, hoping to influence the action. "All I knew was that he was on the top step and the hair on the back of his neck was always up," Randolph said. "He looked like a pit bull. He was always trying to intimidate. He knew the Royals couldn't stand him and he figured, 'I'm going to be a thorn in your ass.' He got off on it. He'd do anything. Throw a pebble or rock toward home plate, try to get in their heads and make a difference. People can debate how much a manager has to do with games, but Billy went into every game wanting to be the difference. He was thinking, 'I'm better than you, I'm going to outwit you, outsmart you.'"

Despite Martin's best trash-talking efforts, the Royals won Game 2, 7–3, as the Yankees committed an astounding five errors. By this time, the excitement and craziness back in New York had reached new levels, fanned as always by the owner, Steinbrenner. The Boss had decided to meddle in the actual on-field tactics by ordering two of his scouts, Jerry Walker and Bobby Cox, to sit in the WMCA radio booth and send instructions to Martin by walkie-talkie as to where to deploy his fielders. Martin took this surprisingly well, at least for public consumption. But the strategy seemed to backfire badly in Game 2, because the Yankees played their worst defensive game of the season. At times, they dropped the ball or threw it away. At others, the Royals would simply hit the ball where the Yankees weren't, almost to mock Steinbrenner's football-like defensive scheming.

The series then shifted for Game 3 to the Bronx, and to a considerably more prominent venue. Politicians and celebrities appeared in the best seats. New York mayor Abe Beame and Secretary of State Henry Kissinger were roundly jeered, while Frank Sinatra and Cary Grant received hearty welcomes. The Royals would face Dock Ellis, who hadn't pitched in ten days and was a man well known for his idiosyncrasies. Ellis's antics were legend. As a minor leaguer, he ran into the stands with a bat to chase after a heckler. He famously pitched a no-hitter in 1970 for the Pirates while hallucinating from a healthy dose of LSD. "The ball was small sometimes, the ball was large sometimes, sometimes I saw the catcher, sometimes I didn't," he recalled in a later interview. He'd been challenged to a fight by Pittsburgh manager Danny Murtaugh during a team meeting. He once threw beanballs at three successive Reds hitters. He was maced by a security guard at Riverfront Stadium in Cincinnati after refusing or failing to show identification. And on this night, Ellis was socked for three runs in the first inning. "I hadn't pitched in a long time and I was overthrowing the ball," Ellis said. "I didn't have anything at all. I was just shoving the ball up there. I was lucky I got out of the inning." Ellis settled down, helped out by a couple of double plays and two would-be base stealers pegged out by Thurman Munson. The Yanks came back with two runs in the fourth on a homer by Chris Chambliss—who was looking for a fastball from Andy Hassler and got a hanging curve instead. They scored three runs in the sixth for the 5–3 victory.

For Game 4, managers Martin and Whitey Herzog then brought back their aces, Hunter and Gura, on three days' rest. They were both clobbered early and the Royals won, 7–4, setting up a dramatic, decisive Game 5, a memorable classic tinged with controversy and, really, the contest that jump-started this fresh rivalry.

Again, the managers went with starters on three days' rest, their number-two guys, Ed Figueroa and Dennis Leonard. Figueroa was a solid pitcher, albeit a little alienated during his years with the Yankees, who never bothered to furnish translators for Spanish-speaking players. Like most starters, he preferred to work on full rest. And like most starters, he was pressured into changing that routine during the postseason. Typically, panicky managers obtain diminishing returns by pushing their starters up a day during the playoffs. And again, neither pitcher fared well. John Mayberry drove home Brett with a two-run homer in the first inning. Leonard didn't get out of the bottom of the first, giving up two runs. The Yankees built and held a 6–3 lead going into the eighth, but Brett's three-run shot off reliever Grant Jackson tied the game. After a rocky series at third base—Brett had committed another key error in Game 5—this one swing established him for the first time as a Yankee killer, a role he would expand and relish.

The Royals entered the top of the ninth inning tied, 6–6, against reliever Dick Tidrow. With two outs, Buck Martinez singled and Al Cowens walked. Jim Wohlford then bounced a slow grounder to third, where Nettles charged, gobbled up the ball, and relayed it to Willie Randolph at second for the force on Cowens. This was a relatively close call—made by future pine tar ump Joe Brinkman—and the Royals felt very strongly that Cowens was safe. There was no challenging such a thing then, no replay review. To this day, many of the Royals feel that Randolph cheated a bit on the play at second to make it appear closer than it was. This was considered an example of the "neighborhood play"—meaning that the second baseman or shortstop was just in the neighborhood of second base on the relay. If Cowens had been called safe, Brett would have come to the plate with the bases loaded and everything might have changed.

The Yanks now came up in the bottom of the ninth, with the place something of a madhouse. Play was delayed five minutes as the grounds crew cleared bottles that had been tossed from the stands onto the outfield. The public address announcer, Bob Sheppard, kept pleading with the fans in his authoritative voice to behave themselves, but they wouldn't heed his entreaties. Rolls of toilet paper continued to stream onto the field. Martin was fuming in the dugout, wanting to get on with the game, afraid even that the umpires might order the Royals off the field and declare a forfeit. Martin never trusted the umps, and did not want to give them any opportunity to prosecute or persecute the Yankees. As it turned out, however, the delay may well have rattled reliever Mark Littell and determined the outcome. Littell, a relatively inexperienced 23-year-old pitcher, remained on the mound during the field cleanup and threw a few warm-up pitches to kill time. In a strange way, he was being iced by the fans. It was getting close to midnight when Chris Chambliss knocked Littell's first pitch of the ninth inning high and over the right-center-field fence for a walk-off homer—the only homer that Littell yielded in the series. Hal McRae chased after the ball, then conceded. Chambliss was already on a tear, having gone 10-for-20 in the five games. The fastball strayed too high over the plate, quite possibly a potential ball one. "I didn't want to be taking. It looked good," Chambliss said. "It was high. It was over the plate. I'm an aggressive guy so I swung at a pitch in the zone that I thought I could get a good swing at."

Chambliss's attempted victory trot around the bases was a more difficult trek than expected. A good portion of the 56,821 fans in attendance had leaped onto the field to celebrate and join Chambliss on his trip. By the time he reached second, the base wasn't there. A fan had just torn the bag from the ground and Chambliss was forced to slap it with his right hand. He was using his forearms to block fans out of his way, as if he were an offensive lineman creating a hole for a running back. Some of his teammates tried to run interference for him, in vain. Randolph remembered getting caught in the madhouse, then having to rescue his own father from the teeming crowd near the railings.

Chambliss continued around the base path, only to crash into an intruder around the shortstop position. He fell to the ground, while a fan grabbed at his helmet from behind. Chambliss scrambled to his feet and somehow managed to weave his way to third base. At this juncture, the journey home became impossible and he just sort of passed by in the general vicinity. "Home plate was completely covered with people," Chambliss said. "I wasn't sure if I tagged it or not. I came in the clubhouse and all the players were talking about whether I got it. I wasn't sure, so I went back out."

Graig Nettles was always the chief rules keeper in the Yankees' clubhouse. He told Chambliss to go out there again and touch home plate where umpire Art Frantz was still standing and waiting, putting his own neck at risk. Chambliss was escorted by two security men back onto the field to touch home and make this victory official, but by then the plate had been rudely removed by a marauding fan. Chambliss merely planted his foot on the ground that previously had housed the five-sided polygon. Meanwhile, the fans continued to rampage on national television, delivering a terrible image of New York City to a national television audience while wrecking the field to the tune of $100,000 in damages.

Chambliss would later talk to the umpires who witnessed this nutty journey, and who told him they considered touching the bases a moot point, considering the scene. "So it was a home run as soon as it went over the fence," Chambliss said. He said the best part of that home run scramble was shaking hands with his first-base coach, Elston Howard, "a big influence on my career." From there, it was all a mess. Chambliss still has the home run ball, which was retrieved by the Yankees. He has the bat, too. "I didn't know for a long time but Graig Nettles is the reason I have the bat. I hit the ball, I probably just dropped [the bat] like I usually do but Nettles had the presence of mind to run on the field and pick up the bat. He took the bat and went back to the dugout. Graig used my bat to protect our gloves and our hats and he's the reason I have the bat today."

It was an iconic walk-off shot, only the second such series-ending homer in the history of postseason baseball at the time (Bill Mazeroski's 1960 home run for the Pirates was the other one, though there have been several more since 1976 in the expanded playoffs). Chambliss was established immediately as a Yankee hero, having driven in eight runs during this series with 11 hits. But this bizarre ending had very real, pine-tar-like possibilities. No doubt if Herzog had been Martin, the Royals' manager would have protested this game. After all, major league rules stated clearly that all bases must be touched in order for any runner to score. Herzog didn't bother, and he wouldn't have won the protest in any case. Instead, he was remarkably gracious in defeat. "I'm sorry we couldn't win," Herzog told reporters after the game. "But I'm happy that the World Series is back in New York. And don't worry, you guys aren't going to be embarrassed."

In actuality, the Yanks were a bit humiliated in a four-game World Series sweep by the Cincinnati Reds. The American League Championship Series had made a lasting impact, however, in the rule book. To make certain there would be no further ambiguity about touching all the bases, the major league governors touched all of theirs. They reacted quickly with a revision that instantly became known as the "Chris Chambliss Rule." The new amendment, in the form of an explanatory comment, was added to Rule 4.09 (b): "An exception will be if fans rush onto the field and physically prevent the runner from touching home plate or the batter from touching first base. In such cases, the umpires shall award the runner the base because of the obstruction by the fans." Suddenly a base runner had an alibi, under special circumstances, for not touching two of the four bases. This was notable for its specificity, if nothing else. What about the occasionally risky journey to second and third base? Didn't Fred Merkle deserve an exception back in 1908, when the poor fellow was waylaid by a field invasion from his path to second base? If he had been extended such an exception, the Giants might have held on to win the pennant against the Cubs and Merkle would not still be baseball's most famous bonehead.

# 7

---

# The Fan

Three decades before David Cone pitched a perfect game for the New York Yankees, he was a lot like the other kids growing up in and around Kansas City, only more so. In his working-class, northeast neighborhood, Cone was a young student of baseball, one of the most rabid supporters of the new Royals franchise. He'd listen to the games on the radio almost every night. His dad, Ed, was a mechanic in the local Swift meat-packing plant, and a big ball fan. The father also happened to be a protective patriarch who shot and wounded with a .22-caliber rifle a knife-wielding neighbor, when that man bashed in the glass front door of the Cones' home and threatened to kill David's brother, Danny.

Ed Cone would watch his three sons—there was a daughter, too, the oldest child—play Wiffle ball in the backyard, and the father sometimes drove the whole family, including the mother, Joan, to games at Royals Stadium down I-435 in the southern end of town. David was born on January 2, 1963, which meant the Royals grew up with him, right through adulthood. They came into the world when he was six years old, inheriting a large chunk of the fan base from the turncoat Athletics. The Cone family was part of that group. David was just out of Little League and starting high school when the Royals were playing all these to-the-death playoff series against the Yankees. He didn't really despise the Yankees, at least not the way he remembered it. David merely wanted the hometown team to succeed, because it seemed like extended family.

"For me it wasn't so much hate," Cone said. "I always had a healthy respect for the Yankees. Even going back to the Kansas City A's, when we were kind of perceived as a farm team way back when for the Yanks. My dad gave me a good background on that history while I was growing up. He respected the Yankees, never hated the Yankees. But certainly we thought the Royals were a team that had to beat the Yankees to put us on the map. We wanted credibility. Even as a city, Kansas City, we were viewed [by outsiders] as the Cowtown. If we could beat the Yankees, that would give it to us. Respect."

David wasn't just a fan, though. He was an athlete. Ed Cone coached his son, nurtured his young career. Father and son, both of them strung tight, went at it on a baseball field on more than one occasion. There was no high school baseball field or team at Rockhurst Academy, the Jesuit school that Cone attended. David was the star quarterback there and played his baseball instead in the Ban Johnson League, a summer session for talented high schoolers and younger college kids. He found himself emulating his hero George Brett at the plate, while imitating some of the Royals' pitchers on the mound. Cone could throw exceptionally hard. At age 16, he auditioned at a local, invitation-only tryout camp at Royals Stadium. At age 18, just out of high school, he was picked in the draft by the Royals and signed by a scout named Carl Blando.

"It was incredible, a dream come true," said Cone, who also, occasionally, foolishly dreamed of being a sportswriter. "I was ready to sign the first contract they sent to me. They offered me $15,000 as a third-round draft choice. I was afraid if I didn't take it right away they would rescind the offer. I couldn't wait to get into the professional life."

Professional life wasn't altogether glamorous at first for Cone, who labored in the minors for five years. He found himself in such places as Fort Myers, Charleston, Memphis, Omaha, and Tidewater. The Royals called him up to spring training once, when he was 19, just to throw batting practice, and he actually had his first chance to meet Brett. "He didn't really know who I was," Cone said. "I think he said, 'So you're from Kansas City, that's great.' That was about it."

In 1983, just a year later, he got a fuller taste of what lay ahead. This happened in a most unfortunate way. He was pitching in a spring-training game and tried to cover home plate after throwing a wild pitch. His legs became tangled with the base runner storming in from third base and he suffered a torn anterior cruciate ligament in his left knee. Cone would miss the entire season of the Pine Tar Game. But because he lived in Kansas City, it was decided he would rehab with the major league team and use its superior facilities. That aided his recovery and his morale considerably. He got a job at a local factory that produced conveyor belts to supplement his very modest income. Cone was now also able finally to establish a real relationship with Brett, who was helpful and encouraging. His affection for the star grew exponentially. In later years, his Kansas City friends nicknamed Cone "George," because of his loyalty to the third baseman.

In 1986, finally, Cone was brought up to the big team in June for real, for the first of two short call-ups that major league players traditionally term "a cup of coffee." He appeared in 11 games altogether that season and pitched 22⅔ innings of relief. His first two outings were something of a disaster. He gave up three hits in his first and only inning against the Twins, mop-up duty. He then fared even worse three days later against Seattle, yielding seven hits and five earned runs in four and two-thirds innings of another lopsided loss. Both these games were played in Kansas City, before friends and family. The pressure was intense. Still, he was earning a big, fat $60,000 salary and Cone viewed this as his dream job.

"It was incredible," he said. "At times, I was intimidated by it, obviously. Not every kid in Kansas City gets to grow up with the Royals during his high school years, especially when they're in the playoffs every year against the Yankees, and then be a part of that team. It was surreal. I was really quiet in the locker room. I only spoke when I was spoken to. I really played the rookie role."

Again, Brett did not disappoint. He invited Cone and all the rookies out to dinner after day games on the road. He talked baseball with them. Cone was in heaven, until he suddenly was traded at the end of the next spring training to New York—the

Mets, not the Yankees. It was one of those big-package deals, a bunch of prospects and marginal players sent in two directions with the hope that one of these guys would turn out to be better than projected. Ed Hearn, a catcher acquired by Kansas City in the trade, was going to be a missing puzzle piece for the Royals, except he got hurt and never reached his potential. Only Cone did. The Royals wouldn't miss him much at first because they were stacked deep with pitching, with a surplus of talent including Danny Jackson, Bud Black, and Bret Saberhagen. "The list went on and on," Cone said. "These things are cyclical. Their number-one draft picks really worked out at the time." So this deal shouldn't have been too stunning to Cone, yet he'd never even considered the possibility of an abrupt departure. The Royals were home to him. The day of that transaction, March 27, 1987, was a devastating and scary moment for the 23-year-old pitcher.

"I'd never even been to New York," Cone said. "I was shocked. I thought I'd at least get a chance to pitch in Kansas City before I was traded. I never really did. I never really got a significant chance. I was surprised, hurt, felt rejected and very intimidated because I was going to the Mets the spring after they'd won the world championship. I thought I would be heading back to Triple A. I'd spent five, six years in the minors and I thought, 'Enough already.' Let me stay in the big leagues, in Kansas City."

Within two years, it was obvious the Royals had made a terrible mistake sending away their hometown pitcher. In 1988, Cone went 20-3 with a 2.22 earned run average for the Mets. He was an All-Star who finished third in the Cy Young voting. The whole New York experience became liberating for Cone—arguably, too liberating. The pent-up Jesuit high schooler in him suddenly displayed a wild side as he wandered into very treacherous waters. Cone drank, he chain-smoked, he played around. "Your ego runs away from you," he told *Sports Illustrated* at the time. "You start thinking, 'Hey, I've got groupies who want to sleep with me just because of who I am.' I got caught up in that." He found himself targeted by three women in an $8.1 million lawsuit claiming he threatened to kill them between games of a 1991 doubleheader.

The same women later claimed that he masturbated in front of them in the bullpen. This was unimaginably great tabloid material. Cone was brilliant, he was temperamental. During one game in 1990, he argued furiously with an umpire while two Atlanta Braves runners circled the bases and scored. He challenged his manager, Bud Harrelson, in the dugout, where they nearly came to blows.

There was no interleague play back then, so he didn't get to pitch again in Kansas City until he was traded by the Mets in August 1992 to the Blue Jays for Jeff Kent. On September 9, Cone finally returned home to face the Royals, again before friends, family, and a lot of ambivalent fans. He beat the Royals, 1–0, giving up just five hits in eight and one-third innings. This was all a bit more than Ewing Kauffman could stand. As a true-blue Kansas City man, the aging owner had real problems with how his own organization had dealt away a great hometown product that it had discovered and developed. When Cone became a free agent after the 1992 season, Kauffman spoke with Cone, told him he was the only pitcher the Royals were targeting. The owner said he would present an offer when Cone "can sit in a room with me and look me in the eye and tell me you want to come home." Kauffman met with the pitcher, told Cone that trading him was the worst move he'd ever made, and signed him to a very different sort of contract than the $15,000 deal he had received as a bonus baby. This time around, Cone would get a $3 million signing bonus, just to kick off a three-year, $18 million deal. All of Cone's behavioral transgressions with the Mets were forgiven. "He basically said, 'Here, take my money,'" Cone said. Needless to say, Cone forged fond memories of Mr. K, who would die less than eight months after completing this deal. "A remarkable man, and the Royals' organization hasn't been the same since he passed away. He was always trying to make the Royals better, bidding on free agents whenever he could. He was always into building the franchise and building the community around. He left his entire wealth to charity in a trust, which tells you what kind of man he was."

Cone settled back into Kansas City life, bought himself Bret Saberhagen's old house for $250,000, a place that might have cost him a million dollars in New York. He pitched two successful years in Kansas City, though the times for baseball were so generally sour that it tainted his tenure there. In 1994, Cone was on his way to a potential Cy Young season, with a 16-5 mark and a 2.94 earned run average in just 23 appearances. Then the players went on strike, the season never resumed, and everything changed. Kauffman was no longer around to pay the bills and the Royals started dumping salaries. They traded Cone, a premier pitcher, back to the Blue Jays at the start of the 1995 season for three long-shot prospects. When Toronto fell out of the American League East race by July, the Jays in turn traded Cone and his salary to the one team that never blinked at such contract numbers, the Yankees.

Here, finally, the Kansas City native found himself in the most traitorous of positions. On April 22, 1996, Cone returned to what was now called Kauffman Stadium, or "The K," to pitch for the Yankees against the Royals. When he took the mound, the sound system graciously blared "Welcome Back, Kotter." He was an established pitcher by then, prepared for such a moment, yet the nerves showed in front of the old gang. Cone walked five batters, allowed four hits, and gave up two runs in a five-inning stint during the Yanks' 6–3 victory. Cone was the winning pitcher. He felt no guilt over the final result. "Wasn't my fault," Cone said. "They were the ones who traded me." Broke his heart twice.

# 8

## The Screw Turns

*"Everyone talks about the Red Sox, but those play-offs against the Royals were as nerve-wracking games as we ever had. We had knock-down, drag-outs. We fought all the time. We didn't like each other. Those guys played real well on turf and it was not easy playing there. Everybody forgets now about that rivalry, but if those games had been in the World Series, they'd be some of the most famous games in baseball history."*
—Willie Randolph

If the 1976 American League Championship Series had been unmatched in its wrenching plot twists, then the 1977 ALCS was arguably even more heartbreaking for loyal supporters in Kansas City. By now, the Royals felt they truly belonged. They had finished the regular season with 102 victories and the best record in baseball. Their staff ERA of 4.02 was tied with the Yankees for best in the American League. Their offense was a neat balance of power and speed. Whitey Herzog and hitting coach Charley Lau had installed their version of "Whiteyball," not that much unlike Billy Beane's more renowned "Moneyball" that was to follow two decades later. The two men emphasized patience, pitch count, and on-base percentage for batters. The Royals had fully earned the home-field advantage in this best-of-five rematch against the

Yanks, and the two teams split 10 games during the year. About the only thing the Royals lacked was a reliable closer like Sparky Lyle, and that shortfall ultimately would prove their undoing.

When the series started this time in the Bronx, the Royals wasted no time in knocking around the sore-shouldered starter, Don Gullett. Hal McRae ripped a two-run homer in the first inning. Freddie Patek added two runs in the second on a double and then John Mayberry slammed a two-run shot in the third for a six-run lead and an eventual 7–2 victory. Since the final three games of this best-of-five series would be played in Kansas City, Game 2 quickly became a must-win for the Yankees. Once again, the Royals went ahead early with a run in the third off Ron Guidry. Cliff Johnson homered in the fifth and Bucky Dent's single gave the Yanks the lead. The Royals tied the game in the sixth when McRae clobbered Randolph at second base to break up a potential double play on Brett's grounder, allowing Patek to score. McRae somehow had the foresight to know this ground ball was coming. Even before Brett's bat struck baseball, McRae was waving his arms around at the runner at second, Patek, instructing him to go home on the next play. It worked for the Royals, but the roughhouse play seemed to awaken the slumbering Bombers, who scored three runs in the bottom of the inning and won Game 2, 6–2, on Guidry's three-hitter. "Turned the whole game around," Thurman Munson said about the play at second. Randolph remembers it as good, hard Yankees-Royals baseball.

"He threw me a freakin' rolling body block," Randolph said. "He slid, rolled, and almost knocked me into left field. And then they called the guy safe. But we knew and understood they would come after us like that. They were not gonna take any prisoners. When stuff like that happened, it happened. And Frank White understood if the situation then came up the other way, he was gonna get it right back. That was unspoken. That was just the way guys played. They came in on you hard, especially in a game like that with so much at stake. McRae had played with the Big Red Machine teams in Cincinnati and had that National League attitude. A lot of the Royals did. George Brett was the same way. Reggie Jackson was like that for us."

The play soon produced yet another new rule change, this one to discourage base runners from bowling over infielders. Rule 7.09 (h), amended in 1978, became unofficially referred to as the "Hal McRae Rule." Randolph, these days, prefers to call it the "Randolph Rule." It seemed every time the Yankees faced the Royals, the rule book changed. This time, league governors decided that no longer would base runners be permitted to travel well past or alongside the bag to nail infielders and prevent relay throws, which in turn forced obvious phantom force plays, or those so-called neighborhood plays.

Randolph resolutely denies he ever was guilty of such short-cuts—though nobody really could blame him, after watching some of the mean, purposeful slides that came his way. "No way," Randolph said, about cheating around the bag. "My force-outs, my double plays, I never went anywhere. I straddled the bag. On the double plays, I was so quick with my arm, I didn't have to cheat. I could stand flat-footed. I was good at getting rid of the ball from the football games I played growing up. I'd go straight up over the bag, come down, and give 'em an elbow or spike 'em—unintentionally, of course. Underneath me wasn't a good place to be. I cut Ozzie Guillen once, stepped on his hand. I think the neighborhood play, that actually started later, when guys were getting away with a little more and the umpires got a little lazier."

McRae's slide at second base just fueled existing resentments. Martin, who had always played the game in the same fashion, insisted McRae's slide was a cheap shot. "When that happened to me as a player I put the ball in the man's face," Martin said. "Randolph didn't do that because he's a gentleman." Herzog shot back, simply, "Martin is full of it." McRae did not apologize one bit. If he wanted to hurt Randolph, he said, he would have cut him around the knees.

In any case, the slumbering Yankees had stirred, even if their left-handed power hitters remained largely neutralized. Once again, Brett made a costly error that allowed two more Yankees to score and put away the game. He would make five errors in the 10 games during the 1976 and 1977 series against New York.

While nobody could ever call into question his Hall of Fame credentials at the plate—"George Brett could fall out of bed on Christmas morning and hit a line drive," John Schuerholz once said—Brett's fielding stats, and his arm in particular, were fairly ordinary. He threw himself at the baseball with abandon at the hot corner, giving up his body when required, yet won only one Gold Glove in 21 years of infield work, most of it at third base. Sabermetrically speaking, his career Rtot/year (total zone, total fielding runs above average per 1,200 innings) ultimately hovered near zero, or average. Although Brett was a combined 14 for 38 from the plate during the 1976 and 1977 ALCS, there is an argument to be made, yet one that is made rarely, that his play at third base may have cost the Royals one or both series.

The 1977 series, tied at one game apiece, moved back to Kansas City for Game 3, and the Yankees now needed to win two of three on the road, on artificial turf. You could often gauge how serious the Yanks were about road games by their evening and late-night habits. During regular-season games in Kansas City, the visitors would often go out to dine and eat heavily at Gates Bar-B-Q, open until midnight on weekends. But the team stayed away from the ribs and sauce during this particular trip. Such abstinence did not immediately pay dividends. Another pitching gem from Dennis Leonard, a four-hit complete game, gave the Royals a 6–2 win and a 2-1 series lead. The Royals were once again within a single victory of their first World Series, with Gura on the mound for Game 4. The Yankees were clinging to a one-run lead with two outs in the fifth, when Martin pulled off one of the most unconventional moves in his idiosyncratic career. He brought in his closer, the Cy Young winner Sparky Lyle, and let him pitch the final five and one-third innings. "I wanted my best pitcher out there," Martin said. This was simply not Lyle's role, yet the reliever somehow managed to allow only two hits and avoid any run-scoring threat over an uncustomary, grueling stretch. Lyle had pitched two and one-third innings the day before in Game 3 and been hammered by the Royals. He'd only gone this long before in emergency, extra-inning situations. Still, years later, after his own lengthy and successful managing career with the minor league Somerset Patriots in New Jersey, Lyle looked back and said he was more than up for the task.

"It didn't matter," Lyle said. "I was ready to go. One of the funny things about that day was, when I was warming up in the bullpen, Billy had called to the coaches there and wondered how I was throwing. And they told him, 'He couldn't get his grandmother out.' So he asked me how I was feeling and I said, 'I feel fine.' Billy said, 'Well, they said you couldn't get your grandmother out,' and I said, 'Well, I'm not facing her.' Back when I pitched a lot of innings in a row, I never tried to overthrow. I just went out there with what I had and made sure I made the pitch. You hear people tell you all the time, it's not how hard, it's where."

Lyle, like Mariano Rivera years later for the Yankees, was a classic closer, brought into games to the delight of fans with an accompanying personal musical number. Rivera's intro was "Enter Sandman." Lyle's was "Pomp and Circumstance." Like Rivera, too, Lyle really only used one pitch. Rivera had the cutter. Lyle employed the slider. Theoretically, he also had a fastball in his arsenal that could top off at around 90 miles per hour, and a lot of batters were waiting on that, sure that Lyle would eventually have to try his straighter pitch if he fell behind in the count. They usually waited forever, because Lyle threw strikes. "They always thought I was going to try to trick 'em, and I never did," Lyle said. "I had too much respect for every hitter I faced to jack with them. Just get 'em out, let 'em think they just missed something, they're gonna get me next time." He threw sliders to the weakest hitters, and he threw sliders to the George Bretts of the world. "I threw that slider in the same spot all the time. I'm thinking I really don't have to move this thing around, because it's off the right knee of a right-handed hitter and it's down and away to a left-handed hitter. Whoever's playing left field I'd just have him play in a little in case they did whack it out there and that made my control really, really good because I'm throwing it to one spot. Muscle memory, that's all it is, and making sure it broke."

That sort of repetitive behavior didn't really allow for much managing from Martin, who fancied himself a pitch caller, among many other things. Normally, Munson wouldn't even bother to signal for a particular pitch or location when Lyle was on the mound. On one occasion, however, after a batter had fouled off several sliders, Lyle was stunned to see his catcher put down a single finger, signaling for a fastball. Lyle shook it off. Munson signaled fastball again. Lyle shook it off. This time, Munson crouched and used his index finger to point sideways toward the dugout, meaning it was Martin who was calling for the fastball. Lyle stepped off the rubber and screamed toward the dugout, "No!"

Martin was not Lyle's favorite manager, in any case. The pitcher much preferred his experiences with Ralph Houk and Dick Williams. "Billy, oh, my God," Lyle said. "There were times I'd hear him talking to a guy who wasn't playing and he'd just promise him the world and had no intention of giving it to him. That was Billy's downfall, and he was like that his whole freakin' career. Nobody knew about it, until you played for him. I'd say it was probably sixty-forty in the clubhouse, guys who liked him and guys who didn't. But forty is a big number. Nettles loved him. Billy left him alone. But scuttlebutt would start going around the clubhouse that he'd tell guys, 'You're gonna be in there tomorrow . . .' Then the guy comes in, he's all jacked up, and Billy had no intention of playing the fucking guy. And maybe he was half drunk that night and forgot about it. Who knows? He'd be blistered."

Most people shared this ambivalence, never knowing if they were getting the charming Billy, the caring Billy, the crude, drunken Billy, or the two-faced Billy. As Marty Appel, the former Yankees public relations man wrote in his memoir, *Now Pitching for the Yankees*, "We never had a bad word between us, and I thought he liked me, but I often had a feeling that as I turned my back to exit his office, he might be smiling at someone else in the room and mouthing, 'What an idiot.'"

Despite his own disdain for the manager, Lyle became Martin's savior in this 1977 series against the Royals. "I was the sort of player, I'm gonna play hard, I don't care if I can't stand the son of a bitch," Lyle said. The reliever nearly hadn't been a Yankee that season after a contractual war with Steinbrenner. Only Ron Guidry's failure to show much talent or desire for the role of closer forced the owner to re-sign Lyle to a three-year, $425,000 deal. In 1977, for about $142,000, he appeared in 72 games, went 13-5, posted a 2.17 ERA with 26 saves, and won the Cy Young award. In Game 4, he just kept getting more effective as the game grew older. "I pitch better the longer I go because my arm gets tired," Lyle said. "When I'm too strong, I try and muscle the ball and you can't muscle that slider. When you do that, it straightens out."

Lyle's unreal performance set up another climactic Game 5 on a Sunday night, with Paul Splittorff on the mound against Guidry, starting on only two days' rest for the first time in his career. When both managers posted the starting lineups, two of the biggest sluggers in the game were missing. Herzog was furious at his first baseman "Big John" Mayberry, who had shown up late for Game 4, violating the manager's cardinal rule: "Show up on time; be ready to play." Mayberry reportedly had been up late the previous night partying, and his play then reflected it. According to Julia Kauffman, people in the organization suspected his problems were due more to drugs than to alcohol, but covered it up. "One of the few times people with the Royals lied about something to the public," she said. Mayberry had struck out twice in Game 4, dropped a foul pop from Mickey Rivers, and bungled a simple relay to first. Herzog replaced Mayberry, finally, in the top of the fifth with John Wathan.

Martin, being Martin, did something even more outrageous. In the biggest game of the season, he benched his star, Reggie Jackson, who was battling a 1-for-15 slump, and replaced Mr. October with Lou Piniella in right field. Martin said he didn't like Jackson's numbers against the left-hander, Splittorff. All Jackson had done during the 1977 regular season was hit 32 homers with 110 RBI, winning a spot on the All-Star team and finishing eighth in the American League Most Valuable Player balloting. Martin and Jackson had a famously acerbic relationship, and this was just the latest chapter.

"He hasn't been swinging well and this guy [Splittorff] has

always bothered him," Martin said. "It's not a decision I'm happy making, but I have to do it. I probably wouldn't in the World Series, but I just had to do it now. If I didn't do it for the ball-club, I shouldn't be managing." Those who knew Martin the best, the beat writers covering the Yankees at the time, gave the manager the benefit of the doubt on this unconventional move. "When Billy did something, even if he could justify it statistically, you always thought there was an undercurrent, that he was get-ting even," said *New York Daily News* reporter Phil Pepe. "But it worked for him. He managed to use Reggie at the right time. Billy was not someone who would consciously do something to adversely affect the team. He sold himself on the idea."

Martin broke the news to Jackson two hours before the first pitch, via coach Elston Howard. All things considered, Jackson demonstrated remarkable restraint in his pregame comments. "Sure, I'm surprised," Jackson said. "You've got to be down, your pride's got to be hurt. But if a man tells me I'm not playing, I don't play. I sit down and pull for the club. I'm not the boss. I'm the right-fielder—sometimes."

The game at Royals Stadium was a tight-wire emotional act from the start. Brett tripled home McRae in the first inning and slid hard into Nettles at third base. It was a standard full-out baseball play, but Nettles kicked at Brett and both benches emp-tied in a nasty melee. Brett scored on an Al Cowens grounder, and the Royals were off and running. Kansas City led 3–1 in the eighth, now within two innings of a World Series, when Martin relented and allowed Jackson to pinch-hit against reliever Doug Bird. Jackson watched one ball, fouled off two pitches, then looped an RBI single to center that cut the lead to one run and set up the outrageous ninth inning.

Herzog didn't trust his closer Mark Littell in such a dicey sit-uation. Instead he brought in starter Dennis Leonard to pitch the ninth and protect the 3–2 lead. Immediately, things began to unravel. Paul Blair's two-strike bloop to center fell in for a sin-gle and Roy White worked a walk. Out came Leonard. In came another starter, Gura. Mickey Rivers, who had stated just the day before that he wished to be traded from the Yankees, singled in the tying run, moving White to third. Out came Gura. In, finally, came Littell to face Willie Randolph. "With the count three and one, I knew Littell didn't want to load the bases for Thurman Munson," Randolph said. "I sat dead red and got the fastball I was looking for." Randolph's sacrifice liner to center scored White with the go-ahead run, and eventually Rivers scored on a Piniella grounder, and yet another bad throw from Brett.

Herzog had gone through five relief pitchers, who yielded four runs in two innings. The Yanks now led, 5–3, and Royals Stadium became a giant mausoleum. Lyle had entered the game with two out in the eighth. With the tying run at the plate in the ninth, Lyle threw yet another inside slider to Freddie Patek on an 0-2 pitch. Patek turned on the pitch, ripped the one-out grounder to third, starting a double play that ended the game and another Royals season. Randolph took the relay from Nettles, pivoted at second base (or close enough), and completed the play with a peg to Chambliss. After what McRae had done to him in Game 2, a neighborhood play was surely justifiable. Randolph insisted later that was not the case. "It was just so quick it looked that way," Randolph said. "That was an around-the-horn job. He was right on top of me." In this instance, it was the less-intimidating Frank White heading toward his knees, but Randolph was not about to take any chances. McRae and Brett were the next two batters, representing the tying and go-ahead runs. Anything might have happened, except it didn't. "I've never been as happy to turn two as I was that day," Randolph said. Patek sat famously in the dugout for several minutes, head down, inconsolable. The television cameras remained on him mercilessly and he became an iconic representation of the star-crossed loser.

Lyle was the winning pitcher for the second straight game. Steinbrenner was thrilled, effusive in his praise for the manager. "Last year in the playoffs and World Series I thought Billy was unsure of himself," the owner said. "I think the job he did in the final game against Kansas City was the finest game of managing under pressure I have ever seen."

As for Jackson and Martin, there was an eerie, temporary détente. Martin called his outfielder "a terrific man," who'd "showed me something, some kind of class." Jackson said Martin had "guts to make that move. Martin would play Hitler if he thought it would help him win." Instead, for the World Series, Martin went with Jackson, who belted three homers in the clinching Game 6 against the Los Angeles Dodgers.

# 9

## One Last Kick
## in the Pants

By now, there was understandably a wide river of frustration teeming through Kansas City when it came to the Yankees. This was not to be confused with the out-and-out hatred toward the pinstriped uniform that could be found in Boston. This was more a hair-pulling, hand-wringing affair. When the Yanks arrived for a hotel stay in Boston, the players might be greeted with profane words and gestures. When they visited Kansas City, they were still often asked for their autographs. Inside the Royals' organization, too, there was grudging respect for the Yankees' established franchise. "If you were going to have a rivalry with someone, who could be better than the Yankees?" said Dean Vogelaar, the Royals' public relations director. But there was genuine animosity brewing among the players themselves, particularly on the Royals' side, and especially from Brett. Brett would tell people back then how much he abhorred the Yankees, and he still tells them now. "To this day, whenever I see Lou Piniella, or Goose Gossage, or one of those Yankees, I tell them how much I hated those guys," Brett said.

Brett won't say that to some of those Yankees, just because he won't talk to them at all. But there was no escaping the Yankees at this time, it seemed. In 1978, the two clubs went at it yet again, a third straight American League Championship Series. In this round, the Royals were little more than an afterthought for the

Yanks, who had come back from so far behind and then won their one-game playoff against the Red Sox on Bucky Dent's homer. The Yankees led the league with a 3.57 ERA and Ron Guidry had achieved one of the greatest pitching seasons in baseball history, with a 25-3 mark and a 1.74 ERA. The Royals had remade their roster considerably from the previous season, amid some uncharacteristic controversy. Ewing Kauffman and Whitey Herzog more or less forced general manager Joe Burke to sell John Mayberry to Toronto in April. Mayberry might have hit 143 homers for Kansas City—including the last one ever slugged at Municipal Stadium in 1972—but the manager privately blamed him for losing the 1977 ALCS and, true or false, there were those background drug rumors. The Royals also released aging Cookie Rojas and made a major deal with St. Louis for closer Al Hrabosky. Andy Hassler, Jim Colborn, and Mark Littell were now all gone, too. In addition, reports surfaced about a feud between Herzog and his celebrity batting coach, Charley Lau, closely aligned with Brett. Still, this was a formidable team built on pitching, speed, and Brett's power in the middle of the lineup. Rookie left-fielder Willie Wilson stole 46 bases and the Royals led the league in doubles, triples, and stolen bases. Leonard was a 21-game winner, Splittorff won 19, and Gura went 16-4 with a 2.72 ERA. Hrabosky anchored the bullpen with 20 saves.

The new Yankees manager, Bob Lemon, faced a tactical problem: Guidry had started and thrown seven innings on three days' rest in that playoff game at Fenway Park on October 2. Now, one day later, the Yankees were opening the ALCS in Kansas City. If Guidry were to get his standard four days' rest, he couldn't start until Game 4 back in New York. If Martin were still managing, in all likelihood, Guidry would have been hurried back sooner than that. But Lemon, a former Royals manager, was in charge now and had brought with him a sense of sanity long missing from the Bronx. He had taken over from Martin in July, when the Yanks were in turmoil and making bad headlines on a daily basis. "You'd get so worn down by all the turmoil, you'd be so physically tired, and you hadn't even been playing," Lou Piniella said, about those days under Martin.

The headlines stopped almost immediately—in large part because of a New York newspaper strike that began in early August. Also, because Lemon's unflappable demeanor was the polar opposite of Martin's. Lemon's ascension was a smooth transition. He retained most of Martin's tactics and even the trappings of the manager's office. He kept the sign on the wall posted by Martin, which Martin himself never could obey: "Company rules. Rule No. 1: The boss is always right. Rule No. 2: If the boss is wrong, see Rule No. 1." Lemon tended to stick closer to a conventional script than Martin, and to avoid hasty hunches. Lemon kept to his natural rotation in the American League Championship Series, and the results did not force him to change his mind. The Yanks routed Leonard and the Royals in Game 1, 7–1, behind two-hit pitching from second-tier guys Jim Beattie and Ken Clay, taking all the pressure off the manager. Kansas City evened things with an easy 10–4 victory in Game 2, and then the whole series spun on Game 3 in New York, Paul Splittorff against Catfish Hunter. Instead of the expected pitching duel, this quickly became a mano a mano affair between Brett and Reggie Jackson. Brett, recovering from an early bout of hemorrhoids, ripped three successive solo homers off Hunter, while Jackson hit a home run, an RBI single, and a sacrifice fly—all off Splittorff, the pitcher whom Jackson supposedly couldn't hit. The Yankees entered the eighth inning with a 4–3 lead and Lemon went to Gossage, who had taken over the closer role so effectively from Lyle during the season. This transition had been awkward, to say the least. Steinbrenner signed Gossage as a free agent in November 1977, only one month after Lyle had bailed out the Yankees against the Royals and was awarded the Cy Young trophy. Lyle was a 33-year-old lefty. Gossage was a 26-year-old righty. On paper—and on paper only—this was the perfect one-two bullpen punch. Gossage had gone from earning $46,800 with the Pirates to signing a six-year contract with the Yanks worth more than $1 million per season.

"I was driving cross-country and heard the news on the radio, somewhere between Arizona and New Jersey," Lyle said. "There was some giant-assed storm chasing me so it wasn't like I could pull off. If I hadn't won the Cy Young the year before, I don't think anything'd be said. George thought he was going to have the best righty-lefty combination in the big leagues, which on paper you would say yes. But when you have two relievers who are used to being in 70-plus games every year, one of 'em's not going to get those innings. And Goose and I were both the same type of pitcher. If we didn't get work, we were horseshit. Plain and simple. Goose, even though we were friends, he didn't know what to say to me when he came to the Yanks. I told him, 'Goose, if I was in the front office and you were available, I'd have got you myself.' That was an opportunity of a lifetime, that's the way I saw it. If we're in the playoffs and we need two more outs to win and he's throwing 97 and I'm throwing an 86-mile-per-hour slider, I'm putting Goose in. I understood professional sports. As it evolved, you see how they're in love with velocity now. I knew I wasn't going to pitch much that year. Only thing I thought was, they really should have traded me first, or in spring training." Instead, Lyle would be dealt a month after the season ended, as part of a package that brought Dave Righetti to the Yanks. Nettles, as often was the case, had the last word on the Lyle trade: "He went from Cy Young to sayonara."

Lyle was a minor role player in the 1978 American League Championship Series, and he certainly wasn't going to get into this pivotal Game 3. The Royals scored two runs off Gossage in the eighth to briefly grab the lead, but Thurman Munson slammed a monster homer off reliever Bird deep into the left-center-field bullpen, ten yards past the 430-foot sign in Death Valley, for two runs in the bottom of the inning and a 5–4 victory. At age 31, after ten seasons spent crouching behind the plate, Munson's body was starting to rebel and his power was the first thing to go. He hadn't clubbed a homer in 54 games, hadn't distinguished himself at all in the series. As *Washington Post* columnist Ken Denlinger put it, "His body looks like something out of an auto graveyard and he has been a mild embarrassment behind the plate and at bat." With a man on first, the Yankee Stadium crowd was just hoping Munson wouldn't hit into a double play and would allow Jackson to get up with a man on base. In fact, the same thoughts were racing through Munson's head.

"We were joking and he said, 'Bet I hit into a double play,'" Jackson said of Munson. "I said, 'Bet you don't.'" He didn't. The pitch from Bird was custom made. The erratic reliever had fallen behind on the count, 2-0, and he simply threw a fat, high, outside fastball. After Munson circled the bases and returned to the dugout, Jackson was one of the first to greet him. The two men had certainly experienced their differences, ever since Jackson declared himself "the straw that stirred the drink." But Jackson was one of the guys on the bench to convince Munson to take a rare curtain call, and the team's most popular player received a heartwarming ovation, one of his last before a tragic airplane death the next season. Munson hadn't really spoken much to reporters all year. He suddenly opened up to the national media afterward in a gush of emotion. The ongoing newspaper strike, apparently, had revived his enthusiasm. "There's a much better feeling on this club this year," Munson said. "It comes from what we've accomplished, from the way we get along with each other in a closely knit group, from the way we know we can work things out. Last year wasn't any fun, even though we won the World Series. Now it's fun. It has nothing to do with Billy Martin. It's not because Billy's gone. It's not because Bob Lemon's here or anything like that. We just go out and play baseball. I have no animosity toward Reggie Jackson. Reggie Jackson has no animosity toward me. I have no animosity toward George Steinbrenner or anybody else. Last year, you [reporters] made such a big thing about my differences with the management and my differences with Reggie. I wasn't playing with a free mind because of the way you stirred things up. Now I'm not playing with a completely free mind because of my physical attributes, but it's fun now."

The Yankees led two games to one, with Guidry on the mound. Steinbrenner was feeling his oats, lacking any filter. He walked into Lemon's office and told his manager, "You sure are lucky. You got lucky the day you met [team president] Al Rosen and me." The Royals were in a deep hole, down two games to one, facing the best pitcher in baseball.

"Guidry is not God," Brett declared, hopefully.

Brett then went out and proved his point, leading off Game 4 with a triple to center field on Guidry's fourth pitch of the game. Brett scored immediately on a single by McRae, before Guidry became God again. He didn't give up another run. The Royals felt cheated once more in the top of the fifth inning, when Willie Wilson was called out trying to steal third base with one out. Wilson insists to this day he was safe, and that he would have scored on Hal McRae's ensuing fly ball—though, of course, there is no way of knowing whether Guidry would have given up that sacrifice fly if Wilson had been called safe. The Yanks had built a 2–1 lead on homers off Leonard by Graig Nettles in the second inning and Roy White in the sixth. White was now in the 14th of his 15 seasons with the Yankees, a man whose role with the team remains to this day greatly underrated. While toiling for many years during the Yankees' dark ages, White was consistently the epitome of professionalism, the steady outfielder who signed all the autographs, guided younger players, and more than held his own at bat. It was a very good and fair thing that his career extended into these glory seasons, and that he tasted the champagne.

A third straight pennant was not yet assured, however. When Amos Otis tomahawked a high fastball off the left-field wall for a double to lead off the ninth, Lemon visited the mound. To the very vocal displeasure of the Yankee Stadium crowd, he pulled Guidry for Gossage. The best starting pitcher in the game that season was replaced by the top reliever. Gossage required 14 pitches to set down in order Clint Hurdle, Darrell Porter, and Pete LaCock. Thousands of Yankee fans ran past guards yet again onto the field and chanted, "Red Sox suck," which seemed to diminish this series with the Royals. There had been a sense of inevitability about the result, and both sides confirmed that notion afterward.

"The third time around and I'll still be seeing the World Series in street clothes," Herzog said. "This is about the 76th time we've played since I've been here—and I think they're two up on us now. We're basically even clubs. We had a better club last year and had three [playoff] games at home. But the Yankees have signed free agents. As a consequence, they're a better team."

Gossage was brutally honest about it. "The Boston playoff was the big game of the year," he said. "We knew we would beat the Royals." The Yanks knew they'd beat the Dodgers, too, and did for their 22nd World Series championship—and their last one for quite some time.

# 10

## The Employee

For five seasons, starting in 1979, Rush Limbaugh worked with the Kansas City Royals, climbing the stubborn organizational ladder to the positions of promotions director and head of group sales and marketing. It was a slow go, actually, a far cry from his future rocket ascension in talk radio. His duties could be humiliating at times and the pay was not at all good. Limbaugh's story, to a degree, demystifies the notion that Ewing Kauffman was the perfect employer, the all-in benefactor, if only because the monetary rewards were so miserly. Still, there were elements to this job that Limbaugh greatly enjoyed, or at least that he came to feel were good for him in retrospect.

Limbaugh had grown up in the medium-sized town of Cape Girardeau, Missouri, less than two hours' drive south of St. Louis on Route 55. He was already dabbling there in radio at age 16 in 1967, using the pseudonym Rusty Sharpe. His father, an attorney, was part owner of a radio station and that connection proved enough to get Limbaugh behind the microphone. "My reason for liking radio was twofold," Limbaugh told Fox News. "I love music and I hated school. And I hated school from second grade on. I'd get up in the morning, get ready to go to school, and I would dread it. I hated it. My mother would have the radio on and the guy on the radio sounded like he was having so much fun. And I knew when his program was over, he wasn't going to go to school. So that's what I wanted to do."

By 1979, however, Limbaugh felt he'd hit something of a dead end. He was hosting a show on a small FM station in Kansas City under a new pseudonym, Jeff Christie, not making the sort of impact he'd expected. Maybe this wasn't his life's work after all. He landed a job with the Royals through a contact in the organization, and hung on for dear life.

"Those years with the Royals, they were the best five years of my life in terms of preparing me for the rest of my life," Limbaugh said, after wrapping up another radio show from his home base in Palm Beach, Florida. "It's not natural to sit in front of a glass-encased studio with a million listeners. I was learning about people back then, learning how people used radio or didn't use radio. I also learned that that type of structure wasn't for me."

His experience in many ways was typical of other employees in the organization under Kauffman. Limbaugh felt useful, felt he had a job there for as long as he wanted. He also felt grossly underpaid. The Royals did not always compensate second-tier employees up to industry standards in larger markets. Limbaugh's salary started at $12,000 and ended in 1983 at $17,000. He remembers that the director of marketing was earning around $40,000 with a car. "Nobody was getting paid much," Limbaugh said. "Upper management was doing all right." After a couple of years, he became frustrated for a number of reasons—the main reason being the number on the front of his paycheck. When friends asked him to go on a trip to Vail, a ski vacation, he couldn't afford it. Limbaugh went in to ask his boss for a $3,000 raise. He said it would make a big difference in his life. "If you want $3,000 more, then work $3,000 more," he was told. No raise. By 1982, he grew so desperate that Limbaugh very nearly accepted a marketing job for Guy's Food potato chips. That decision might have changed the course of radio talk show history. "I'm sure there are a lot of people who wish I had taken it," Limbaugh said.

He stuck with the Royals instead, tried to figure out how to sell tickets. "As a marketing guy, I was constantly studying the numbers," he said. "The big trick was once you get them to come once to your stadium, how do you get them to come out twice? I became fascinated with how the success of a team can define the whole town. When we were winning, the whole city loved us." There were problems for Limbaugh, though, besides the salary. He was in charge of the pregame ceremonies, the national anthem, the first pitch. He often had to beg players to participate in festivities that did not appeal to them. They traditionally hate that sort of thing, yet another drain on their limited free time. "The job I had was perfect for players to make fun of me," Limbaugh said. He once described his role to the radio audience as, "The front office grunt that came down and bugged 'em for autographs for sponsors, and I was the joke. Every baseball in the dugout was thrown out at me when I forgot a baseball for the first pitch one night. So, yeah, I was a lovable doofus."

He became the object of myriad practical jokes. During the 1981 playoffs, a tense time for everyone, some players told him that Dick Howser was very tight with the actor Burt Reynolds, and that Limbaugh should ask Howser to ask Reynolds to throw out the first ball. He went into Howser's office, bugged the manager about Reynolds, and Howser went ballistic, screaming and throwing things. "You think I have time now for your stupid stuff?" Howser railed. There had never been any Howser-Reynolds connection, it turned out. This was merely another cruel setup by the players.

"Rush was a good guy, just a duck out of water with us," said Dean Vogelaar, the public relations director. "In person, away from the microphone, he wasn't so sure of himself in those days. People would walk into his office, he'd have every newsmagazine spread out over his desk. Nobody really knew what to make of him." Limbaugh says he was trying to change the culture a bit. Ironically enough, he was lobbying as a progressive back then, in terms of game-time entertainment. "They were still playing organ music all the time," Limbaugh said. "I was thinking, 'You can't have some Liberace imitator as your entertainment.' I started playing R&B music and it made some people nervous. They thought the crowd in Kansas City would rather hear country. But they let me do it."

Limbaugh had virtually no interaction with Kauffman, who kept his distance from employees low in the franchise's chain of command. "He ran Marion Labs differently," Limbaugh said. "The salespeople there were pampered. They would enjoy trips to his home, have dinner with him. He didn't meet with the sales-people from the Royals. It was a strict corporate structure. But Mr. K was still seen as a beloved figure. The Kauffmans were royalty."

One time, and one time only, Limbaugh was summoned to Kauffman's ballpark suite. Nobody had any idea what this was about. Herk Robinson, Limbaugh's superior and the club's future general manager, was scared to death that Limbaugh would say or do something that might prove a disaster. "He was petrified," Limbaugh said. It turned out that Kauffman merely wanted to know whether Limbaugh thought it was a good idea to invite Pearl Bailey to sing the anthem. Kauffman was anxious that her appearance might offend people—not because she was black, but because she was so closely associated with Broadway and New York. Bailey had sung "The Star-Spangled Banner" at Shea Stadium before Game 5 of the 1969 World Series and, according to Sports Illustrated writer Paul Zimmerman, later set the all-time record for the longest version of the anthem by carrying on for two minutes, 28 seconds, before a Yankees-Dodgers World Series game in 1978. Kansas City had its own rich music tradition. Jazz artists like Count Basie and Charlie Parker either were native to the place or had come to adopt the city. Bringing a celebrity singer to Kansas City was a little like importing cheese to Wisconsin. But in this case, very good cheese. "I told him I thought it would be great, an event unto itself," Limbaugh said.

There were some considerable perks in all of this for Limbaugh. For one thing, he enjoyed an insider's vantage point whenever the New York Yankees came to town. He started his job just after the Yankees had beaten the Royals in a third straight American League Championship Series, and nurtured a large civic grudge.

"I remember it as huge, as someone from Kansas City would," Limbaugh said. "From our perspective, we're this small, Midwest town and back in the day you would look outside our stadium, past I-70, and see the livestock grazing. Now here come the big, bad Yankees. These were the Darth Vaders from the Northeast.

ABC had a contract with Howard Cosell and that just rallied the whole town against the Yankees, against Cosell. Everybody thought, 'These Yankees, they're making fun of us. They think they have better restaurants, a higher culture.' They'd come in six times during the regular season, and you could not buy a ticket. Those games were the way the Royals' organization judged itself. It was electric, exciting. The rivalry had good guys and it had villains like Reggie Jackson. Beating them was everything. When you work for a baseball team, you're usually working eighteen hours a day as the norm, and you can't wait for the season to be over. But that was not applicable in those games against the Yankees."

So he had those series with the Yankees to reward him, and Limbaugh also forged a friendship with the Royals' brightest star, George Brett. Limbaugh had come to know eccentric pitcher Nelson Briles even before hooking on with the Royals, and Briles knew Brett. Then it turned out, surprisingly, that Brett recognized Limbaugh from his Kansas City radio show. "Here I was at a Podunk radio station, but he knew me," Limbaugh said. "And it kind of evolved from there, I don't know why. Brett was always running interference for me. He treated me great. And then we would play flag football with the Chiefs' staff every Thursday, and we went out for dinner."

By the end of a very shaky 1983 season, Limbaugh was more than ready to leave, as were a lot of other employees. Kauffman had sold a chunk of the team and a drug scandal was taking hold.

"That kind of tumult was unfamiliar to everybody," Limbaugh said. "It had been a well-oiled, smooth-running machine. Sure, it had some personnel problems, but everybody liked each other, there were no problem people. It was like being on a championship team. Most people don't get to feel what that feels like. To be on the plane coming and going with these players, to be in the locker room, ninety-nine percent won't get to experience it. But then everybody started worrying about their jobs, which nobody had ever worried about before."

After 1983, Limbaugh went back to radio, to KMBZ in Kansas City, where Mormon ownership soon became uncomfortable with his brand of bombastic talk show heat. "I was breaking new ground, simple political commentary," Limbaugh said. "The local media columnist for the *Kansas City Star* was actually writing columns about me. That was considered bad, very bad, controversial. I was fired for using the word 'therefore' too often. It cluttered the minds of the listeners."

It was on to Sacramento for him then, and a very different career arc. "When I finally got to New York, Brett and the people with the Royals couldn't believe it," Limbaugh said. "They thought I was smart, maybe not in their same area of expertise. But they didn't expect this." He kept in touch with Brett. They played golf together. Limbaugh came down for Brett's final game in Arlington, Texas, on October 3, 1993. He drove to the ballpark on the team bus, then announced, "There's someone I got to see down here." He headed for the stadium suite of George W. Bush, general managing partner of the Rangers about to run for governor. Then Limbaugh talked more with Brett.

"I met a lot of people in my time," Limbaugh said of Brett. "He's one of the best."

Limbaugh, of course, went on to host his provocative, conservative syndicated radio show with audiences estimated as large as 14 million listeners nationwide. The actual numbers are hard to acquire, since Arbitron has never really measured audiences at the 600 or so stations on which he is carried. Regardless, everyone knows his name, his bellow. As Royals personnel will tell you, and as Limbaugh freely admits, nobody in Kansas City saw it coming.

"I remember him literally spelling his name out for me in the Stadium Club, where we ate," Julia Kauffman said. "He actually worked his way up to get to the promotions stuff. But he's a nice guy."

Julia Kauffman bumped into Limbaugh in New York City years later at Elaine's restaurant, at a small party. He was a famous man by then. "He treated me like I was his best friend," she said. "I remember thinking, 'You're a pretty down-to-earth guy.' I ignore the radio stuff, that's all to make money. It's bullshit, like the Kardashians, or the 'Housewives of this or that.' It's all staged."

# 11

# Can't Lose 'Em All

Something outrageous happened in 1979: The Yankees and Royals didn't play each other in the American League Championship Series. In fact, neither team won its division. These two clubs were so in sync, they both somehow shared a down season. The Baltimore Orioles ran away with the American League East, while the Yanks mourned the loss of Thurman Munson in a small-plane crash that August. The whole Yankees team assembled for Munson's funeral in Canton, where the great catcher's ornery father showed up and told anyone who would listen that he had been a better ballplayer than his son. It was a disorienting experience, and season, for everyone involved. Meanwhile, the California Angels nudged the Royals in the West by three games.

This anomaly was immediately remedied the following season, when both the Yanks and Royals put together some of their most impressive work. The Yankees, now managed by Dick Howser, won more than a hundred games with yet another strong finish. They stood at 75-50 after a 3–1 loss to Oakland on August 26. The Yanks then began a 28-9 binge that kept the Orioles at bay and obliterated everyone else in the division. Reggie Jackson batted .300, with 41 homers and 111 RBI. Tommy John (22-9) and Guidry (17-10) made for an enviable one-two punch at the top of the rotation. Maybe Guidry was no longer quite God, but now John was such an effective workhorse (he threw 265⅓ innings in 1980) that it didn't seem to matter. Gossage (2.27 ERA, 33 saves) was still a reliable closer.

That didn't necessarily mean everything was roses in New York. The newspaper strike was long settled and the headlines had resumed. Howser didn't carry anyone's water and feuded quietly with Steinbrenner on a regular basis. This was different from Billy Martin's clashes with the Boss. Howser refused to suffer irrationality. He also had a significantly broader experiential background than Martin and wasn't necessarily wedded to the pinstripes. Howser had spent three years playing shortstop for Florida State University, where he twice was an All-American shortstop. "From my dad's viewpoint, he had an opportunity through higher education and he was very grateful for it, always appreciative," said Jana Howser, one of his twin daughters who became executive vice president of the National College Baseball Hall of Fame in Lubbock, Texas. He was signed by the Kansas City Athletics in 1958, and three years later was named *The Sporting News* Rookie of the Year. That first pro season, Howser also met his future wife, Michelle Metzger, whose family coincidentally were good friends with the Kauffmans. After his retirement in 1968 (when he was earning about $16,500 from the Yankees), Howser became third-base coach with the Yanks for ten seasons, from 1969 to 1978. He was then hired in 1979 to be the head baseball coach at his old school, Florida State. After one year there, Steinbrenner called Howser and asked him to return, to become manager of the Yankees.

"That wasn't an easy decision for him, going back to the Yankees and leaving Florida State," Jana Howser said. "There was a big discussion around the house." So this was a job for Howser, not a lifetime commitment, and he was more than willing to forfeit his post in the name of sanity, if push came to heave. Howser refused to order Jackson to shave his facial hair, no matter how it annoyed Steinbrenner. When the phone rang in his office after games, while the press was assembled, Howser would very publicly inform the owner he was too busy to converse. There were other things that bugged Steinbrenner about Howser, too. Big things, little things. "He was a master at getting under George's skin, taking little shots at him," said Bill Madden, the Yankee beat writer at the *New York Daily News*. When infielder Eric Soderholm got a big hit to win a game, Howser couldn't resist commenting, "There are people around here who gave up on him. I wasn't one of them." Steinbrenner, who had criticized Soderholm, took direct offense at these words as the war between owner and manager escalated. Steinbrenner also didn't like the way Howser reacted to controversial plays on the field. The owner expected his managers to charge at the umpires, literally and figuratively kick up some dust. Howser, knowing full well this rarely did any good, chose to view things more often from the dugout, a disapproving Buddha on the bench.

The Royals that season, typically, were a more collegial bunch. Jim Frey succeeded Whitey Herzog as manager and the Royals had reloaded for 1980. They played their own stretch of amazing baseball, though it arrived earlier in the season. Kansas City owned a relatively modest mark of 47-33 at the All-Star break, then went 36-11 through August 27. An eight-game losing streak in late September served as a cautionary signal, but the Royals were well ahead in the standings and Kansas City righted things by winning five of the last six games. Center-fielder Willie Wilson batted .326 with 230 hits, stole 79 bases, and scored 133 runs. He also won a Gold Glove. After all the problems the Royals had endured from erratic closers, they successfully had moved homegrown Dan Quisenberry, 27, into the critical slot. That season, Quisenberry amassed 12 victories and 33 saves out of the bullpen. Dennis Leonard won 20 games. Larry Gura, 18-10, posted a 2.95 ERA.

Brett was the biggest story of 1980, though, as he chased the .400 mark. He wasn't even close in early July, then began a hot streak for the ages. On August 17, he went four-for-four against Toronto and pushed his average to .401. Brett was still around the .400 mark through the end of the month, even as pitchers gave him little to hit. He hurt his hand in Cleveland, and a modest 4-for-27 slump in September eventually doomed the quest. But he finished the regular season with ten hits in his final 19 at-bats for a .390 average. He accomplished all this despite three visits during the season to the disabled list for nagging injuries to his heel, hand, and ankle. Brett drove in 118 runs in just 117 games, becoming the first player since Joe DiMaggio in 1948 to total more RBI than games played in a season.

All this set the stage for the fourth playoff meeting in five years between the Yankees and Royals. The patient Kansas City populace had grown understandably impatient by now. The players, too, were sick to death of losing. "They always seemed to rise to the occasion," Willie Wilson would recall. "They always got the key hit. We would hit a ball hard, but right at someone." After three successive setbacks, the slow burn was gaining heat finally. "In Kansas City, the hatred toward us wasn't as blatantly bad as it was in Boston, but they didn't like you anyway just because you beat them so often," Guidry said. "It got worse and worse the more times you went there, because you'd beaten them again the last time. And then beaten them again."

The fans demonstrated good faith nonetheless, showing up in force, 42,598 strong, at Royals Stadium for Game 1. They were rewarded with a blowout 7–2 victory. Brett doubled off Guidry and homered off reliever Ron Davis. Gura got the win. In a best-of-five series, the Yankees very badly needed to win Game 2 on the road, and the pitching matchup favored the Royals, with Leonard against Rudy May.

There always seemed to be one particular game in these series between Kansas City and New York that determined the final result; often, it was one particular play. In 1980, that moment arrived earlier than usual in the series, in the eighth inning of Game 2. Once again, the Royals broke out in front, this time on three runs in the bottom of the third. Darrell Porter and Frank White singled, and Wilson laced a ground-ball triple off May to right field, scoring both runners. Then Wilson scored on a double by U. L. Washington. In the top of the fifth, Graig Nettles huffed and puffed his way to an inside-the-park homer before Willie Randolph doubled home Bobby Brown to make it 3–2. That set up the fateful, pivotal play in the top of the eighth, which finally would allow the Royals to push their boulder to the summit.

With one out, Randolph lined a single to right. After Leonard struck out Bobby Murcer, Bob Watson drilled a double to left. Randolph had been ordered by third-base coach Mike Ferraro to steal on that pitch. He stumbled a bit as he broke for second base, with his right foot planted awkwardly on the artificial turf and his left foot on the dirt. Ferraro waved Randolph home anyway, even though Wilson played the carom perfectly off the wall. Wilson's relay from the outfield went over the head of Washington, the shortstop, to Brett at third base. "I didn't try to throw it as hard as I could," Wilson said. "I just wanted to throw to an area." Brett fired a perfect strike to Porter at the plate. Randolph tried to knock over Porter, roll into him, to no avail. He became the third out and the Royals would win this game by a run.

As might be imagined, Steinbrenner did not take this course of events in stride. A close-up of the owner on a television broadcast showed him leaping out of his seat, screaming obscenities aimed at his coach, Ferraro. After the game, on his way to the visitors' clubhouse, Steinbrenner snapped to reporters, "My players didn't lose this one." When it was mentioned to him that Randolph had slipped on the base paths, Steinbrenner countered, "That's what the third-base coach doesn't see. He hasn't seen it all year." Ferraro insisted it was the right call, that if he held Randolph at third the Royals just would have walked the next batter, Jackson, intentionally. Statistically speaking, Ferraro was likely correct. Third-base coaches are often too cautious sending home runners from third with two outs, for fear they will be second-guessed. The odds of that runner being knocked in by the next batter are generally no greater than 30 percent, while the chances of beating a tight relay play at the plate are typically greater. Steinbrenner, however, was in no mood for statistical analysis. "Maybe they do walk Jackson, but then you've got Oscar Gamble coming up with the bases loaded," Steinbrenner said. "We're going to win this thing anyway. Kansas City is running scared."

Nobody was running scared, it turned out. Not Howser, who refused to fire Ferraro. And not the Royals, who closed out the series in Game 3 with a 4–2 road win in the Bronx for the sweep. When Tommy John left the game for Gossage with two outs in the top of the seventh, Kansas City was down a run and had Wilson on second base. An infield single by Washington moved Wilson to third and brought up Brett. In retrospect, Gossage should have been more careful with the Royals' slugger, pitched around him, and perhaps loaded the bases. Instead, the reliever went at Brett, as was his habit, as would always be his habit, and paid the steepest price: a three-run shot off a 1-2 fastball, clocked at 98 miles per hour, that sat right there in the middle of the plate. "Power versus power," Gossage said about his stubborn competition with Brett. "I like to feel I'm the best. He likes to feel he's the best. If you're gonna get beat, you can't get beat by a better guy. I mean a better hitter." Yankee Stadium grew so quiet after that homer, you could hear the number-4 train rumbling behind the outfield wall. Brett turned to Al Zych, the Royals' longtime equipment manager, who for years had been driving a beat-up 1964 Chevy. Thinking ahead finally to World Series shares, Brett told Zych, "There, Al. Now you can get rid of that piece of junk and buy yourself a decent car." Quisenberry closed out the game and the ALCS. The Royals were able to celebrate a pennant, at last, right there at home plate in the Bronx.

Minutes later, Steinbrenner was stomping around the locker room, saying over and over to the players, "Good season. Thanks a lot. See you next year." The owner gave no such assurance to the disobedient Howser, who was already thinking in terms of an exit. The manager would be coerced by Steinbrenner into staging an awkward farewell press conference and then began considering his career options. He even pondered walking away from the game for a while. Instead, he ended up in Kansas City the following season, the start of a successful managing tenure that would include a crowning championship there. "We thought he was retiring," Jana Howser said. "I remember him saying after he was fired, 'I've been fortunate to do what other people only dream of doing, and for that I'm thankful.' He never pointed a finger at anyone. Then Ewing Kauffman and John Schuerholz were calling him and talking him into unretiring."

Back in 1980, after his Yankees had lost the American League Championship Series, Howser was clearly in no panic. "I'm fairly young. I'm in good health," Howser said. "We won 103 games this year and we had a lot of injuries. We got six runs in three games in the playoffs and that's not our game." Howser and some of the players then went to pay a visit to the Royals' clubhouse. This had been a long time coming for Kansas City, and the Yanks respected that notion. "These guys went through this three times with us," Randolph said. "I've got a few friends over there. I know how they're feeling right now."

That good feeling didn't last long enough in Kansas City, and didn't quite make up for all that had come before. "Somehow, it wasn't the same as the earlier playoff years," Rush Limbaugh said. "It wasn't quite as intense, when we almost felt robbed." The Royals went on to lose the World Series in six games, to a Philadelphia Phillies team every bit as starved for a title. It was quite literally a painful series for Brett, who was suffering terribly from a case of hemorrhoids that dogged him during the season. Heading into the bottom of the sixth in Game 2 against the Phillies, he could take no more. After singling twice already in the game, he informed Frey this had become something of an emergency situation. He was replaced by Dave Chalk at third base, and then Brett immediately caught a flight back to Kansas City for minor surgery, performed by Dr. John Heryer. Brett was back in the lineup for Game 3 and hit a homer. He batted .375 for the Series. No matter. For Brett, this was still a truly humiliating experience. He prided himself on playing through pain, and on performing at his best under the greatest pressure and on the biggest stages. All prior evidence pointed to those prime-time attributes. It had taken him all these years to reach the World Series, and then suddenly he was being mocked by hecklers in Philadelphia for the cruel betrayal of a vein in his lower rectum. He tried to joke away his misery with the quip, "My problems are all behind me." It wasn't enough. Brett became the "Hemorrhoid Guy" in the minds of the ignorant, and in the small brains of casual fans who couldn't come close to spelling the word. Worse, the ailment wouldn't go away. The next February, Brett left the Royals' spring-training camp in Fort Myers, returned again to Kansas City, and underwent more surgery under Heryer's knife. Brett would hear silly jokes and taunts from hecklers for two more years, until those same fans found something else to scream about and define him.

"Every city I went to, I was the Hemorrhoid Guy," Brett said.

"And you get these people sitting by the on-deck circle, the first at-bat they don't say anything, and then they get a few beers in them and start making hemorrhoid jokes. Well, I've heard every hemorrhoid joke in the world. My best response is, 'Now I have a perfect asshole, and you *are* a perfect asshole.' But from October 1980, to July 24, 1983, that's what I heard. And then from July 24, 1983, to now, I'm the Pine Tar Guy. So it's really the greatest thing that ever happened to me. Thank you, Billy Martin. Thank you, Graig Nettles."

Not quite yet, though.

# 12

## Big Apple Circus

By 1983, the New York Yankees had devolved from the Bronx Zoo into a crass, three-ring spectacle. The stuff that went on inside Pete Sheehy's clubhouse was now beyond comprehension at times, and certainly beyond the imagination of today's fan. These events were not as mundane or uninspired as the illegal use of performance-enhancing drugs or other modern plagues. Instead, the manager, Billy Martin, smashed a urinal one day, delivered a profane threat against a reporter the next, and could soon be seen passing notes during a game to a girlfriend in the front row from the visitors' dugout. The star outfielder, Dave Winfield, killed a seagull in plain view. The owner fired the manager's best buddy for spite, in part because nobody picked up the telephone on time. On it went like this, a runaway train of a team that somehow remained in pennant contention for most of the season. Meanwhile, that 60-40 split in the Yankees' clubhouse favoring Martin in 1977, as estimated by Sparky Lyle, was now more like 40-60.

The chaos trickled down directly from the owner's box. It is true that George Steinbrenner's Yankees captured seven World Series championships, a remarkable achievement. It is often forgotten, however, that this fabled franchise under his reign suffered the longest drought without a title since Babe Ruth arrived in tidy gift wrapping from Boston. The Yanks went title-less for 18 seasons, from 1979 to 1996. In the mid-to-late seventies, the Bombers had been an oddly successful concoction of arrogance and egos. They captured three pennants in a row, two championships, and somehow emerged from all the nonsense and the noise when it mattered most. By the 1980s, though, they were nine parts lunacy and only one part winning. In 1981, the Yanks had captured the pennant, knocking off the A's in the American League Championship Series. But they blew a two-game lead in the World Series, and this infuriated Steinbrenner so much that he issued a cringe-worthy public statement: "I want to sincerely apologize to the people of New York and to the fans of the New York Yankees everywhere for the performance of the Yankee team in the World Series. I also want to assure you that we will be at work immediately to prepare for 1982." Goose Gossage heard about this statement and decided right then and there he would play out his contract and leave the Yankees after the 1983 season. He couldn't take it anymore. "I made up my mind in that '81 World Series, with George meddling," Gossage said. "He was off the charts, getting in fights on the elevator, all the distractions, yelling at Dave Righetti, 'This is the biggest game of your life, don't fuck it up!' Just leave us alone, George. I was disheartened."

The Bombers struggled to a 79-83 record in 1982 with three different managers: Bob Lemon, Gene Michael, and Clyde King. This meant, inevitably, that Steinbrenner would turn back the following season to his most poisonous and cruel addiction, Billy Martin. Steinbrenner considered Martin "a baseball genius," though he knew all too well about Martin's many problems mixing alcohol with a fabled temper. Steinbrenner felt the Yankees required shock therapy, and Martin was just the jolt needed. "Believe me, this will be different because Billy and I will communicate better with each other," Steinbrenner assured the media when he rehired Martin on January 11, 1983. Then the owner immediately rubbed salt in the agreement when he okayed a mockup of Martin screaming at an umpire for the cover of the media guide, without asking his offended manager. This was Martin's third of five stints as the Yankees' manager, and there would be big problems from the start. For one thing, Thurman Munson was gone. Even when Reggie Jackson was at his peak of self-aggrandizing behavior, Munson had held the clubhouse together for Martin, been his most loyal soldier. Now there were mostly older imports or younger Yankees who owed nothing to Martin, who were not part of his two pennant-winning seasons. Don Baylor and Ken Griffey were experienced and sophisticated enough to view Martin's shenanigans as outrageous. Here was a manager, after all, who had lost his job with the Yanks the last time around for getting into a fight with a marshmallow salesman.

Already early in the 1983 season, Martin came storming into the clubhouse one day, threatening to throw *New York Post* sportswriter Henry Hecht into the whirlpool. This was an ancient feud, dating back to Billy I and Billy II. When Martin was fired by Steinbrenner in 1978, Hecht wrote an aptly acerbic column, "Goodbye and Good Riddance," in which he called the manager "a pathetic figure, self-destructive, childish, a man who will go to pieces if he can't get another job managing." Martin on this occasion in 1983 called Hecht "a scrounge" and ordered his players not to speak any longer with the reporter. "This guy got me fired twice and he's trying to get me fired again," Martin said. "Any of you guys who talk to this little scrounge, don't talk to me."

"You can come into the clubhouse," Martin then told Hecht, "but don't try to come into my office. If you do, I'll dump you in the whirlpool. If you were a big enough man, I'd dump you right now. What do you think of that?"

"You can imagine what I think of you," Hecht answered.

"Yeah, I know," Martin said. "I read the shit every day."

Martin still had his allies in the clubhouse, chief among them Graig Nettles and Willie Randolph. The longer-serving Yankees tended to back up Martin. They remembered winning with him in 1977, and they remembered him when he was fearless and closer to the top of his game. He had demonstrated loyalty to them, too.

"It's not that Billy was the best manager I played for," Randolph said. "He was alienating his own players at the time, and there were players who hated him. I didn't think he walked on water, but he was my first big-league manager and he'd played my position and I played it like he did. He taught me a lot of things, skill-set stuff. He always protected me. Billy made us feel that it was us against the world, all the time. That's why we fought, because it was part of the team's DNA. I feel funny now when

I'm among my former teammates, because some of them will say terrible things about him and I won't. They'll say, 'How can you defend him? He was a greasy cocksucker.' To each his own, I guess. It's not that he was great, but for that one year or two he was the best manager for the team."

As Randolph wrote in his own memoir, "Some managers you win for, and some you win despite them, or maybe even to spite them. It was clear to me that Billy was devoted to the game, that he'd paid enormous personal sacrifices to it, and it just seemed to me that the universe should somehow be fair and get out of Billy's way and allow him to succeed. Billy treated me fairly, and I wanted the baseball gods to do the same."

Not everyone maintained that reservoir of goodwill for Martin. They saw him at this juncture mostly as an oft-drunken clown, a baseball man well past his prime and purpose. Almost immediately after the whirlpool threat, Baylor and Griffey talked to Hecht. They had no quarrel with the writer, and little respect for the wacky Martin. The roster was a terribly mixed bag, creating a divided locker room.

"The managers are always going to come and go before the everyday players, and we knew that," Ron Guidry said. "Billy was always tough to play for, but everybody's a professional and whenever Billy was with us, we had good competitive clubs. The trouble with Billy and Steinbrenner was that one wanted it done his way, the other wanted it the other way. It's pretty tough doing it both ways."

Because of these rifts, there were also problems with Martin's coaching staff in 1983. Steinbrenner wasn't going to let Martin run this team without tight supervision. The owner wouldn't allow Martin to appoint all the coaches, instead insisting that straight-arrow Jeff Torborg and veteran Don Zimmer be part of the staff. Martin viewed Torborg, in particular, with great suspicion, as a spy for Steinbrenner. He also resented the so-called special adviser, Clyde King, who was considered another secret agent for the owner. After a while, Martin wouldn't even speak to the club's public relations director, Ken Nigro, who wasn't sure exactly what he had said to annoy Martin. Before each game,

Nigro would have to get the lineup from Torborg instead of the manager. "Might have been one comment I made about Bert Campaneris," Nigro said looking back about this one-sided feud.

Martin became isolated in a bunker of his own making. He trusted virtually nobody on the staff except his former teammates, Yogi Berra, the first-base coach, and Mickey Mantle, who would pop in during spring training as a celebrity instructor. Martin also had one other tried-and-true ally in the clubhouse, Art Fowler, a journeyman relief pitcher in the fifties and sixties and his longtime drinking buddy. Fowler followed Martin around as the pitching coach wherever Martin was hired, beginning with the Twins in 1969. Fowler was there by Martin's side in Minnesota, Texas, New York, and Oakland. In good times and bad, in bars and in the dugouts, Fowler was Smee to Martin's Captain Hook. But in New York, where Steinbrenner called the shots, Fowler's job security was forever in question. When the owner wanted to punish his manager, he would simply dump Fowler, at least for a while.

On top of such unhelpful staffing matters, Martin's personal life was not at all in order. "Billy was on the verge of a nervous breakdown that whole season," *New York Daily News* beat writer Bill Madden remembered. The manager was married at the time to his third wife, Heather Ervolino, yet that proved to be a relatively brief commitment and Martin was not a faithful husband by any stretch.

The 1983 season was surely eventful, and Martin would be a big part of virtually every tabloid headline. The team was in transition yet again, not necessarily in a good way. "I remember early on, not a lot was going on with us on the field," Guidry said. "It was fun watching Don Mattingly and Dave Righetti start to develop, but that was about it." The starting rotation that season would include Bob Shirley (5.08 ERA), Jay Howell (5.38), and Matt Keough (5.17). By early June, the Yanks were mired in a slump and appeared to be slipping out of the pennant race. Steinbrenner ordered a mandatory workout for his players, a decree that Martin ignored. The manager instead suggested only a voluntary session, and put his least favorite coach, Torborg, in charge of the nonevent. In Milwaukee on June 11 during a 6–2 loss that dropped the Yanks to 29-27, matters unraveled terribly. Martin sat on a towel on the top step of the dugout, near the corner, so he could pluck notes from the sandal of his girlfriend and future wife, Jill, sitting nearby in the stands and wearing a yellow sundress. Martin hardly seemed to notice that his starter, Guidry, was getting lit up in the fourth and sixth innings. This scene created a real problem for Don Carney, the producer in charge of the WPIX–Channel 11 Yankee broadcasts. Carney did not wish to put this spectacle on television back home in New York, and ordered cameras to point away from Martin as often as possible. Martin's unprofessional, lovestruck behavior continued the next day, another loss in Milwaukee. Eventually, inevitably, reluctantly, this misbehavior was reported by the writers covering the team. Madden went to Steinbrenner for comment, and the owner suggested he would likely replace the popular manager with the even more popular Yogi Berra, defusing potential fan anger. When Martin discovered that Madden had written about the incident, he could be heard screaming in the clubhouse about the reporter, "Does he know I'm married? I'm married!"

This nonsense was almost immediately followed by a urinal-smashing tantrum by Martin in Cleveland during a 9–6 loss on a Tuesday night. It happened during his angry foray into the clubhouse in the fifth inning, with the Yanks down 6–1 and the stupid urinal staring Martin defiantly in the face. "None of the players did it," Martin later confessed. "I called [Indians owner] Gabe Paul and offered to pay for it." Steinbrenner flew into Cleveland two days later to confer with Martin and his agent, Eddie Sapir, amid rumors that this was a pro forma firing ritual, and that Berra would be installed. Martin somehow survived—maybe because the Yanks routed the Indians in the last two games of the series, or maybe because Sapir was a master of pouring cold water on Steinbrenner's steaming cerebrum. Martin merely promised Steinbrenner he would stop the silliness and instill discipline in this faltering team. Camera crews at the Stouffer Hotel who were waiting to report on the manager's demise were treated instead to Sapir's declaration, "Reports of the girl were unfounded! Billy has been vindicated!" Steinbrenner insisted on his pound of flesh, however. He fired Art Fowler, Billy's running mate. Torborg would now share pitching coach duties with Sammy Ellis, an unusual and awkward platoon.

The sacking of Fowler set the scene for the next ugly event, on June 17, when the club returned to Yankee Stadium for a three-game stand against the Brewers. Martin was fuming about Fowler's dismissal and, by the look and smell of him, had done some serious drinking before arriving for work in the afternoon. When he emerged from his office into the clubhouse, he spotted a young woman intern from the *New York Times*, Deborah Henschel, the only reporter there. She was in the wrong spot at the wrong time, for sure, and Martin reportedly delivered some vile sexual insults at her. Henschel and the *Times* corporate relations department protested to Steinbrenner, who then launched his own investigation.

This was a farcical adventure, the height of insanity, in what soon became known in the *Village Voice* as the "anterior/posterior" probe. Steinbrenner summoned three witnesses to testify about Martin's clubhouse tirade, with the aim to discover exactly which insult Martin had hurled. If Martin had told Henschel to perform fellatio on him, Steinbrenner would fire the manager and make Berra the manager. If, however, as Martin claimed, he had merely told Henschel that "the *New York Times* can kiss my ass," or perhaps, "Get your ass out of here," then all would be forgiven. George Frazier, the pitcher, Mark Letendre, a trainer, and Zimmer were in the clubhouse at the time. They told Steinbrenner what they heard, or what they thought they heard, or what they thought Steinbrenner wanted them to have heard. Zimmer mostly confessed he hadn't heard anything, because he was at the other end of the room. Clearly, there was no cause for Henschel to lie about such a thing. In any case, Steinbrenner absolved Martin. The triumphant manager sat with reporters the next day and further disparaged the poor young victim: "She was dressed like a hussy, with a slit in her dress up to her ass," he said.

Ugh. It was awful, but Martin still had a job and the season sputtered forward, even picking up steam. The Yankees actually started to win some games. On the Fourth of July, which also happened to be George Steinbrenner's 53rd birthday, Dave Righetti threw a no-hitter, the first by a Yankee since Don Larsen's perfect game during the 1956 World Series. The Yankees were the Yankees again, sort of, hanging around near the top of the American League East.

# 13

## When the Royals
## Were Not So Royal

Nobody's perfect, not even those exemplary, steady Kansas City Royals. The 1983 season was hardly the Royals' finest hour, scandalized from start to finish, almost Yankee-like in flavor. The previous off-season had begun ominously enough for Dick Howser and his batting coach, Rocky Colavito, who were both sentenced to 90 days in jail by a local municipal court judge, Leonard S. Hughes. This unlikely development occurred because of an incident back on August 19, 1982, when Colavito was leaving Royals Stadium around 11:00 p.m. after a conventional 3–0 victory over the White Sox. The Kansas City coach was driving with his teenaged son when his car was struck by another auto leaving the parking lot. Colavito and the other driver, David Roach, began arguing. Howser, following in his own car, joined what became a heated shoving match as two local policemen arrived on the scene. This at the time made quite the splash in Kansas City, and Ewing Kauffman was not thrilled at the fuss when he read about it in the newspaper. He called Dean Vogelaar, the Royals' public relations director, and set up a meeting with Howser for 8:30 the next morning in the owner's office at Marion Labs. Vogelaar accompanied the chastened manager into Kauffman's office and prepared to leave the two men there. Kauffman told Vogelaar to stay. "This won't take long," Kauffman said, before turning to Howser. "Dick, I have been reading about my manager on pages other than in the sports section. I don't like to read about my manager on those pages. Do you understand?"

Howser said he did, in fact, understand. This had been even a greater embarrassment to him than it had been to Kauffman.

"Okay, let's talk about the club," Kauffman told Howser. The dress-down required all of thirty seconds. Kauffman's message had been delivered and Howser would not repeat such an indiscretion.

Eventually, after the Royals finished their 1982 season in second place, Howser and Colavito went to court. They were charged and found guilty of interfering with a police officer after a traffic accident, though their attorney, Michael Waldeck, argued they were actually victims of overzealous enforcement. Howser was fined $100; Colavito, $250. Roach was originally charged with drunk driving, according to the Associated Press, though that charge was dropped when he agreed to attend an alcohol-counseling program. This was, clearly, a different, more lenient time in regard to DUIs. Howser and Colavito appealed their sentences and had them reduced to six months' probation. So the manager and his batting coach actually began the 1983 season on probation, which hardly represented the customary, family-friendly image preferred by this franchise.

That blip, unfortunately, was just the beginning. Troubles dogged the Royals on and off the field. The roster and the organization had collected a surprising number of oddball characters. Some of them were benignly quirky, others poisonous. The future Hall of Famer and full-time operator, Gaylord Perry, fell into the former category. Still full of silly mischief, Perry had signed as a free agent with the Royals after his release from Seattle on July 6 at the age of 44. If only his Vaseline balls were the Royals' biggest problem, the club would have been just fine. But there were many other more serious sporting and ethical setbacks.

Brett, red hot at the time, suffered a broken toe on June 7 and went on the disabled list for three weeks. Kansas City slumped during a 10-16 stretch in June and July. Howser juggled his outfield, tried to shake things up. Wilson, still a swift base stealer but not quite the same force at the plate, was shifted to center field and fractured a knuckle in August. Amos Otis went to right field and became little more than a part-timer. Pat Sheridan and Leon Roberts platooned in left. The reliable middle infielders Frank White and U. L. Washington struggled at the plate. White's batting average dropped 38 points from 1982. Shortstop U. L. Washington's average plummeted 50 points. The starting rotation wasn't very good after the club's ace, Dennis Leonard, went out for the season with a knee injury on May 28. Larry Gura's earned run average rocketed to 4.90 and he lost 18 games. The greatest disaster of all, though, was Vida Blue.

Blue, a popular Cy Young and Most Valuable Player winner for the Oakland A's in his prime, was acquired in March 1982 in a multiplayer deal with the San Francisco Giants. Kauffman had coveted Blue for years, tried to pry him from Charlie Finley. But this was no longer the same electric starter who'd won 107 games over six seasons for the A's. It was one trade Schuerholz would have loved to take back. He gave up Atlee Hammaker, who in 1983 posted the best earned run average, 2.25, in the National League. Blue, meanwhile, was effective enough during his first season in Kansas City, then fell apart in 1983. He was 0-5 with a 6.01 ERA in 19 appearances, including 14 starts. Worse, much worse, Blue, plus stalwart Wilson, outfielder Jerry Martin, and first baseman Willie Aikens, became the targets of a federal drug probe during the season involving as many as ten Royals. Suddenly, Kauffman's Disneyesque franchise had turned into something dark and troubled.

"When the scandal broke, the law enforcement officials addressed our club during the 1983 season," Vogelaar said. "The real impact didn't hit until after the season, when they were charged. John Schuerholz dealt with it every single day, until we got to spring training the next season. It was a very un-Kansas-City-like year for us."

This was 1983, not 1998, so the federal investigation into the Royals' clubhouse had nothing to do with steroids or any other performance-enhancing drugs. Instead, it focused on the use and distribution of cocaine—a scourge that haunted most major sports in the eighties. Cocaine use among athletes would gain tragic infamy with the death of Maryland basketball star Len Bias in 1986. The National Basketball Association, in particular, was enduring troubles along this line and instituted a stringent drug program as part of an agreement between the owners and players' association. Black athletes, fairly or not, were facing a real image problem.

Blue was something of a tragic figure in this regard, an unfortunate pioneer blazing the wrong trail for other immensely talented, addictive personalities who were to come, such as Darryl Strawberry and Dwight Gooden of the Mets. Blue had been one of baseball's great attractions in his day, with Oakland and then with San Francisco. He could throw a baseball 100 miles per hour, his curveball was very nearly unhittable, and he was a charismatic charmer. "Blue throws smoke, and he throws it for strikes," Joe DiMaggio once said after watching him pitch in Oakland. "What more does he need?"

He required money, for one thing. With the A's, Blue battled the skinflint owner Charlie Finley for years over salaries, until Finley tried to sell him to the rich Yankees in 1976 and trade him to the Reds in 1977. During those two seasons, Blue was earning a yearly salary under $150,000 (he was paid only about $28,000 when he won the Cy Young award in 1971). Commissioner Bowie Kuhn vetoed both deals, saying they would be bad for baseball. By the time the Royals finally obtained Blue, he was heavily into cocaine and had been for some time, according to his own, later accounts. Eventually, as a result of investigations, he pleaded guilty to a federal misdemeanor charge of possessing cocaine and would spend three months in a Fort Worth, Texas, correctional facility. "Getting involved in drugs was bad judgment, the worst mistake I ever made," Blue said. He later testified in the Pittsburgh drug trials of 1985, in which seven men were found guilty of distributing cocaine and such famous players as Willie Mays and Willie Stargell were mentioned in testimony for allegedly handing out amphetamines.

Wilson reported that he tried cocaine for the first time around November 1982, introduced to the euphoric drug by Blue, whose connection was a local fan, Mark Liebl. There was a big party scene back then in the wealthy neighborhoods around Kansas City, with high-powered professionals coming and going. The players themselves didn't really snort cocaine together; the social pairings were almost random. Doctors with lawyers. Lawyers with ballplayers. Wilson said his flirtation with the drug lasted a short time, just over the winter and not into the busy spring-training season. But then a former teammate, the late Al Cowens, asked Wilson to score some drugs for him, and Wilson obliged—or tried to oblige. He called Liebl, who told Wilson he couldn't help the player. Investigators had tapped Liebl's phone. Wilson's 20-second call would prove to be his legal undoing. He first got a clue of this on July 25, the day after the Pine Tar Game, when he was heading to a doctor's appointment back in Kansas City for an examination of a sore shoulder that was hurt during the Sunday game against the Yankees. The road trip was done, the pine tar repercussions were just starting to take root. Suddenly, Wilson was pulled over in his car by two members of the Kansas Bureau of Investigation in a dark sedan who demanded to know whether he knew Liebl. Wilson pleaded ignorance and the two men told him they would keep in touch. Later in the day, Wilson heard on the radio that several Royals were being investigated for drugs, and that one of them was a "superstar." Wilson remembered thinking, naively, "Who is the superstar?" It was him, of course. Wilson would come to understand later that Blue, not Liebl, had been caught first and turned on everybody else. Liebl pleaded guilty to distribution charges and served nearly two and a half years in a Fort Worth correctional facility. Blue eventually apologized to Wilson, who forgave the pitcher. At the time, the outfielder figured he would get probation and a fine, nothing serious. That was typical in these cases. After all, he hadn't actually obtained any drugs during the phone call.

That's not how it turned out. The judge in the case, Federal Magistrate J. Milton Sullivant, delivered a stern sermon to Wilson, the 1982 batting champion, about his "special place in our society," then sent him to prison for 90 days on the misdemeanor drug charge of attempt to possess. The outspoken Wilson was not happy with the sentence, or with the judge's sermon. "That's a responsibility I never asked for," Wilson said. "I didn't sign a contract to take care of anybody else's kids or to be a role model for anybody else."

After serving 81 days in jail, waxing and washing floors, avoiding further trouble, Wilson was released and a bit more remorseful. "I hated the way it came out, like I was a junkie in the street," he said. "I made one phone call, and that was it. I'm not saying I didn't try [cocaine], but I was not on it when the thing was going on. But it was still my fault. I'm not mad at the judge, he was doing his job. I'm not mad at the FBI. They were doing their job. It was basically my fault. Once I figured that out in prison, I was all right."

The Royals had no patience for this scandal, certainly not with Blue, a relatively new arrival. He wasn't a homegrown star and he really couldn't pitch very well anymore. "Dad didn't have any tolerance for drugs," Jana Howser said. "None of us in the family did." Schuerholz released Blue on August 5, 1983. Jerry Martin was also released, and spent 90 days in a federal penitentiary. The Royals would trade Aikens to Toronto after the season. Wilson, however, was a mainstay in his eighth season with the Royals. Nobody really knew what to do with the star outfielder, least of all Kauffman. The owner understood about parking-lot brawls and batting slumps. He could deal with those. The prescription drug magnate, however, couldn't wrap his mind around cocaine use quite so easily.

Kauffman very much wanted to forgive Wilson, however. Though he was still suspended from baseball, Wilson would be invited to spring training in 1984. Kauffman instructed him to bring his whole family. There was one uncomfortable meeting among Kauffman, Wilson, and Wilson's wife. Kauffman told Wilson that the other players involved in this scandal were no longer Royals. "Here is what I'm going to do," Kauffman said to Wilson. "I'm going to give you a new contract. But . . . if . . . you . . . ever . . . do . . . that . . . again, you will feel the wrath of Mr. K." Eventually the Royals welcomed their outfielder back to the team in May 1984, after his one-year suspension was lifted by Bowie Kuhn.

Wilson would tell people his brief drug experimentation phase was due to the pressures of the sport and the constant public spotlight. He'd struck out twelve times in the 1980 World Series. He was skewered in 1982 for sitting out the last day of the season to protect his batting-title lead over Robin Yount. "Before I played baseball, I never smoked or drank or took drugs," he told *Sports Illustrated*. "People think the game is glamorous, but I never wanted the attention—good or bad."

This mess was all brewing in the background in 1983, not made public yet, but the organization was freaking out a bit. Dan Quisenberry, the team's prolific closer and joker, would quip at the end of the season, "I'm surprised we didn't make more trades with the Yankees. Half our players are already in stripes." Kauffman decided to be proactive about the whole sordid affair. He began plans for a program, Project Choice, which he would found for the city's public school kids. Students at Westport High School, and some select students at other city schools, were asked to sign a contract to promise they would stay off drugs, avoid teenaged pregnancy, maintain decent grades, and graduate on schedule. If they stuck to the bargain, Kauffman would pay their college tuitions. It was a wonderful idea, accomplishing a great deal to clear the team's image in the minds of local residents, and it changed the dialogue during coming years. In the summer of 1983, however, when the Royals headed to Yankee Stadium for a four-game set, there was little but scandal and frustration fermenting in the bowels of the franchise.

# 14

## The Talent
## and the Temper

George Brett, like many men in this game, could be crass
and could be charming. It depended on the mood, on the
moment, on how the game was going, on the mix of alcohol at a
party, on whether he was dealing with a Yankee or a Royal. Life
in the public light can be both revealing and deceptive. The same
crude fellow captured on YouTube carrying on a rather detailed
monologue about pooping in his pants was the same gentleman
who had once pulled up in a horse carriage to the New York hotel
where the Kauffman family was staying, and drove Muriel and
her daughter, Julia, all through Manhattan after a heartbreaking defeat. That magical, chivalrous event happened in the early
morning. More astounding, it occurred on October 15, 1976,
just hours after the Yankees had clinched the American League
Championship Series with Chambliss's homer.

"We were commiserating back at the hotel about how we'd
been victims of a bad call, how [Cowens] had been safe by a
mile at second base," Julia Kauffman said. "Daddy went to bed,
because he always went to bed early. And all of a sudden at three-
thirty or four o'clock in the morning, here comes George, in a
Central Park carriage. He must have been at a party. And he's
got the reins and he takes mother and I and the two policemen
who were watching us all through Manhattan. He buys McDonald's for everyone. And we come back through Manhattan, and I

remember thinking, 'Julia, you better capture this in your brain, because the sun is rising and you're in a carriage with George Brett driving.'"

George Brett, that seething bull in a china shop on July 24, 1983, still comes to Julia Kauffman's house to this day for tea and conversation on a regular basis. He behaves himself like a true gentleman. "He signs baseballs, I give them away," Julia Kauffman said. "It's funny to think about, I know, George Brett drinking a pot of tea, with a cozy warming it. But it's a serious cup of tea. He becomes totally different."

Brett will not be remembered for sipping tea, of course, but rather for a competitive knife's edge that served him well on most occasions but at times drove him right over the cliff. He came by his vaunted temper through nature and nurture, his dad being at least half responsible for both. Pushy fathers have always been a big part of baseball, from Mutt Mantle, a metal miner with an obsessive vision for his son Mickey; to John Piersall, the driven dad who pushed his boy Jimmy several steps too far, toward madness. Major League Baseball is largely guilty of feeding this ravenous monster. Golden, talented children are identified and promoted at an early age, then quite often forced to make a career commitment right out of high school. Sometimes these urgent, half-educated decisions have worked out well in the end. More often, they have not. In George Brett's case, the relationship with his father, Jack, was unusual in at least one respect: George was not that golden chosen child in his family. Far from it. The twist here was that Jack Brett hardly bothered with George, who was supposedly a hopeless case. George's motivation in this instance derived, ironically, from his father's dismissiveness and lack of respect.

There were four Brett boys. Ken and Bobby were considered the "good sons," the high achievers in school who would certainly be successful in one way or another. Ken was the kid destined for the greatest things, a superstar athlete at El Segundo High School in California, a top student, and then the fourth pick overall by the Boston Red Sox in the 1966 draft. Until Boston selected Ken in the draft, Jack had always hoped he would succeed Mantle as the Yankees' center-fielder. John, the oldest son, and George, the youngest, were viewed as the family's slackers. George was the lazy kid with the T-shirt floating outside his pants, his sneakers flopping on his sockless feet. Jack forever felt George required a good, loud lecture and maybe a kick in those pants.

The Bretts lived not far from LAX airport, in a modest, well-kept home that was run in good-cop, bad-cop fashion. Ethel, the mom, cuddled and coddled the boys, particularly George. Jack was the bad cop. He was a World War II veteran, shot in action, the family provider. He had made sacrifices, shunting aside potentially glamorous career paths to study accountancy, to become eventually a finance director for the Datsun car company. When the boys all played baseball down the hill at Rec Park, Ethel would work the concession stand while Jack announced the game. Jack thoroughly believed Ken, not George, was the family's great hope back then, its road to fame and wealth. Oddly, he never really seemed to change his mind—even after George's career blossomed into something extraordinary and it became clear to others that nobody on the planet cared more about this sport, or worked harder at it. Eleven years before his death from cancer in May 1992, Jack summed up life with George in the Brett household this way during an interview with *Sports Illustrated*'s John Garrity:

Maybe I neglected George. I don't think I pushed him into sports so much, although I thought that would be his one salvation. Because when you can't read, when you can't write . . . when you don't have those skills developed to the point of other children of the same age . . . the parent begins to say, "Well, what the hell can this kid do?" We used to just sit there, look at him and say, "Poor George. Poor George. What's going to happen to him?" 'Cause he took shop and phys ed. Auto mechanics. No hard courses. Ken took four years of Spanish, four years of English, four years of biology. He would devote his time to study. Nobody had to prompt him. With George—oh God, it was an issue daily. It was always, "George, did you do your homework?" And he'd say, "I have no homework." He probably didn't. He was taking shop.

That sort of derisiveness never quite disappeared. It was still evident after George started smashing baseballs in all directions like nobody else in the business. In his dad's eyes, George could never be as good as his older brother—even after Ken's arm betrayed him, and Ken became a journeyman pitcher for ten different teams, with an 83-85 career win-loss record. There was the time, George told reporters, when Ken homered during a game in which he was pitching. George happened to go oh-for-three on the same day, just one game. On the phone, Jack was yelling at George, "You're getting outhit by your brother, and he's a pitcher!" When George finished the 1980 season at .390 instead of .400, his father rebuked him with, "Do you mean to tell me you couldn't have gotten five more bleeping hits?" Right up to the end, until Jack's death, the father wondered what was wrong with George, why his batting average was slipping below .300 at age 38 and 39. When George went hitless, Jack would inquire impatiently, "Well did you at least hit the ball hard?"

So George Brett had good reason to be angry at the world, and to be resentful of his father. "I hated my dad," he confessed in that *Sports Illustrated* story. "He'd say, '*Bobby* wouldn't do this,' or 'Kemer [Ken] wouldn't do that.' I was intimidated. I was scared to death of him. I remember I got out of the car in my uniform, my head hanging and the next thing I felt was a foot coming right up my ass! For embarrassing the family. That's probably where I got my hemorrhoids."

But this much was also true: Whenever George was angry or out of control, he was likely raging because of something to do with baseball, the one activity he'd come to love above all others. He was no slacker in this sport, no tourist. Brett was all in. In 1981, during a tough one-run loss to Texas in Kansas City, Brett injured his ankle while sliding home and was in a foul mood leaving the stadium on the way to the hospital for an exam. When a UPI photographer, Tom Gralish, tried to take his picture, Brett smacked him on the head with a crutch and swiped at the camera. Lord, how he hated injuries. Brett's temper was legend already at this stage. A former *Kansas City Times* news-side reporter remembered being assigned to a local charity basketball event in

Ewing Kauffman, self-made pharmaceutical magnate, became the founding father of the Royals when he established the model expansion team in 1969 and opened Royals Stadium four years later. (Baseball Hall of Fame)

George Steinbrenner poses in front of Yankee Stadium, where he was often stalked by reporters as he entered and left the place. More often than not, he was happy to furnish them with back-page headlines. (*New York Daily News*)

Billy Martin is downright congenial while discussing plans in his office before the 1976 American League Championship Series against upstart Kansas City. (*New York Daily News*)

It is high, it is far, it is gone. Chris Chambliss celebrates his walk-off homer that will give the Yanks a 7–6 victory over the Royals in deciding Game 5 of the 1976 ALCS. But first . . . (*New York Daily News*)

Chambliss has to fight his way around the basepath, battling with fans who should be called for interference. (*New York Daily News*)

Yogi Berra, George Steinbrenner, and Billy Martin embrace like the best of friends after Chambliss's homer gives the Yanks their first pennant in a dozen years. (*New York Daily News*)

Hal McRae takes out Willie Randolph at second base with a body block in the 1977 ALCS. The hit was so nasty that Major League Baseball amended its rulebook to ban similar incidents.
(*New York Daily News*)

Still wearing his uniform, Billy Martin talks to the press in July 1978, just days after souring relations with Steinbrenner forced the manager to resign.
(*New York Daily News*)

Yet again, in October 1979, Martin is fired by Steinbrenner and replaced by Dick Howser, who reluctantly leaves a secure college coaching post at North Carolina State to join the circus.
(*New York Daily News*)

John Schuerholz, longtime Royals executive, oversaw a much calmer, saner baseball realm in Kansas City. Schuerholz resented the big-spending Yankees but never stopped trying to beat them. (Baseball Hall of Fame)

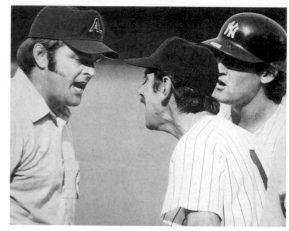

Whenever Billy Martin argued with umps, or the world in general, Graig Nettles was at his side. (*New York Daily News*)

Dick Howser put up with the madness in New York, then found a happier home back in Kansas City after Steinbrenner fired him at the conclusion of the 1980 season. (Baseball Hall of Fame)

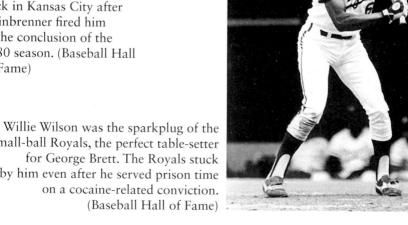

Willie Wilson was the sparkplug of the small-ball Royals, the perfect table-setter for George Brett. The Royals stuck by him even after he served prison time on a cocaine-related conviction. (Baseball Hall of Fame)

Goose Gossage throws another 100 miles-per-hour fastball, challenging anyone and everyone—including George Brett—to hit his best pitch. Brett took the dare on July 24, 1983, ripping a homer in the top of the ninth over the right-field wall at Yankee Stadium. (*New York Daily News*)

Umpire Tim McClelland measures the pine tar on Brett's bat against the 17-inch width of home plate, while Billy Martin waits for the umps to call one, finally, his way. (Associated Press)

For some reason, Brett doesn't approve when his homer is ruled an illegal hit and he's called out, ending the game. That's umpire Joe Brinkman with the headlock on the Royal's neck. (Associated Press)

It was left to Lee MacPhail, the American League president, to overturn the umpires' decision and reinstate Brett's home run. Steinbrenner told him he'd better move from Manhattan to Kansas City. (Baseball Hall of Fame)

Bob Fishel, trusted adviser to MacPhail, was wise enough to prepare affidavits from the original pine tar umps. They testified that Brett touched all bases on his home run trot. When Billy Martin appealed on those grounds at the start of the August 18 resumption, he was foiled by Fishel's foresight. (Baseball Hall of Fame)

Infamous attorney Roy Cohn (second from right), who represented the Yankees in the pine tar court hearings, hangs out with Studio 54 owners Steve Rubell and Ian Schrager, in all their glory days. (*New York Daily News*)

George Brett holds his precious bat. Note pine tar levels. (Baseball Hall of Fame)

While the Yankees may rule the Hall of Fame in Cooperstown, there is still room for this display of Brett's seven-grain pine tar bat—albeit wiped clean to legal limits. (Filip Bondy)

Rush Limbaugh may be a big deal on radio now, but in 1983 he was just the Kansas City Royals' promotions director, scrambling to find someone to throw out the first pitch at each ball game. (*New York Daily News*)

David Cone, a homegrown Kansas City star and huge Royals fan, pitches his perfect game for the pinstriped enemy in 1999. (*New York Daily News*)

Dean Taylor, a Royals executive for decades, was the man most responsible for researching and drafting the appeal of the umpires' pine tar ruling. He's kept a copy of that letter to Lee MacPhail, for posterity. (Dean Taylor)

which Brett suddenly started screaming at the referees over a call, a meaningless whistle. When the reporter approached Brett about this afterward, the star yelled crudely at him, "What's wrong? Didn't get laid today?" It was only the next day when it became apparent why Brett was in such a rage. He had broken a bone in his hand during the exhibition basketball game and the injury would force him out of the Royals' lineup. That temper stuck with Brett, never left him. Years later, he got in a shoving match on the team flight with Willie Wilson, after a tough loss in Boston. As recently as November 2013, not long after being named vice president of baseball operations for the Royals, Brett was forced to issue a public apology for a tirade he launched at a particularly aggressive, persistent autograph seeker at Kansas City International Airport. "Hopefully I've learned a very valuable lesson," he said. "You can wake up in the morning and be in a good mood or you can wake in the morning and be in a bad mood. This has made me want to wake up in the morning and be in a good mood every day."

That wasn't likely to happen, but he could live with his own short fuse as long as he was around baseball and around players who cared as much as he did. They had to love the game, live the game. "This guy was a remarkable athlete, who would pitch batting practice both left-handed and right-handed," John Schuerholz said. "Whether he was a rookie in Billings, or a perennial All-Star, every time he had a baseball uniform on him, he had a great joy about him. I wouldn't want to be on the opposite side of him, but luckily I happened to be his general manager, watching him grow."

In this very separate universe of baseball, Brett found father figures who were more attentive, more supportive, than his own dad. He had a high school coach, John Stevenson, who understood that George didn't have to be exactly like his brother Ken, that he was an incomparable athlete in his own right. George could be 165 pounds, maybe five feet ten inches, and still own an otherworldly, ambidextrous coordination that made him different from the others, a superstar. There was a scout, Rosey Gilhousen, who signed him with the Royals, even after Jack threw the guy out of the Bretts' home during the first day of negotiations, because the contract wasn't good enough. "I don't think when you did anything with my father, it was easy," George said. There was Whitey Herzog, his manager in Kansas City. When Brett was inducted into the Hall of Fame in 1999, he spoke about what Herzog had meant to him. "I remember his first day, when he came over to manage the Kansas City Royals [in 1975]," Brett said. "He said, 'George, you're playing third and you're hitting third every day as long as I'm managing.'" Before that, under Jack McKeon, Brett didn't exactly know his role. He'd be batting first or sixth or seventh. Herzog showed that kind of confidence in this special player and then invited Brett over to his house once every summer for a home-cooked meal. The pair would go hunting, fishing, golfing. They'd do the things that a father would do with a favorite son, not with a slacker.

And then there was his favorite hitting coach, Charley Lau. In Brett's long career, Lau would come as close as anyone to the perfect father surrogate, the patient mentor. Brett wasn't accustomed to asking for help, never looked for a counselor or adviser. He'd been taught by Jack long before then that self-motivation and self-learning were sacred, that improvement came from within. When Brett struggled, he simply blamed himself. He had appeared vaguely promising in the minor leagues, but frankly nothing special. Brett batted .284 on the Class AAA Omaha Royals in 1973, with just eight homers in 117 games. When he was called up from the farm team in 1974, Brett was hitting .266. He figured he should know his place in the Kansas City clubhouse, keep quiet, and be thankful he was being given a chance in the major leagues. He didn't bother Lau. Instead, Lau approached Brett just before the All-Star break in 1974, when Brett was batting .242 and struggling mightily. Lau put his arm around the kid and said, "George, I think you got a chance to hit, but you're gonna have to change a few things." For two days during that break, they worked on Brett's stance, on his thought process. They worked on going with the pitch to all fields, on leading with his hands, on relaxing at the plate. "Too much tension is like a cancer," Lau told him. Brett came out of the break, collected four hits in his next 13 times at bat, and figured that he was now a Zen master of the batter's box, that this minor tune-up was all he required. Lau told him it wasn't that easy. They kept working at it, looking at videos of other players, taking extra batting practice every day. "I think for as long as Charley Lau was our hitting coach, he and I had extra batting practice, three o'clock on the road, four o'clock at home," Brett said. Some days, Brett remembered, it was just five swings. Some days it was ten, enough to reinforce the muscle memory and learn a new lesson. Years later, when he was inducted into the Hall, Brett made a point of calling out Lau, thanking him for "molding me as a ballplayer and making today possible."

In the absence of Ken, who was busy on other major league teams, George also found himself hanging with a big brother figure, Hal McRae, seven years his senior, who took Brett under his veteran wing in the Royals' clubhouse. "He's the one that taught me how to play the game of baseball," Brett said. "He led by example. He ran balls out, he slid into second, tried to break up double plays. He stretched singles to doubles, doubles to triples. He would do whatever it took to win a ballgame, and he wasn't in a hurry to go home when it was over. He was willing to sit in his locker, have a few cold ones, and discuss the game for as long as it took." McRae wasn't this way just with Brett. He helped mentor others as well and was a calming influence on Willie Wilson, who also possessed a terrible temper on top of a burgeoning persecution complex. Wilson, in his own memoir, admits, "If I was Jackie Robinson, black people would not be playing baseball right now. I would have ruined it for everybody." So McRae would take Wilson aside, tell him to cut the nonsense, and he'd help build Brett's confidence, too.

This was a lasting friendship that had been sorely tested in 1976, through no fault of either man. The American League batting race between them that season wound down to the very last game against Minnesota on October 3 at Royals Stadium, and then to their very last at-bats in the ninth inning. It was a relatively meaningless game, since Kansas City already had clinched first place in the American League West and the Twins were five games behind. Even the outcome of this very game was more or less decided. Brett stepped to the plate with one out, his team trailing 5–2, knowing he required a hit to move fractionally ahead of McRae, who was on deck. Brett lofted a fly to left field, where Steve Brye had been positioned extremely deep by manager Gene Mauch. Brye didn't make the catch, badly misplaying the ball as Brett bounded around the bases for an inside-the-park homer. McRae, now requiring a hit to win the title, grounded out to short. He then made a couple of obscene gestures directed toward the Twins' dugout, leading Mauch to confront him on the field. In the clubhouse after the game, McRae charged that the Twins had rigged the whole thing so that the white player would beat the African American. "Things have been like this for a long time," McRae said. "They're changing gradually. They shouldn't be this way, but I can accept it. I know what happened. It's been too good a season for me to say too much, but I know they let that ball fall on purpose."

A similar uncomfortable batting race between teammates would take place in 1984, when Don Mattingly nudged out his Yankee teammate Dave Winfield, .343 to .340, on the final day. Winfield felt during that September most fans were cheering for Mattingly—though Winfield, too, shrugged his shoulders at such an inevitability.

Mauch and Brye flatly denied any conspiracy against McRae. The Twins' manager termed the controversy, "The worst thing that's happened to me in 35 years in baseball." Rod Carew of the Twins, who had been in the same race right up to the final day and finished at .331, also backed his own manager and outfielder. "That's a bunch of crap when they talk about racial stuff," he said. Brett finished at .333, with McRae at .332. The whole thing might have driven a wedge between the friends. But somehow the two men demonstrated no animosity toward each other. Brett, just 23 years old at the time, was deferential, even horrified, at the way things had ended. "I think maybe the Twins made me a present of the batting championship," he said. "And if they did, I feel just as bad about it as Hal does." As the Royals advanced to the American League Championship Series, reporters continued to ask both men about the matter. McRae repeated that he held no grudge toward Brett, while the third baseman said he would love to share the batting title with his teammate. The whole affair seemed to bring the two men closer together, not push them farther apart.

By the time Brett made his 1999 induction speech in Cooperstown, his father had passed on. Jack died of cancer in 1992 at age 68. Brett's brother Ken was already diagnosed with brain cancer and would lose his six-year fight in 2003, at age 55. Everybody knew how George would treat Ken in that induction oration, with reverence and love; how he would cite his mentors, from Herzog to Lau to McRae. But George needed to address Jack, too, and no one could dare guess how that would turn out. George wasn't sure, either, until the last minute. He was fighting off tears at the thought of it, until he finally uttered what amounted to a very personal eulogy.

"To my father who passed away in 1992, prior to me getting 3,000 hits and right after I had gotten married: He's never seen his grandchildren. At least my three boys. But growing up, sometimes I misunderstood your tough and dominant ways, Dad. But as I've grown up, I have realized what your goals were: for me and my brothers never to be content, and to be tough competitors. I think we all learned well from you. Thank you."

If that wasn't entirely a profession of love, his speech represented a modicum of forgiveness. Jack had created George, had made him larger than life by treating him as something much smaller than that. George took it from there, became a grand and historically important athletic figure. How grand? How important? The debate about whether George Brett was the greatest hitter of his generation is necessarily open-ended. As always, it depends on one's definition of great, and of generation. If you're talking about pure power hitting, then Reggie Jackson and Mike Schmidt easily surpassed Brett. If you're talking about a *Moneyball* sort of litmus test, on-base percentages and all that, then Brett fell well short of Wade Boggs, Rod Carew, and Tony Gwynn. Sabermetrics do not do Brett many favors, largely because he did not like to walk. He preferred to swing at all pitches, good or bad. Brett drew only 1,096 bases on balls in 11,625 plate appearances—or just one walk every 10.6 appearances. By comparison, Boggs and Carl Yastrzemski (who overlapped Brett for less than half his career) walked once every 6.5 plate appearances. Schmidt's ratio was 6.7; Jackson's, 8.3. Later on, Barry Bonds, who didn't quite qualify as the same generation as Brett and had other obvious issues as well, remarkably averaged one walk every 4.9 plate appearances—27 percent of those walks intentional. Among Brett's contemporary stars, only Robin Yount, at 12.7, posted a higher rate of plate appearances per walk. Schmidt was also a better-fielding third baseman by a considerable margin, with ten Gold Gloves to just one for Brett. But that's a positional argument, not an offensive consideration. If you're going by clutch, situational hitting, it would seem Brett has no peers. That isn't just general observation, either. Since statisticians began recording such numbers, he holds the record for the highest batting average during a season with runners on base, at .469, in 1980.

The more conventional numbers are on Brett's side, which is perhaps why he received a higher percentage of Hall of Fame votes from the Baseball Writers Association (98.19) than any other nonpitcher of his generation. He hit over .300 in 11 of his 21 seasons, winning the batting crown on three occasions. He amassed more than 100 RBI during four of his seasons, totaling 1,596 RBI altogether. He knocked more than 20 homers during eight of his seasons, playing at home in a pitcher's park. He was a 13-time All-Star and a one-time MVP with 3,154 lifetime hits and a career batting average of .305 (Schmidt finished at a relatively humble .267). Brett did this all for a single franchise, his Royals, which also surely aided him with Hall of Fame voters. Loyalists like Brett, Schmidt, Gwynn, and Yastrzemski—and still later, Chipper Jones and Derek Jeter—were becoming far rarer in the age of free agency. If Brett had played his home baseball games in Yankee Stadium, Fenway Park, or Wrigley Field, instead of at The K, there is no telling the enormity of his legacy, or how many homers he might have knocked.

Many Hall of Famers, such as Jackson, were dominant players at their positions for a set period of time. Many others, like Boggs, were slow-and-steady amassers of numbers. Brett was both the tortoise and the hare. Beyond all that, the mind's eye told you that Brett was the greatest batter of them all for his time, that he could hit any pitch in any direction for any distance. "No doubt in my opinion," the late Bobby Murcer once said. "George Brett does it all. Hits for average. Hits for power. Hits everything. He's the best hitter I've ever seen since I've been watching baseball." You might have to go back to Stan Musial, another star who plied his trade in Missouri, to find someone able to do what Brett did. Musial never threw a historic tantrum on the field, but then, he never was called out for pine tar on his bat after knocking a homer against his most hated rivals, against the manager who mocked his brother from the dugout. And he never had a father like Jack.

# 15

## The Game

A baseball team writes an evolving, organic narrative during the course of a season, forever a moving target. On Sunday, July 24, 1983, the Yankees were out of their early-season doldrums and feeling pretty good about themselves. There were nagging injuries, certainly. Pitcher Rudy May, outfielder Ken Griffey, and second baseman Willie Randolph were all on the disabled list. Catcher Butch Wynegar was out with a pulled groin muscle, while shortstop Andre Robertson had a bruised hand. But team captain Graig Nettles was back from a bruised shoulder and the Yankees' roster, as was its tradition under George Steinbrenner, was deep enough to handle such minor setbacks. One day earlier, on Saturday, Ron Guidry beat Kansas City while throwing a one-run complete game. The Yanks had won eight of their last nine games and were finishing up this successful home stand, having played themselves right back into the thick of one of the tightest pennant races in memory. Only three games now separated first-place Toronto from fifth-place Milwaukee in the American League East. At 52-40, the Yanks sat in fourth, two games back of the Blue Jays. Despite all the chaos and nonsense that had dotted this Yankees season, they were right there in the hunt.

The Royals were right there, too, though less deservedly. The American League West, lacking a superior team, was very nearly as tight as the East. The White Sox, 48-45, were the leaders, followed by Texas, 48-47, and California, 47-48. Kansas City, like the Yankees, sat fourth. Also like the Yankees, the Royals were just two games back, at 44-45. All season long, they'd been hanging around the .500 mark, going nowhere in particular, up or down. They were relatively healthy, though the chemistry on the team was just not quite right. That drug scandal was building behind the scenes in the clubhouse. The Royals' aging rotation was failing them a bit. Only Bud Black and Paul Splittorff would finish the season with earned run averages under 4.25. Gaylord Perry was now 44 years old. Vida Blue, 33, was a full-blown wreck. Steve Renko, 38, finished 1983 with a 6-11 mark and a 4.30 ERA. Larry Gura, 35, was on his way to an 11-18 record and a 4.90 ERA. Still, the Royals featured an impressive offensive lineup. Despite a recent slump, Brett entered the game batting .352 with 19 homers. Hal McRae, the designated hitter, was hitting .327 on July 24, while Willie Mays Aikens (who never particularly appreciated that middle name) was at .324.

This was the final meeting of the season between the Yanks and Royals, a typically close series that New York led, 6–5. Dick Howser started Black, arguably the most dependable arm in his rotation. The lefty was not a strikeout pitcher, and he had zero complete games to his credit at this juncture of the season. But his best stuff moved hard away from right-handed hitters and he'd generally been tough on the Yanks. Shane Rawley started for New York. He owned a strong, live arm and two complete-game victories over the Royals in 1983, both in Kansas City. Eight of his nine victories were complete games and he was known to work quickly, sometimes too quickly. Rawley had a reputation for suffering one really bad inning per game. It is a disease that has afflicted many pitchers over the years. More than two decades later, for example, it became the fateful trademark of A. J. Burnett, an overpriced free agent in the Bronx. Nobody knew when that one disastrous inning would arrive for Rawley, but it was sure to rear its ugly head by the sixth or seventh. Those one bad innings had added up to Rawley's 9-8 record and a 4.00 ERA going into this game. He'd pitched well against the Royals, however, with a lifetime record of 5-2 and a 2.92 ERA.

Willie Wilson started in center field for Kansas City, which was now his regular position after being shifted from left. Amos Otis was not thrilled when he was exiled to right field, suffering a hitting funk of sorts, but the shift by Howser made sense for a number of reasons. Wilson had more speed and could run down balls in the gap at pitcher-friendly Royals Stadium. Otis owned the better arm, a more critical weapon in right. Howser used Aikens as a pinch-hitter off the bench in this game and started the following lineup:

Willie Wilson, center field
U. L. Washington, shortstop
George Brett, third base
Hal McRae, designated hitter
Amos Otis, right field
John Wathan, first base
Leon Roberts, left field
Frank White, second base
Don Slaught, catcher

Billy Martin dropped struggling Dave Winfield from the cleanup spot to the number-five position. The manager thrived on hunches and had no reservations about tinkering with his lineup, ever. Players' hurt feelings were never his concern. When his Tigers went into a stubborn tailspin back in 1972, Martin decided to pull the lineup order out of a hat. The pitcher would bat ninth. Everybody else's spot would be determined by luck of the draw. That was how the slugger Norm Cash came to bat leadoff, for only the second and final time in his long career.

On July 24, 1983, Martin was not quite so desperate, yet he started the right-handed Steve Balboni at first base against the left-handed Black, in place of left-handed Don Mattingly. Hard to believe in retrospect, but the manager was still platooning these two young players, uncertain which prospect would prove more worthy in the long run. It was quickly becoming clear that Mattingly was far more promising. He was an extraordinary fielder, a contact hitter with line-drive power to both fields, almost Brett-like in that way. It was tremendous fun watching the 22-year-old emerge from nowhere. He was still wearing uniform number 46 at this time, but his swing already looked as formidable and flexible as it would in later years, when he wore number 23.

Bye Bye Balboni, as he was nicknamed for his tape-measure homers, had been considerably less impressive. He was a remarkable power hitter at the Triple A level, knocking 32 homers in 83 games for the Yankees' farm team in Columbus. He was an abysmal failure, however, every time he was called up to New York. Balboni, destined to become a Royal the following season, simply couldn't hit a major league curveball. Opposing pitchers had figured that out quickly enough, and it seemed an odd move by Martin to start Balboni against Black's filthy breaking stuff. Campaneris, meanwhile, started at second in place of the injured Randolph. Campaneris was Martin's proud reclamation project. The former A's star had unretired at age 41, and was somehow slapping the ball around to the tune of a .347 batting average. He'd been particularly hot of late, with nine hits in his previous 19 at-bats.

Martin's lineup:

> Bert Campaneris, second base
> Graig Nettles, third base
> Lou Piniella, right field
> Don Baylor, designated hitter
> Dave Winfield, center field
> Steve Kemp, left field
> Steve Balboni, first base
> Roy Smalley, shortstop
> Rick Cerone, catcher

The Royals always drew a decent crowd in the Bronx, and the midsummer series was no exception. This was scheduled for a four-day, four-game set, but severe thunderstorms canceled the game on Thursday, and famously truncated the scheduled Diana Ross concert that evening in Central Park. The Yankees therefore lost a good part of the day's gate when they were forced to reschedule the rainout as part of a Friday twinight doubleheader. On both Friday and Saturday, the games had attracted more than

40,000 fans. Sunday, however, produced miserable weather from the start. There was a hard rain in the morning. The sky was slate gray, and this would be an unusually raw summer's day, with temperatures peaking at only 71 degrees. The left-field bleachers were closed off for lack of demand and a good part of the upper deck was completely deserted. The threat of rain showers lingered, so the tarp stayed on the infield before the game and there was no outdoor batting practice. Bob Sheppard, the Yankees' public address announcer and unofficial voice of God, started things off by introducing the Marine Color Guard band and an old mainstay, John Amirante, to perform the anthem.

Wilson led off by fouling out to Balboni at first base. Washington arrived at the plate, chewing on a toothpick as he often did. This was an odd routine, not particularly attractive even by baseball's slovenly standards. There had been a pitcher, Sam Jones, who played for six different teams in the 1950s and 1960s, who demonstrated this same habit until he became nicknamed, simply, Toothpick Jones. But it was not common practice to walk to the plate with a sliver of wood in one's mouth. The Royals, in general, carried an informal air about them. Unlike the Yankees, virtually every player on Kansas City competed with his two top buttons unbuttoned on his jersey, Washington included. In any case, Washington was not having a good season. He was striking out too often and seemed to be swinging for the fences—not exactly the sort of behavior expected from a shortstop. He struck out again for the second out in the first inning, which brought up Brett, hitless in his last ten at-bats. He ended that minislump immediately with a clean single up the middle, before he was stranded there at first.

The game continued in this fashion, innocuously enough, nothing special. Martin was typically wound tight, leg up on the top step of the dugout, glaring intently at every unfavorable ball or strike call from umpire Tim McClelland behind the plate. Howser, by contrast, sat back and watched from the bench. The Royals scored a run in the top of the second, when White's grounder to Campaneris forced Roberts at second base and allowed Wathan to score from third. The Royals might have had a big inning, if not for an unexpectedly brilliant diving catch of Otis's sharp grounder down the line by Balboni, the giant first baseman. That was the sort of play expected from Mattingly, not Balboni.

The Yanks tied it up in the bottom of the second on a solo, one-out homer by Winfield off Black's fat 0-1 fastball. Winfield had been struggling and his average was down to an uncharacteristic .252. But no pitcher ever wanted Winfield to uncoil himself completely like this, and the powerful outfielder absolutely destroyed an outside pitch. His line shot carried some 470 feet to left center, over the Yankees' bullpen and straight into the stadium's Monument Park.

It was clear by the third inning that Rawley was just rearing back and throwing fastballs, not particularly confident in his other pitches. He walked McRae, which was once a dangerous thing to do. In his prime, back in 1976, McRae stole 22 bases. He still owned above-average speed at age 38, but wasn't frisky enough to try something stupid. McRae was always a good, smart baseball man. In the bottom of the third, Wilson demonstrated his own speed by running down Smalley's blooper. He made an impressive diving catch, but hurt his left shoulder on the play and eventually would have to leave the game. This was the injury that led to his doctor's appointment back in Kansas City the next day, and to Wilson's brief roadside interrogation by the Kansas Bureau of Investigation.

When Wathan lined a single to center to lead off the fourth, pitching coach Sammy Ellis came out to talk with Rawley on the mound, reminding him to keep an eye on the runner. Ellis was not one of Martin's favorite coaches—not at all a drinking buddy, like the deposed Art Fowler—but this was simple protocol and the manager would send Ellis scurrying to the mound whenever necessary. Among Rawley's weaknesses was the inability to hold potential base stealers close to the bag. His big kick and stride were a problem. Sure enough, Howser called for a hit and run, figuring Wathan might steal second if necessary. Roberts's single moved Wathan to third, though Roberts was thrown out at second on a smart cutoff play by Nettles. Few players were as baseball-wise as Nettles, then 38 years old, even if he had lost some range at third and some points on his batting average. He had recently shaved off his mustache, superstitiously, to break out of a bad stretch. White then drove in his second RBI with an infield single, a sharp hit knocked down by Nettles along the third-base line. Wathan, who owned surprising speed for a catcher/first baseman, scored his second run and the Royals now led, 2–1. When Slaught ripped a single to left for Kansas City's seventh hit, Martin signaled to his bullpen for Dale Murray to get up and start throwing. He'd seen Rawley blow up before, and was on guard.

Wilson, his shoulder still aching, walked to the plate with two men on, one out, and a chance to do some real damage. He surprised everyone with an attempted bunt that bounced off the plate and straight up into his body. McClelland behind the plate was blocked from making a call. Instead, Joe Brinkman at second base indicated that Wilson was not out, that the ball had struck him while he was still in the batter's box and this was merely a foul ball. This call did not go over well with Martin, who sprang from the dugout, headed for Brinkman, and assumed his favorite role of outraged victim. Brinkman wouldn't budge on the matter. Rawley hung in there and fanned Wilson—a leadoff man who led the Royals in strikeouts, not a good thing. Washington then lofted a tricky fly to right field, where Piniella circled under the ball clumsily, then fell and somehow made the catch at the warning track, still rolling around.

The old aphorism in baseball is that the player who makes the great catch to end an inning always seems to lead off at bat the next inning. In reality, surely, the odds are one in nine. In this case, Piniella came to the plate first after what would have to be called more of a circus catch than a great one. Piniella was always a fussy hitter in the batter's box; someone who changed stances at the drop of a cap. He was a devoted student of hitting and would discuss that fine art with anyone willing to talk at length on the subject. It was clear already he was headed for some sort of coaching or managerial role, though Piniella, an original Royal and now age 39, was still denying he had any interest in any such postplaying career. He was a colorful fellow, beloved by the press corps. He had a temper as a player, too, much like Brett. Piniella once stood on the bag at second at Yankee Stadium and, in clear view of everyone, signaled a middle finger to the official scorer up in the press box who had inexplicably called his double an error. On this occasion, he pulled a ball hard off Black that curled foul into the seats to the left of the pole. Then he grounded out. Black was in a groove, his pitches breaking low while he induced three straight ground outs from the meat of the Yankee lineup—Piniella, Baylor, and Winfield.

Brett led off the fifth inning with a groundout, and was now just 3-for-16 in this series. After McRae flied out to second, Otis was up—and up to no good. The Royals' right-fielder was famous for calling time out just as the pitcher was starting his delivery. Since Rawley was such a fast worker, Otis had done this to slow down Rawley already earlier in the game. He did it again, then laced a liner to right-center that tailed away from Winfield. Rawley got Wathan to pop out, however, ending the threat.

In the bottom of the fifth, Kemp flied out, Balboni looked foolish again while striking out, and Smalley was stranded at first after his single because of a diving save by Brett on a bullet down the line from Rick Cerone. Nothing doing for the Yankees. Rawley took the mound in the sixth, flagging and ragged. After Roberts grounded out, White and Slaught both slammed long triples to the wall for a 3–1 Kansas City lead. Slaught had attempted a suicide squeeze before his three-base hit, diving at the ball to make contact with his bat to rescue the runner, White, coming home from third. The Yanks would have been better off if the bunt had succeeded. Rawley was now imploding in familiar fashion. Martin trotted out decisively from the dugout after this tenth hit by the Royals, signaling for reliever Murray.

Murray had recently become a very reliable middle reliever, improving dramatically since Ellis convinced him to pitch exclusively out of the stretch. Oddly enough, Murray still warmed up in the bullpen with a full delivery, then switched to the stretch in games. He'd also shed about six pounds with the help of the young Yankees trainer Gene Monahan. Whatever worked, worked. It was often a mental thing with these pitchers, who occasionally required a confidence boost. Murray struck out pinch-hitter Pat

Sheridan, who was replacing the injured Wilson, and then got Washington on a grounder to short.

Down by two runs, the Yanks stormed back in the bottom of the sixth. Campaneris, a persistent pest, singled through the hole in the left side of the infield to lead off, then moved to second on a one-out single by Piniella. Black was clearly more vulnerable in the later innings. He'd thrown only 72 innings in his first 11 starts, which back in 1983 was an indication of a pitcher who couldn't finish what he started. Howser signaled for right-handed reliever Mike Armstrong to get up in the bullpen, not a second too soon. Black left his first pitch to Baylor out over the plate, and the red-hot batter slammed it for a triple to left-center on one hop off the wall. Campaneris and Piniella both scored, tying the game. Howser called for lefty Don Hood to start throwing, but stuck with Black for another batter, Winfield. This was a costly hunch, allowing the fatigued Black to face the right-handed batter Winfield. The Yankee outfielder ripped a hard shot off Black that handcuffed Brett at third base and went for an RBI single. Winfield was thrown out trying to stretch that hit into a double, but the Yanks now were ahead, 4–3.

Brett led off the seventh, massaging his bat handle as was his habit and then stepping into the batter's box. He singled off the tip of Murray's glove, his second hit of the game. Brett's slump was history. McRae grounded into a double play, however, on one of Murray's dipping forkballs, and Otis struck out.

Howser finally brought in Armstrong, one batter too late, to start the seventh. Since a righty was now on the mound, Martin tabbed Mattingly to pinch-hit for Balboni. Mattingly was on a nine-game hitting streak, and would only get one or two at-bats to continue that streak. This fact actually became important, potentially complicating baseball's fastidious record books, because of what followed. In the sort of at-bat that would become very familiar over the years, Mattingly went inside-out on a pitch and drove the ball to left field. His liner was caught this time for the first out. The sun was now peeking from behind the clouds a bit, finally, as Armstrong coaxed both Smalley and Campaneris to fly out to end the inning.

Time was running low for the Royals in the eighth inning, as Wathan blooped out to Campaneris at second. Aikens pinch-hit for Roberts and lofted a fly to left. Suddenly the sun was a real problem for Kemp, who lost sight of the ball momentarily before flipping down his tinted glasses and making the clumsy catch. White then tried to get on with a two-out bunt that was handled with surprising dexterity by the big pitcher. Murray caught the ball bare-handed and threw out the speedy White at first.

It was now the bottom of the eighth, and Nettles was leading off. Throughout his 11 years with the Yankees, Nettles always wore the number 9 jersey. It wasn't until he was traded to the Padres at the end of spring training in 1984 that the Yankees moved to retire the number in honor of Roger Maris. Nettles walked, just as Sheppard announced paid attendance that day at 33,944. Certainly, there weren't that many fans in the ballpark. Piniella then did something he almost never did: He tried to bunt. He might have been a great student of hitting, but Piniella was just awful at this. His stab at the ball was so pathetic that he laughed at himself, right there in the batter's box. The Yankees traditionally were not a small-ball team, and bunting was never a priority. Every spring, the broadcaster and former Yankees shortstop Phil Rizzuto would go down to Fort Lauderdale to the team's spring-training facilities and work with batters on bunting. And every summer, they would fail him miserably. It was a great frustration to Rizzuto, who would regularly express his indignity in the announcers' booth. Eventually, Piniella flied out to center without advancing Nettles. Baylor popped to second, also failing to move along Nettles. Winfield's broken-bat, line single to center sent Nettles to third, before Kemp popped out to Brett for the third out. The Yankees' failure to score this insurance run would come back to haunt them, and make for a fine tale.

# 16

## The Ninth

*"I wanted that pitch to be buried in his neck. He beat me. I don't know how he got the barrel of his bat on that ball."*

—Goose Gossage

George Brett knew about the pine tar, and he had a fairly good notion about the rule. Despite some hedging that day and in years to come, Brett understood full well that his precious seven-grain bat was in violation of the pine tar rule. There is a witness to his premeditation. Dean Vogelaar, the Royals' public relations director at the time, was at the batting cage with Brett just days earlier in Toronto, before the Royals headed to New York for their next series. "I'd probably remember this moment better than George," Vogelaar said. "George showed me the bat. He showed me the pine tar on it. He was going to keep using it, he said, but had some concern about it. He wondered how much longer he would be able to get away with it."

Umpires had warned him, and there was no hiding the fact that Brett was a complete pine tar mess, Exhibit A in a baseball court of law. Most batters have certain habits they rely on when they step to the plate. Sometimes these are superstitious rituals, sometimes these are muscle memory cues. Brett routinely massaged the barrel of his bat before placing his left foot first into the batter's box. The pine tar would get all over his left hand and then he often would tip his batting helmet with that hand and the helmet would get all gunked up from the pine tar. That stuff was everywhere, all over Brett, a launderer's nightmare. So there may have been some cold-blooded calculation involved in the unlawful use of this bat, even if the crime was ultimately petty. And while Brett might have known he was guilty of stretching the rules in this matter, he seemed largely unaware of the potential consequences for such misconduct.

Brett's bat only grew more illegal during this weekend series against the Yankees, from additional pine tar applications. The home team actually supplied Brett with the stuff as part of the pregame routine. Pete Sheehy, equipment manager for the Yankees since 1927, delivered a can of pine tar to the Royals on that fateful Sunday morning, along with rosin bags and other sticky tools of the trade. Sheehy had begun providing pine tar to teams around the early 1970s, when it suddenly came into fashion. "Babe and the others, they didn't use such stuff as pine tar and batting gloves and things like that," Sheehy said, with some disdain. "They just swung the bat."

Bats were still being swung on this summer Sunday afternoon, from both sides of the plate. It was now the fateful ninth inning, the Yanks were up by a fragile 4–3 score. If this game were played today, then surely the bullpen closer would be called in to pitch the ninth. Goose Gossage hadn't appeared the day before and had only thrown to two batters in the previous three days. He was at this time arguably the best reliever in the game, working on the final year of a $458,000-per-season (plus bonuses) contract, and about to earn about three times that from the Padres. Just before this very game, Gossage warned reporters he would likely test his worth in the free agent market at the end of the season. "I'm not saying I won't be back, but I'm not saying I will," he said. "I just want to go somewhere fun."

Billy Martin at first stubbornly ignored Gossage in the ninth inning of this game. The manager never had the same sort of trust in Gossage he once placed in Lyle. Instead, during the eighth inning, Martin ordered the right-handed Jay Howell and the lefty Bob Shirley to warm up in the bullpen. Then when the ninth inning began, Martin decided to keep Murray in the game.

Don Slaught led off, grounding out to Roy Smalley. Pat Sheridan then laced a sharp liner down the right-field line. Don Mattingly timed his jump perfectly, catching the ball at the apex of his leap. It was yet further proof that this was the team's first baseman of the future. The Yanks were now within one out of closing out this victory, taking the series, 3–1, and winning for the ninth time in ten games. Better still for the home side, the next batter, U. L. Washington, was 1-for-17 in this series. Washington fouled off a rather desperate bunt attempt, then managed a seeing-eye grounder that rolled through the middle of the infield, just beyond Smalley's reach. This brought up Brett, obviously not the guy that Martin wanted at the plate in this instance. Martin now signaled for Gossage, the fireballing right-hander, to pitch to the left-handed slugger—not pitch around him.

The other leading man in the Pine Tar Game, Rich Gossage, had a very different relationship than Brett with his own father. In this Colorado Springs family, Jake Gossage was always one of Rich's two biggest supporters at Little League games—the other being Rich's mother, Sue. "They never missed a game," Gossage would say, in his 2008 Hall of Fame induction speech. "I had a dream of playing in the big leagues. My dad would always say I was going to be there someday and I would say, 'Oh, Dad, don't say that,' because deep down I just didn't believe it would happen." The boy was given the nickname "Goose" by a friend who simply morphed the previously shortened name, "Goss." Growing up in a tight, loving family, Rich Gossage lived a childhood filled with cherished baseball memories. While Jake Gossage doled out unceasing praise to his son, Rich received cutting critiques from his brother Jack, who would tell him during front-yard pitching sessions, "You're not throwing very hard. You're throwing like a sissy." Rich, tears in his eyes, would try to throw harder. "That's where my wild delivery came from, all arms and legs, flailing, coming right at you," he said.

The Gossages lived far from any Major League Baseball team at the time, since the Colorado Rockies wouldn't come to Denver until 1993. Instead, they would gather around the television to watch the Game of the Week, or sometimes *Home Run Derby*, a TV show that ran its course long before Brett came to the plate this day. "But George Brett knows about *Home Run Derby*," Gossage said. "He hit a few off me. People ask me who was the greatest hitter I ever faced; hands-down it was George Brett. I can't imagine Ted Williams being that much better than Brett. My God, he was phenomenal. I faced a lot of great hitters on their way out: Frank Robinson, Al Kaline . . . but George Brett, in his prime, he was hands-down the best. And he was a Yankee killer. He hit a couple shots heard round the world off me."

Back when Gossage was growing up, watching *Home Run Derby*, Mickey Mantle was in his estimation the best hitter around, and the Yankees were his favorite team. Jake Gossage died when Rich was a junior in high school and couldn't be around when their big league dream came true, when a scout named Bill Kimble convinced the White Sox to draft Rich in the ninth round of the 1970 draft and offer him a modest signing bonus of $5,000. Gossage suddenly was scared about what would come next. "I felt like the whole weight of the world was on my shoulders when I signed that contract," Gossage said. "I'd given up my scholarship to go to college and had no idea what I had gotten myself into." He'd never even been out of the state of Colorado. Rich drove his brother's Jeep to a hunting spot where he and his father used to go on occasion. "I sat there all day and cried," Gossage said. When he was promoted to Appleton in the Midwest League, Gossage struggled so badly that the manager there recommended his release. He had enough supporters among the coaches and fans to survive that crisis and then thrived in 1971 under a new manager, Joe Sparks. By 1972, he was pitching for the White Sox and learning about off-speed stuff from the team's artful pitching coach, Johnny Sain. He had other influences in his career as well, some nonpitchers like Chuck Tanner, Dick Allen, Thurman Munson, and Bobby Murcer. Gossage grew close to several teammates on the Yankees, and would invite many of them to come out to his spread amid the mountains of Colorado for some beer guzzling and deer-hunting expeditions in November. There, in a rich, grassy valley, Randolph, Baylor, and Ken Griffey, Sr., would ride horses, sleep under the stars, and cook over a campfire with Gossage, plus some of the pitcher's relatives and friends. Gossage was generous with his hospitality and his time. He didn't always treat the media respectfully. He was a great quote, yet he could be discourteous. Once, he agreed to write a book with Marty Appel and had the poor fellow fly out to Colorado, only to inform the would-be author that he'd changed his mind—without offering money for Appel's flight of inconvenience. But with fellow ball-players, Gossage would talk about families and he'd talk baseball. He enjoyed sharing his life and lifestyle, even with the cynical city slickers.

On the mound, Gossage was considerably less welcoming. He developed a pitch that approached 100 miles per hour, grew a Fu Manchu mustache, and perfected a glare that intimidated batters nearly as much as the fastball. It was not fun being hit by a Gossage pitch, though he would later admit to purposely drilling only three batters in his career—Ron Gant, Al Bumbry, and Andres Galarraga. "They had it coming," Gossage said. When he was first paired with Martin after signing as a free agent with the Yankees in 1978, there was immediate friction between the two. The manager wanted Gossage to throw at a batter that first spring, with intent to hit the man as revenge for one slight or another. Gossage owned a mean fastball, but harbored no such inner anger. "Why should I hit somebody?" he asked.

After he was done pitching, looking back, he compared his career to "a kid getting on his favorite ride at Disney World and not getting off for 22 years." That's what Gossage said when it was all over. He didn't always enjoy his times in New York, however, wasn't always a big fan of the nuttiness that came with Martin and George Steinbrenner. He once referred to the owner famously, during a clubhouse tirade, as "the fat man." While Gossage was on that Disney World ride of his, there were plenty of unpleasant bumps along the way. The Pine Tar Game was one of the nastier thuds.

On July 24, 1983, Gossage was in his 12th major league season and still very much in his prime. He had a 2.05 ERA coming into this game, and would finish the season at 2.27, with a 13-5 mark, 22 saves, and 90 strikeouts in 87⅓ innings. He gave up only five homers in 1983. So there was plenty of well-earned confidence and arrogance. Many pitchers would have walked Brett in that situation—even with the tying run on first. They might have pitched to him defensively, ceding the base on balls if necessary. Gossage wasn't one of those pitchers. His feisty attitude was statistically understandable, or at least defensible. In his career against Gossage, Brett went 10-for-35, for a .286 average, with an on-base percentage of .364, three homers, and 11 runs batted in. This was far better than most hitters fared against the reliever, but it still in theory gave Gossage about a 63.6 percent chance of retiring Brett.

"That was Goose, he wanted to go mano a mano," Randolph said. "He was not backing down. He had so much confidence, he always figured, 'I got this guy.' That was his mentality. And that's why he's in the Hall of Fame."

Not all the great pitchers thought this way. Some were more tactical. Watching from the dugout, Ron Guidry that day figured he would probably have found a way to throw four balls to Brett and face the next batter, Hal McRae, with two outs and two men on. It would have meant moving the tying run to second base, yet it also would have meant avoiding the world's most virulent Yankee killer. "George was the toughest I ever faced," Guidry said. "By far the best. You hoped to God when you faced Kansas City you found out George was in a slump, swinging at bad pitches. Batters can get themselves out that way more than not. But when George was hot, I don't care who you are, you're not gonna get him out. The thing is, he's only gonna hit four times a game. You're thinking if you don't give him a lot to hit, he won't hurt you. But when George was hitting, he hit everything. He hit bad pitches. He hit them for home runs. So you had to be extra careful. There were not too many games when I let him beat me in a game. If we were losing 10–0, I'd pitch to him. What's 11–0? But there were times I didn't let George beat me, 'cause I knew he could. This looked like it might have been one of those times. One of my standing rules was if I'm going to make someone a hero, it's not going to be the guy who's in the newspaper every day."

Gossage was more fearless, and arguably more foolish. He threw a first-pitch fastball, high and outside. Brett went the other way with it, driving the ball hard down the left-field line before it hooked slightly foul. That shot should have been a warning flare to Gossage, who ignored the signal. Gossage's second pitch, another fastball, was too high, a ball for certain. Rick Cerone, the catcher, had set his mitt low and inside as a target. Gossage wanted this fastball, estimated at 98 miles per hour, to be "buried in his neck," but the pitch sailed a bit too far over the plate. Brett never hesitated, because there was no time for a tentative swing against Gossage. With most pitchers, a batter had about a quarter of a second to react to the pitch once he identified its speed, location, and trajectory. Against Gossage, that time frame was even tighter. Brett tomahawked the baseball into the lower deck in right field, about nine rows back behind the 353-foot sign, jogging memories of his three-run shot against Gossage in the 1980 playoffs. For the record, the baseball struck Brett's bat at the heart of the barrel, above the pine tar. From then on, however, everything was different. All sanity left the building.

As Brett loped around the bases, a long-planned Yankees plot was hatched, a challenge unveiled. It was clear that Brett's favorite Louisville Slugger was stained with pine tar far above the 18-inch mark permitted by archaic Rule 1.10 (c). Still, somebody had to notice that fact and make a fuss about it, or the umpires would have continued to ignore the crime. Graig Nettles and Don Zimmer, then the third-base coach, must share in the glory when it comes to alerting Martin about the matter.

Nettles was a mischief maker of the first order, and a serious clubhouse character. Taken in the proper doses, he could be a valuable aid to most reporters, a timely quote. "He was very clever, a great wit," said Phil Pepe of the *New York Daily News*. Nettles would think of a line, refine it, then call over Pepe or one of the other New York writers to try it out. Nicknamed "Puff" for his quick, almost magical exits from the clubhouse, Nettles wrote "E-5" (error, third baseman) on his own glove—a nice self-deprecating touch. He could be generous to teammates and their families, like the time he successfully lobbied Neil Diamond—who had been Thurman Munson's favorite singer—to include the late Munson's name in a rendition of "Done Too Soon." Nettles also could be horrifically politically incorrect, and said things about ethnic groups that offended reporters. One Jewish writer refused to interview Nettles ever again after the third baseman reportedly called him "a Jew cocksucker."

"Graig was a very, very bright and articulate guy," Willie Randolph would write in his own memoir. "He used his wit as a weapon, a whip and a welcome mat—and sometimes as an un-welcome mat." The nasty stuff, unfortunately, was not that uncommon around major league environs. Vic Ziegel, the late Jewish sports columnist at the *News*, would tell the story of a chance meeting on the street with a reserve Yankees catcher and a few teammates in Fort Lauderdale, during spring training. "Hey, Vic," the inebriated player shouted, "how did Hitler miss you?" Nettles never went that far. He was far too smart and nuanced for that, not so mean.

Nettles had spotted the offending smudges on Brett's bat during a series two weeks earlier in Kansas City. "The same thing happened to Thurman Munson a long time before in Minnesota, except it was just an RBI single he lost," Nettles said. "I told Billy about it in Kansas City." Nettles knew all too well about tainted bats. His own bat split open during a game on September 7, 1974, at Shea Stadium and sprayed out a half dozen Superballs. He'd knocked a homer with the same bat earlier in the game against the Tigers, but the single is what gave him away. "Now, that's an illegal bat in my opinion," Brett said much later, still harboring a grudge. "Filling your bat with cork or Superballs is probably not the right thing to do."

Brett didn't know how to cork a bat, never even tried. But Nettles detailed the pine tar rule to his wily manager, Martin, who was waiting for just the right moment to issue a challenge. By the time that perfect moment arrived with the home run, both Nettles and Martin had forgotten about the pine tar. Contrary to many accounts, it was actually Zimmer who reminded the Yankees' manager. Nettles was busy, manning third base at the time.

Zimmer was in the dugout. "You don't say anything when the guy doesn't get a hit," Zimmer said. "[But after the homer,] I told Billy, 'Go out there—that thing's illegal.'" Years later, whenever Zimmer met Brett, the coach would laugh and say, "What did I start?" He started a lot. Martin walked out on the field, a poker player with a pair of aces in the hole. He pointed to the bat, kept pointing at it. "Get the bat!" he instructed catcher Rick Cerone. "Get the bat!" The umpire crew that day consisted of Tim McClelland at home plate, crew chief Joe Brinkman, Drew Coble, and Nick Bremigan. Bremigan was given the bat at first. McClelland, a very large, imposing figure, at the time was in his rookie season in the American League and not yet a full-timer, still considered "a vacation umpire," filling in for others. It was not a sure thing that the umpires would even agree to examine the bat. The Cleveland Indians' manager, Mike Ferraro, would later point out that this same crew refused his request the previous month to inspect Jim Rice's bat for pine tar. "I went to Joe Brinkman, who was the crew chief, and told him I'd like him to check the bat with home plate," Ferraro told the *New York Times*. "He said he didn't have to if he didn't want to. And he didn't."

This time, with Martin in their faces, the same umps became more curious. "Bremigan knew the rule book as well as anyone I've ever known," McClelland said. Bremigan explained the specifics of the obscure pine tar rule to the whole crew. McClelland didn't have a ruler or tape measure that day—it was not part of the umpires' regulation equipment—so he dropped the bat down on home plate, which is 17 inches across.

The pine tar extended anywhere from 22 to 24 inches from the end of the bat, nearly a half foot past the permitted distance. While all this was going on, Brett was receiving congratulations from teammates about his home run, then alternately pacing and sitting in the dugout, wondering what the umpires were going to do next. Soon he was looking out from the top step, unbelieving.

"At first I thought they were going to call me out for a corked bat, 'cause I never heard of any rules about excessive pine tar on a bat," Brett said, though that clearly was not quite the truth. He just never had heard that a batter could be called out for such a thing. His teammate, second baseman Frank White, leaned over on the bench and told Brett that something vaguely similar had once happened to John Mayberry ten years earlier. White warned Brett this was all about the pine tar, and could very well become serious. "We're in New York," White told Brett. "Billy's got all the umpires out in the center of the field, our manager's still on the bench, and I just don't think we have a chance."

It was indeed strange that Dick Howser wasn't reacting at first to this bizarre scene played out directly in front of him. Maybe he was simply too rational to deal with such lunacy on a visceral level. This sort of passive posture from the manager, though deceiving, was exactly the sort of thing that had driven Steinbrenner to fire the fellow. Howser was level-headed to a fault. "He had been with the Yankees, he'd worked with Billy," Jana Howser said. "Dad didn't throw his knowledge of the rules in people's faces."

Even McClelland thought Howser's inaction was odd. "What I thought was weird was that no one from Kansas City even came out to see what I was doing measuring the bat," the umpire later told the *Belleville (N.J.) Times.* "Dick Howser was sitting there, but he didn't come out to see what was what. Once I realized there was more pine tar on the bat than the rules allowed, the call was simple."

Martin just kept pointing at the bat. Nettles jogged in to join the fun. The four umpires purposefully walked away from Martin and huddled. As the umpires dispersed, debate turned to the question of which umpire would make the call. They understood to some extent the stir this would create. Brinkman offered, but McClelland said he would perform the duty. Brett was now working himself into a frenzy on the bench, preparing for his historic charge. Brett told White, "If they call me out for too much pine tar, I'll go out and I'll kill one of those SOBs." Not that he would, or could. Brett posed no real threat. During speaking appearances in the Midwest, McClelland liked to point out that at this moment in Yankee Stadium the umpire stood six-foot-six, 250 pounds, wearing shin guards and a chest protector, carrying a mask in one hand and a bat in the other. "What's he going to do to me?" McClelland asked rhetorically. McClelland later liked to

make a fine distinction about his ruling. He didn't call out Brett
for "an illegal bat." He called Brett out for "an illegally batted
ball," ending the game. Brett at the time certainly was in no mood
to consider such distinctions.

"McClelland starts looking for me and he points to me and
calls me out and I'm heading out there," Brett said. "I blanked
out. I still got a sore neck from Brinkman's headlock, though it's
getting better. To hit a home run off Goose was a big thrill, and
then to have it taken away off a trivial portion of the rule book,
I just lost it. I looked like my father chasing me around after I
brought home my report card."

John Wathan was sitting on one side of Brett in the dugout,
coach Jose Rodriguez on the other. They both tried to hold him
back, then chased after Brett along with Howser, Rocky Colavito,
and utility outfielder Joe Simpson, hoping to stop Brett from
reaching the umpires. "I was quicker than him," Wathan said.
"But I didn't get him. I never saw a guy run that fast out of anger."

There was no real destination point in mind, just pure, uncorked
rage. Brett somehow avoided bumping into McClelland by cutting slightly to his right. Brinkman grabbed him from behind in
that headlock. Simpson and Leon Roberts, his teammates, caught
up to Brett and began delicate negotiations with Brinkman.

"I went out there to make sure he didn't do something bad and
then I told Brinkman to let George go," Simpson said. "You don't
want to see a teammate in a headlock like that."

Brinkman looked at Simpson and asked, "You got him? You
sure?" The umpire was skeptical and wanted to avoid a full-
blown physical confrontation. "There was real fear in Brinkman's
eyes, because he didn't know what George would do," said Simpson, who later became a commentator on Atlanta Braves games.
Brinkman released Brett, finally, reluctantly. After escaping the
headlock, Brett kept pushing at Brinkman, from the front this
time. Rodriguez held on particularly tight. Brett yelled a stream
of obscenities aimed at McClelland. "It was mostly, 'That's bullshit,' or, 'That's horseshit,'" Simpson said. "And believe it or not,
there's a difference. I'm not sure when baseball began to differen-
tiate those two, but it had."

"Bullshit" simply meant the call was wrong. That word was generally tolerated by umpires. "Horseshit," however, implied general incompetency, and was immediate grounds for ejection. Brett was implying both. The call was both bullshit and horseshit. His arms flapped so wildly that a Royals minor league affiliate in Northwest Arkansas would soon order and distribute to its fans a Brett "bobble-arms" doll.

The Yanks weren't a party to this rumble, merely observers. This was a unique, one-team melee around home plate, then again when the jumble of angry men approached the dugout as Brett grabbed his cap and glove. The manager was now fully engaged, angry, ready for a fight. "I recall very vividly watching it on TV, like it was five minutes ago," Jana Howser said. "I saw the look on his face. That was so atypical of his disposition. He was really an easy person to talk to. That was the one time I saw him so hot. The escalation of events upset him more than anything."

The whole outburst—from the moment Brett was called out by McClelland until he gave up and walked into the runway toward the clubhouse—lasted two minutes, ten seconds. Brett did not yet realize the lasting impact of his extraordinary tantrum, though he soon would. "Right after the game I didn't think that much of it, to be honest," he said. "But I remember getting back to my hotel room and calling one of my brothers to tell him what happened. He said, 'Oh, I know, I was watching another game on TV and they broke in and showed what happened.'"

Back in Kansas City, Ewing Kauffman was very peacefully watching these events transpire on a television in his sprawling Prairie Mission mansion. "For some reason I was with my parents in their house that day," Julia Kauffman recalled. "We were all watching the game. Well, maybe I wasn't actually watching the game. I was with my mother, and she had me doing things, and we weren't really watching it. Ewing was watching, though." Soon enough, he was instructing his family members, with a quiet sense of urgency, "Get in here. Get in here."

Julia saw what had happened and quickly got herself into a real snit, like Brett. "I was furious, beside myself," she said. "A lot of the anger was just the great rivalry we had with the Yankees. Then the phones started to ring with people who knew our unlisted number." These callers were fuming, too. They were wondering what Kauffman thought of this pine tar nonsense, and what he intended to do about it. "What I remember the most," Julia Kauffman said, "was Daddy, so calm, saying, 'Quit worrying. We're going to appeal this and we're going to win.' And that was the end of it. He just went on like nothing had happened. He wasn't mad or anything."

Other viewers in Kansas City, however, were growing angrier by the moment. They were being jobbed by the big, bad Yankees yet again. "I'm watching it on TV," Rush Limbaugh said. "I'm watching the body language of McClelland listening to Martin seriously. Then they cut to the Royals, they were high-fiving in the dugout, they had no idea. They thought there was no way anything was going to happen. I'm at home, thinking, 'Yes, there's a way.' I was totally captivated by it. Everybody thought it was a ridiculous call."

Those on-site in the Bronx realized the impact of Brett's outburst immediately. "That was the maddest human being I ever saw in my life," Gossage said. "Maddest baseball player I've ever seen, for sure. I was out there laughing my head off. I thought it was hilarious." Watching from the press box, a Yankees public relations intern, Tom Consentino, looked down, saw Brett charging home plate like a one-man herd of elephants, and considered himself very fortunate indeed. Just three days earlier, Consentino had performed a favor for the Long Island newspaper *Newsday*, setting up an interview between Brett and an elementary school kid who had been selected as part of that newspaper's school program. Brett had been reluctant at first, even grouchy, but then graciously spent more than an hour at the Stadium talking with the young student before the Thursday game was officially postponed due to rain. That version of Brett had looked nothing like this maniac down below, this steaming locomotive. Imagine if that poor kid had been scheduled for a postgame interview on Sunday. This edition of Brett was outraged and stripped down to his bare, competitive soul. "If you can envision his visage coming out of the dugout in full bull-like charge, with veins sticking out of his neck and eyes glazed over, that's the kind of competitor he was," John Schuerholz said. "At the same time, you have to remember this same man had a joyful countenance whenever he was playing baseball, when he was a rookie in Billings, or a perennial All-Star in the majors. Every time he had a baseball uniform on him, he had a great joy about him. I see him now, he has the same smile, the same delight. But this Pine Tar Game, it was against the Yankees and against Billy Martin, the guy who planned this attack. George was set up for this. Martin expected him to do something destructive like this to hurt his team."

The fans at Yankee Stadium, vastly entertained by this whole scene, began jeering the Royals. To emphasize that this was a done deal, that the Yankees had won the game, the soundboard operator switched on Frank Sinatra's version of "New York, New York," which remains a tradition today in the Bronx after the final out. The chaos, however, was not entirely settled on and around the field, since the whereabouts of the offending bat was now an issue.

In order to measure the bat, McClelland first needed to identify Brett's precious, seven-grain, wooden club as the culprit and get his hands on it. This turned out to be relatively easy. Merritt Riley, then a 17-year-old batboy for the visiting team at Yankee Stadium, would later blame himself, unfairly, for that. On the eve of the 30th anniversary of the Pine Tar Game, in 2013, Merritt, a New York City policeman, told the *Wall Street Journal* that it was all his fault. Riley was supposed to grab Brett's bat after the homer and run back with it to the dugout. There, it would be placed in a rack, where it theoretically—though, in truth, doubtfully—might be lost among the other timber. After Brett's homer, however, Riley just stopped and stared. The Royals' star had come to know Merritt over the years and always treated him with particular goodwill, dubbing him, "Spaulding," after a bratty kid in the movie *Caddyshack*. Riley waited at the plate, watched Brett round the bases, and then, against all protocol, gave Brett a high-five as he crossed home plate. As Riley belatedly headed for the dugout with the bat, Martin came out to demand the measurement and catcher Rick Cerone seized the club. He gave it back to Riley for a moment because, Cerone said, "I forgot what I was supposed to check the bat for." But Martin came out to appeal and McClelland grabbed the bat again from Riley. The batboy returned to the Royals' dugout at that time, beginning to understand he had become a small part of history, and worrying for his existence. Howser screamed at him. Brett was pacing. When the game ended, Riley went to the Yankees' clubhouse for about 45 minutes until the heat died down. Wathan said Riley should be fired. "We hid him for a while," said Lou Cucuzza, the clubhouse manager at the time (his son, Lou Jr., later became the visiting clubhouse manager). "The Yankees surely weren't mad at him." He was, after all, a Yankees employee. Finally, Riley returned to the Royals' side, where Brett first asked, "Why the fuck didn't you pick up the bat?" Brett was just kidding, it turned out. He figured the umps were going to get the bat anyway, one way or another. He was probably right. This event did not really spin around the batboy. It had a momentum all its own. Besides, it wasn't just Riley who failed to react quickly. McRae was on deck and might have retrieved the bat, but he was mesmerized, too, by the circumstances.

Back in the dugout, one quick-thinking Royals teammate figured he could hide the evidence so that the umpires' decision might be successfully appealed, or maybe so that Brett's bat could be quietly untarred. Not surprisingly, that conniving teammate was Gaylord Perry, the future Hall of Famer who somehow doctored balls for 21 years before he finally was caught with Vaseline under his cap. Perry was so unrepentant and shamelessly commercial that he had already entitled his 1974 autobiography *Me and the Spitter: An Autobiographical Confession*. Perry had learned the fine art of the spitball while with the Giants in 1964, from his teammate Bob Shaw. Upon application (literally), Perry's ERA dropped from 4.03 in 1963 to 2.75 in 1964. He honed the pitch and his reputation carefully, fully hoping that his illegal skills would burrow into the heads of opposing batters. Among those hitters who were driven most insane was Reggie Jackson, who struck out 22 times against Perry. After one such embarrassing at-bat, Jackson returned to the dugout, retrieved a container of some unidentified liquid, and splashed it all over the field while arguing that Perry might as well throw this stuff on the baseball as well. Perry's forkballs/spitters were so unpredictable, and the baseballs so greasy, his catchers often had trouble throwing the balls back to the mound. He was finally nailed for Vaseline under the cap on August 23, 1982, while pitching for Seattle against the Red Sox, ejected, and then suspended for ten days. The Royals signed him as a free agent the next season. "He should be in the Hall of Fame with a tube of K-Y Jelly attached to his plaque," manager Gene Mauch once said. Eventually, in 1991, Perry was elected to the Hall without the jelly jar attached. He will always be viewed, however, as a man with many agendas. And on this day in July at Yankee Stadium, Perry had his eye on the baseball bat.

"Gaylord Perry, being the man of foreign substance that he is, got the bat and twisted it out of my hands," McClelland said. Perry then began a baton relay to teammates so they could hide the evidence. "It seemed like the tunnel from the dugout to the clubhouse was like a vacuum cleaner, like everybody was getting sucked into there," Simpson said. Eventually, two umpires and several stadium security guards cornered Kansas City pitcher Steve Renko in the runway. Renko gave up his prize, this historic piece of wood, to Brinkman.

Brett was still fuming after the event, sitting at his locker, considering the ramifications. Just for starters, he now had 19 homers on the season, not 20. Rick Cerone, the Yankee catcher, had been credited with a putout. Brett was asked what he would do if the American League suspended him for attacking an umpire— though Brinkman said he personally thought Brett's outraged behavior did not necessarily warrant such punishment. "If they suspend me, I'll quit," Brett said.

His manager, Howser, was in an equally lousy mood, likening the call to the famous Brinks Robbery. "I haven't even seen the bat," Howser said. "It's like, who's got the gold? The CIA might be in on it. It might be in the think tank somewhere in the Pentagon. I don't like to rip Brinkman, but I'm going to. Everywhere we go, the guy's haunting us. You get Gossage versus Brett and you see what happens. I saw a 450-foot home run. For a game to be decided by this . . . I don't know."

Howser was not exactly built for this crazy stuff. He took it out a bit on Brett in the clubhouse, snapped at him about taking better care of his bat. How could Brett let the pine tar accumulate to such heights? Brett had a rational explanation ready for his manager, then for the New York reporters who surrounded him afterward on the scent of a great tale. If such a controversial play had happened to a star today, he'd likely go hide in the trainer's room until the next day. Brett was a mensch, though. He talked.

"You can't keep all the tar on the bottom, or it gets sticky and you lose the feeling you want to get," Brett said. "In the past, I've had some umpires warn me, 'George, your pine tar is getting pretty high,' and I would fix it. But I used the same bat the whole series and nobody said anything to me. I thought you just couldn't have the tar above the label. I hit the home run about twenty-nine or twenty-nine and a half inches from the bottom. There's no way it touched the pine tar."

Vogelaar knew he had a potential public relations disaster on his hands with both Brett and Howser boiling mad—at each other, at the umpires, at the Yankees, at the world. "Had this happened against any other team, I don't know if it would have had the same impact on George and Dick," Vogelaar said. "But both were hyperventilating. I kept the clubhouse closed a few minutes extra. Dick was shouting at me. This in itself wasn't that unusual. He'd holler and scream after some games, describe some play to me. Then, in the past, by the time the media came in, he was calm. This time, though, it was different. Something had to happen, he kept saying. He wanted me to do something. Finally I said, 'Let me call Bob Fishel.'" Fishel was the public relations director for the American League, the assistant to president Lee MacPhail. Maybe a protest could be filed.

On the first-base side of the stadium, where the Yankees dressed, the mood was considerably more buoyant. The Bombers packed and dressed for an 11-game road trip to Texas, Chicago, and Toronto. Martin, truly jubilant for one of the few times this season, walked past Gossage, who had somehow just been credited with his 12th save of the season. "Billy," Gossage said, "I really don't know how he hit that pitch."

"What pitch?" Martin said. Later, in his office, Martin smiled and said he would have argued the call if he were in Howser's shoes, but then accepted it. This was utter nonsense, and he knew it. Martin swiveled in his chair. "Well," he said, "it turned out to be a wonderful Sunday."

# 17

## The Rules Nerd

Dean Taylor, the man who first confronted and unraveled the pine tar ruling, grew up in Roseburg, a small town in southern Oregon, oddly dreaming about running a baseball team. Taylor, a focused and fastidious fellow, would go to bed listening to the games from Los Angeles on KFI, the 50,000-watt radio station. He followed the Dodgers in the National League and for some fateful reason began to root for the Royals in the American League. Taylor wanted to be part of this world in one fashion or another, and eventually found a way. Walter O'Malley, the Dodgers' owner, had helped to inspire and establish in 1966 a sports administration program at Ohio University, where for the first time graduate students under Dr. James Mason would be trained to work in professional sports. After earning an economics degree from Claremont McKenna College in 1973, Taylor entered the graduate program in Athens, and went a step further upon earning his master's degree: He and a college friend, Mike Manning, actually founded an independent minor league team in New Westminster, British Columbia, Canada.

It wasn't as hard back then as it sounds now. For his senior thesis, Taylor had researched and laid out a plan for the operation of a minor league franchise, which included his vision for promotion, hiring of staff, advertising, ticket sales, and recruitment of players. After some poking around, Taylor and Manning were told by Bob Richmond, president of the Northwest League, that his organization was expanding from six to eight teams during Christmas vacation of 1973–74. All Taylor and Manning needed to do was travel to Walla Walla, Washington, attend that session, make a presentation, and submit an application. "Here we were, just 22-year-old kids, but the franchise fee might have been $500 and back in those days you could start a team with $25,000 total," Taylor said. He had some backup, too, for a budget that inched toward $80,000 after all expenses were totaled. Taylor had married the daughter of Bill Forrest, head of a wood-processing firm back in Oregon. Taylor's father-in-law agreed to help finance the ambitious enterprise. This would be a labor of love for all concerned, not of fiscal responsibility, and Taylor paid himself about $750 per month for all his considerable troubles. Taylor and Manning unsuccessfully scouted potential home ballparks in the Washington State towns of Yakima, Wenatchee, and Olympia. They then headed north across the border, eventually settling upon Queen's Park Stadium in New Westminster, Canada.

Next, the roster required filling. The two young founders placed ads throughout Washington, Oregon, and California trumpeting their tryout camps. They signed their own players, hired a 48-year-old player-manager, Frosty Kennedy, and a pitching coach. They then held a local "Name the Team" contest. Four entrants came up with the winning name, Frasers, which was a reference to the Fraser River that flowed nearby. Debbie Kroeker, an elementary student at Surrey School, was given a pair of season tickets and a Canadian savings bond, because her winning entry had been drawn first. Her photo, standing next to Taylor, was on the front page of the local newspaper, *The Columbian*, on February 15, 1974, a feel-good welcome. The New Westminster Frasers were now officially a baseball team. "I didn't feel at all intimidated by my age," Taylor said. "In many ways it helped me relate to the players. Even though we were pretty young, Mike Manning and I felt pretty confident in our abilities."

That confidence was soon sorely tested. Kennedy, a distant relation to the famous Massachusetts clan, abruptly left the Frasers before the season after a blowup over a pair of cleats that he billed to the club. Frosty was a character, to put it mildly. In 1956, he hit 60 homers for the Plainview Ponies of the Class B

Southwestern League, a feat that earned him a place in Cooperstown. In 1953, when Plainview was still in the Class C West Texas–Mexico League, he batted .410. Maybe these were the low minors, but such an accomplishment was enough for Frosty to boast in a 1985 interview, "I'm the greatest player ever. Babe Ruth hit 60 homers but never batted .400. Ted Williams and a lot of other guys batted .400 but never hit sixty homers. I did both." Among his antics, he was known to wad up tobacco chaw while rounding the bases and roll it toward the opponents' dugout. Jim McConnell, a Whittier, California, newspaperman, reported that Kennedy was fuming over the whole cleats affair with the Frasers. "I figured if they were gonna argue over a $49 pair of shoes, they weren't ready to have me around," Frosty told McConnell. "One thing ya gotta know. Wherever Frosty goes, he goes first class."

So Taylor had to find a new manager, and there was also still the thorny, political process of acquiring approval for billboards within the stadium, a proposal that surprisingly met with great resistance. The New Westminster City Council deadlocked three to three on the matter, a negative outcome that meant that Taylor was not permitted to post signage in the stadium and would lose considerable revenue, nearly $10,000. Alderman Ken Wright, voting against the proposal, said that if the council had approved such a deal, then the New Westminster Bruins junior hockey team would likely demand the same right. Where would the madness end?

The Frasers hemorrhaged considerable money. The weather was typically too wet in the Pacific Northwest, cutting into attendance. The team was mired in last place. By midseason, an article in the *Columbian* began, "The only thing that leaks in the Frasers' club office is red ink." Taylor's wife, Jeanne, was not pleased with the lack of support from the local politicians. "We're still hoping to make it in New Westminster," she told the newspaper. "My daddy told us to take a few licks if we had to, but don't give up the ship." That ship was ultimately abandoned. The Frasers finished the season at 34-50, their only year of existence. They later became the rather humorous subjects of a Canadian nonfiction book and theater play.

Taylor moved the team next year to Boise, where it was affiliated with the Oakland A's and fared considerably better while being managed by Tom Trebelhorn. When a minor league team becomes an affiliated farm club like this, the major league franchise helps out with workers' compensation insurance, payroll taxes, and many other financial headaches. Taylor eventually took a sabbatical from his beloved baseball enterprises, enrolling in the army as a field artillery officer in Lawton, Oklahoma. He was a gunnery instructor, an expert on plotting the course of various launched missiles, taking into account weather, atmospheric conditions, and the rotation of the earth. Taylor then returned to administrative duties in the minors with the Reds' farm club in Eugene, from 1978 to 1980. He was considering a six-year commitment in the U.S. Army reserves when he received a phone call on Election Day, 1980, from a young executive, John Schuerholz, in Kansas City. Schuerholz had just been promoted to vice president of player personnel. Everybody was bumped up along with him, because the Royals, after all, were not the Yankees and operated under a rational, corporate model. Job candidates didn't pop out of the woodwork, and employees weren't fired on a whim. Somewhere at the lower end of middle management, Dick Balderson, future general manager of the Mariners, had been promoted from assistant minor league director to minor league director. That left a job vacancy for a number-two guy in the Royals' farm system. Taylor had been recommended by Chief Bender, farm director for the Reds, for that job of administrative assistant. Taylor told Schuerholz he grew up loving the Royals and would come there for exactly the same salary he was earning in Eugene, $17,600. As Rush Limbaugh also had testified, few Royals employees, other than the players, were getting rich with the Royals.

On July 24, 1983, Pine Tar Day, Taylor was an assistant director of scouting development for the Royals, and had organizational matters to consider that prevented him from attending the baseball game in the Bronx. But Taylor watched the game on television at his Kansas City home, where he saw Brett's famous tantrum and all that followed. "I'm sort of a rules buff," Taylor said.

"So my main thought process was to go to the rule book, validate or invalidate the umpire's decision. I went to Rule 110, though now [since amended] you don't see the same thing. Looking at it, it basically addressed the pine tar and eighteen-inch rule. It was clear in there the penalty for violation was limited to the bat being removed from the game. The light went on over my head and I thought the umpires had misinterpreted the rules, mixed up 101 with 606, considered pine tar to be an illegal bat. It was fairly obvious in my mind we had a decent chance of getting it overturned."

Rule 1.10 (b) was more complicated than merely a simple prohibitionist act. It stated in full: "The bat handle, for not more than 18 inches from the end, may be covered or treated with any material (including pine tar) to improve the grip. Any such material, including pine tar, which extends past the 18-inch limitation, in the umpire's judgment, shall cause the bat to be removed from the game. No such material shall improve the reaction or distance factor of the bat."

The key phrase here was "improve the reaction or distance factor of the bat," which was not the case. And if that was not true, then Rule 2.00 ("An illegally batted ball is . . . one hit with a bat which does not conform to Rule 1.10") and Rule 606 ("A batter is out for illegal action when . . . he hits an illegally batted ball") could not be invoked. The ball had not been struck illegally. It was just the bat that was illegal. There was also a Rule 4.23, entitled "Doctored Bats," that stated, "The use of pine tar in itself shall not be considered doctoring the bat. The 18-inch rule pertaining to the use of pine tar still applies, but violation of the 18-inch rule will not be cause for ejection or suspension." That rule, in itself, would not prohibit an umpire from calling a player out for using a bat with an illegal application of pine tar. But it could be cited, nonetheless, as another example that breaking the 18-inch barrier was not exactly a cardinal offense and did not mandate such drastic measures.

That wasn't the end of Taylor's research. He delved into baseball history, tried to find all the instances in which batters were called out, or not. He read and reread the rules. Rule 606 (d) discussed the altering or tampering of bats, specifically those filled with illegal substances, or flattened out, or hollowed, or nailed, or covered with substances such as paraffin or wax that might harden the club. In cases like those, a player using such a bat would be called out and ejected from the game. But that wasn't what pine tar was all about. Pine tar wouldn't boost the journey of a batted ball. Pine tar was just a dirty, sticky substance that Calvin Griffith didn't appreciate.

There had been precedents on both sides, so they didn't really help or hinder Taylor's case. Back in 1975, before the pine tar rule was specifically written into the books, two incidents had produced two very different results. As Graig Nettles correctly remembered, Thurman Munson was actually called out during a game on July 19, 1975, in the very first inning of a 2–1 loss to Minnesota. Munson singled home Roy White, then was deemed out when Twins manager Frank Quilici demonstrated to umpire Art Frantz that his bat had too much pine tar on the handle. The call arguably cost the Yankees that game. Bill Virdon, the Yanks' soon-to-be-fired manager after this 15th loss in 21 games, argued the call with umpires to no avail. Munson aimed his wrath not at Frantz but at Minnesota catcher Glenn Borgmann. Munson felt there was a catcher's code of honor, and that Borgmann had broken that code by ratting out the bat to Quilici. According to Major League Baseball historian John Thorn, "This was before the rule was on the books, so it may have been a special instruction to the umpires that was codified in the following year." In any case, Virdon made one huge mistake: He never appealed Frantz's ruling to the new American League president, Lee MacPhail, who therefore did not validate or veto the call.

Interestingly, Frantz's pine tar ruling created several copycat appeals in minor league games. Research by Shane Tourtellote of *Hardball Times* found that the Orlando Twins, Minnesota's Double-A farm team, protested a bat just one day after the Munson incident. Tom Poquette of the Jacksonville Suns lost an RBI single and was actually ejected from the game. Just three days after that, future Yankee manager Bob Lemon, then with the Richmond Braves, attempted a similar appeal during a game against the Pawtucket Red Sox, but umpire Steve Fields refused to measure the pine tar on the bat. A further appeal to the International League was denied.

Taylor was much more focused on the game that took place September 7, 1975, and directly involved the Royals. Here was a real precedent and argument to be made. Facing the Angels in Anaheim that Sunday afternoon, John Mayberry had knocked two homers with a bat that was clearly pine tarred beyond the 18-inch mark. The Royals won their eighth straight game, 8–7, and the umpire crew that day refused to disqualify Mayberry's homers because of the bat. Dick Williams, the Angels' feisty manager, then protested the umpires' noncall to MacPhail. The American League president denied Williams's protest, ruling the intent of the law had nothing to do with impact on the ball, or on the game. This was just a technical matter that didn't affect the outcome. If the baseball had been discolored by the pine tar from the bat, that in itself did not add feet, or even inches, to the projectile's flight over the wall. This was a question of tidiness, of bat hygiene, more than anything.

That was more than enough evidence for Taylor, who called Schuerholz at his home in the evening, telling the general manager there was a very good chance the umpires had misapplied the rules. Schuerholz instructed Taylor to write it all up, put his notes together, and meet at the general manager's office the next morning. Schuerholz did a little bit of his own research, found an American League regulation that indicated the use of pine tar should not be considered doctoring the bat. "It was then we knew the whole thing tied together," Taylor said. Taylor sat at one desk, Schuerholz at his own, and the pair crafted the letter of protest, a three-page document. They submitted it to MacPhail's office using what amounted to a primitive fax machine, a telecopier, with a cover letter. Personal computers were just coming out and the Royals didn't have any on their desktops. Like the Yankees, the Royals largely relied on Teletype machines for their news. Taylor mailed a hard copy to MacPhail as a backup but kept the original for himself. He still has that historic document, written in uppercase letters, in the Royals' office where he works as assis-

FILIP BONDY

tant general manager. As might be expected, it is an amalgam of
Taylor's straightforward rules approach and Schuerholz's sense
of outrage at the call itself, at Billy Martin's behavior, and at the
Yankees in general. It was typed in all capital letters, as if for
emphasis. Early on, it is all Taylor:

CLEARLY, THE INTENT OF RULE 1.10 (b) WAS TO PRO-
VIDE THE UMPIRE WITH THE POWER TO REMOVE
SAID BAT FROM THE GAME, IF IN HIS JUDGMENT THE
18" RULE HAD NOT BEEN FOLLOWED. THERE IS NO
OUT TO BE CHARGED OR NO OTHER PENALTY LEV-
ELED EXCEPT REMOVAL OF THE BAT IN QUESTION
ACCORDING TO RULE 1.10 (b).
   SINCE NEITHER HOME PLATE UMPIRE TIM MC-
CLELLAND NOR CREW CHIEF JOE BRINKMAN DISAL-
LOWED THE USE OF THE BAT IN QUESTION AT THE
TIME OF THE AT BAT, OR IN ANY PREVIOUS AT BAT AND
BY STRICT AND LITERAL INTERPRETATION OF RULE
1.10 (b) REGARDING THE PENALTY FOR USE OF A BAT
VIOLATING THE PINE TAR PROVISIONS AND AMERI-
CAN LEAGUE REGULATION 4.23, IT IS OUR POSITION
THAT THE DECISION OF THE UMPIRES TO DECLARE
GEORGE BRETT OUT IS OUTSIDE OF THE SCOPE OF
THE OFFICIAL PLAYING RULES AND THE AMERICAN
LEAGUE REGULATION PREVIOUSLY REFERENCED.

Later on, however, there is definitely more Schuerholz:

IN CONCLUSION, IT IS OUR POSITION THAT THE
COMBINATION OF BILLY MARTIN'S INCOMPLETE
KNOWLEDGE AND COMPREHENSION OF THE OFFI-
CIAL BASEBALL RULES STATED ABOVE AND HIS FORE-
BODING AND INTIMIDATING MANNER, CREATED
CONFUSION IN THE MINDS OF THE UMPIRES WHO
MISINTERPRETED THE INTENT AND SPIRIT OF THESE
SAME RULES.

More than 30 years later, Schuerholz can still muster some of that outrage over Martin's ploy that day, and about the ruling on the field.

"The way the regulation was written, it was about soiling the ball," Schuerholz said. "If anybody thinks pine tar on the bat can affect flight of ball, he's nuts. Billy Martin had this nefarious plan. But right and justice were on our side and everything turned out the right way."

Righteousness didn't just instantly transpire, however. The baseball gods did not descend from the pristine clouds above Cooperstown or an Iowa cornfield to pronounce Brett's clout a homer. The protest was telexed into the very mortal hands of league president Lee MacPhail and his right-hand man, Bob Fishel. These two New Yorkers and former Yankees employees were the ones who would mull over the matter and deliver a verdict. Considering the process, it was odd that Taylor and Schuerholz were so confident this was such a sure thing.

# 18

# In the Spirit
# of the Rules

Leland Stanford MacPhail, Jr., was always a reasonable and judicious man, a peace negotiator among the belligerent nutcases who dotted his world. MacPhail surely understood excess and irrationality, because he had been raised by a father, Larry, who was a terrifying baseball genius. Larry MacPhail had been an insightful front office executive with the Cincinnati Reds, Brooklyn Dodgers, and New York Yankees, bringing with him relatively fresh notions such as night baseball (albeit cloned from the Kansas City Monarchs) and televised regular-season games. His relationship with Dodgers manager Leo Durocher in many ways became the dysfunctional model for the later feuds featuring George Steinbrenner and Billy Martin. There was no telling how many times Larry MacPhail fired Durocher, or how many times Larry MacPhail rehired Durocher. "There is a thin line between genius and insanity," Durocher once said. "And in Larry's case it was so thin you could see him drifting back and forth."

By all accounts, Larry was a short-tempered man and a fearsome drunk. As the alcohol took hold, his dreaded behavior at victory celebrations—and there were many, to his credit—became grossly disruptive. Larry MacPhail had his share of barroom brawls, only they were sometimes staged in fanciful ballrooms. The most renowned of these fisticuffs was the so-called Battle of the Biltmore Hotel, Larry MacPhail's last stand in the world of baseball. This was 1947, MacPhail was 57 years old, and he was de facto owner of the Yankees. His team had just won the World Series in seven games over the Brooklyn Dodgers on a Monday afternoon. Immediately afterward in the Bronx clubhouse, champagne was guzzled and MacPhail was telling everyone that he planned to leave the sport on top, immediately, and with a bang. When the party moved to the Biltmore in the evening, MacPhail took it upon himself to punch out George Weiss, the team's general manager and MacPhail's longtime nemesis. Reporters suddenly had something to write about besides a mere World Series championship.

Larry MacPhail's temper tantrums continued throughout his lengthy retirement. He was not a renaissance man. In a 1945 document that came to light before a 2015 auction in Long Island, Larry MacPhail wrote to a committee studying baseball's color line: "There are few, if any, negro players who could qualify for play in the major leagues at this time. A major league player must have something besides natural ability. . . . I have no hesitancy in saying that the Yankees have no intention of signing negro players under contract or reservation to negro clubs." His son, Lee, remained close to his father somehow, right to Larry's dying days, demonstrating enormous patience for a grumpy old man. Right until his own death in 2012, Lee would tell the story about being stopped by a traffic cop in Miami during spring training, with his father as a passenger in the backseat. Larry got out of the car and berated the policeman for having the nerve to stop his son. "That father of yours is going to get you in a lot of trouble someday," the cop finally warned Lee. It was one of Lee's favorite stories.

"My grandfather was bombastic, flamboyant, a genius when sober, brilliant when he had one drink and a raving lunatic when he had too many," former baseball executive Andy MacPhail, Lee's son, told the *Baltimore Sun*. Meanwhile, Andy called his father "mild-mannered, low-key, a consensus builder. He was the most fair-minded man I ever met."

So there was a very real, innate conflict of personality in that family, though there was also love and admiration. When he escaped Steinbrenner and became president of the American

League, Lee hung a picture of his father on the wall next to the desk in his office. "He was very aggressive and very colorful," Lee told the *Bergen Record*, describing the man in that picture. "It's been said that if children have very loud, boisterous parents, that they go the other way, but I'm not sure. I just know that my basic nature is different than his."

The MacPhails agreed upon one thing, however: They loved baseball. Lee always wanted to get into the sport, follow his dad's heavy footprints. But Larry thought his son shouldn't make that decision lightly or prematurely and that Lee should experience life's other offerings first. Defying all logic, Larry MacPhail set up his son after graduation from Swarthmore College in a very different business—pig farming in Florence, South Carolina. "How my grandfather thought that would dissuade him from wanting to enter baseball is an enduring mystery in my family," Andy MacPhail said. If that was Larry's goal, then it surely failed. Lee served in the navy and fought briefly in the Pacific at the close of World War II, then returned to the States to get on with his inevitable career choice. He would come to think of his years spent in the Yankees' farm system as the greatest fun, bathed in the golden glow of nostalgia.

"The best jobs I've had in baseball were in the minor leagues," Lee MacPhail said. "I've always enjoyed player development, seeing players grow from 18-year-old kids into major league stars." In 1946, he became general manager of the Yankees' Triple-A team in Kansas City, while his father was still the Yanks' top executive in New York. He remembered being at a Blanton, Missouri, tryout camp, where some teenager named Mickey Mantle showed up with his father, Mutt. Lee MacPhail played a real role in constructing the dynastic Yankee clubs of the 1950s, yet when he became general manager of the Yankees, he couldn't quite bring a pennant to New York. He never enjoyed the success he later had as general manager of the Orioles. He tried mightily, though. MacPhail personally made the trip to Canton, Ohio, to sign draftee Thurman Munson in 1968. There, in the Munson home, MacPhail handled the signing himself in awkward surroundings, with Thurman's father lying on a sofa in his underwear, chiming in only, "He ain't too good on pop fouls, ya know." Ultimately in 1973, MacPhail took over from Joe Cronin as president of the American League. He might have been commissioner, if he owned the ambition. Back in 1969, Michael Burke, then president of the Yanks, called up MacPhail, his general manager, in the middle of the night to see if he had any interest in succeeding General William Eckert. Also on the phone line: a Wall Street attorney and National League counsel, Bowie Kuhn. MacPhail wanted nothing to do with the post. "I hadn't had the formal education in law that the job required," he said. "I wasn't a lawyer."

At the start of 1983, before the pine tar controversy fell into his lap, MacPhail was planning a simple retirement of sorts at age 65 and after 42 years in baseball. He was thinking of spending more time, finally, with his patient wife, Gwen, at their homes in New York and Florida. That didn't quite work out. While the 26 owners debated furiously about whether to renew Bowie Kuhn's contract when it expired in August (Kuhn would be allowed to remain as commissioner for another season, before he was replaced by Peter Ueberroth), they unanimously asked the popular MacPhail to become president of the Players Relations Committee. "Much to my surprise they started zeroing in on me," MacPhail said. "They wanted a baseball man, and partly because I was planning to retire, that made me available."

So MacPhail was still a busy man, even before Brett's homer. He had made some important rulings in the past. A year earlier, in August 1982, the American League president handed down that ten-game suspension of Gaylord Perry for doctoring a baseball against the Boston Red Sox. It was like a judge finally nailing Al Capone after decades of renowned wrongdoing. But this one on the pine tar would be a ruling for the ages, and MacPhail knew it. He also knew that he'd get the best counsel possible from his chief adviser, Bob Fishel.

Crazy? Bob Fishel knew about crazy, from the looniest employers of them all, Bill Veeck and George Steinbrenner. Like MacPhail, his very sane boss in the American League office, Fishel was a measured, button-down guy operating in a world of spontaneous combustion. "He had the highest moral standards," said Marty Appel, who worked with Fishel in the Yankees' public relations department during the seventies. "He had a real instinct for doing the right thing, despite working for some scoundrels."

MacPhail had learned to rely on Fishel in many baseball matters over the years when they were with the Yankees. Fishel would take extensive notes on players, statistics that wouldn't show up in the box scores, such as good and bad fielding plays. He'd first learned his craft in St. Louis from Veeck, baseball's most mischievous owner, a rascal of the first order. Fishel was Veeck's public relations man with the Browns, and played a key role in one of the most outrageous episodes in major league history. When Veeck decided it was about time for a midget to bat for his team, in order to draw a base on balls, Fishel actually was the one who signed Eddie Gaedel in the backseat of Veeck's Packard. Fishel also was responsible for supervising Grandstand Manager Day, which allowed fans in the stands to hold up signs that suggested strategies such as, "Bunt," "Hit and Run," and "Steal." This was a similar, albeit less-sophisticated system, suggested later by Kauffman for the Royals. Working for Veeck was the ultimate challenge for the straitlaced Fishel, but he learned to loosen up a bit and have some fun. When the Browns relocated to Baltimore, Fishel thought his career in baseball was done. He moved to Cleveland to work in an ad agency, where there were Fishel-types galore. Not everyone wants to be surrounded in the workplace by doppelgangers, however. The siren call of baseball sounded again and Fishel left after just six months for New York in 1954 to become head of the Yankees' public relations department. Fishel always figured he was hired by George Weiss because he was Jewish, and because many of the beat writers at the time were also Jewish. Fishel wasn't a religious fellow, but maybe Weiss thought he could relate better, culturally speaking, to these yahoo reporters who were making the general manager's life miserable.

Fishel stayed at that public relations post for two decades and several regimes in the Bronx. Ownership changed from Dan Topping and Del Webb, to CBS, to George Steinbrenner. All of them, even Steinbrenner, recognized Fishel as an incredibly effective employee. Fishel was an old-school guy, a small fellow with thick glasses who was meticulously groomed and parted his hair down the middle. He kept an electric shaver in his desk and, if summoned to a late-afternoon meeting with the elegant Burke, he would perform a touch-up trim just for the occasion. Fishel was never married. He viewed the Yankees and baseball officials all around the country as his family. He knew the birthdays of the Yankees' employees and made sure to acknowledge them. He would send out hundreds of Christmas and holiday cards to people in the business. In person, he would address an associate in a throwback, gentlemanly, almost British manner as "old man." He had a great personal touch, doling out advice to anyone, and they'd listen because it was good advice coming from a benevolent father figure. When George Brett was flirting with the .400 batting mark in 1980 (still at .401 on September 4), Fishel immediately recognized the mounting pressure. National media types began following the story, smothering the Royals' third baseman with the sort of attention rarely seen in Kansas City. Bumper stickers sprouted around the city urging "George Brett for President." Ted Williams, the last batter to hit .400, offered praise, which only ramped up the pressure. "He's a helluva hitter with a lot going for him," Williams said. "He's strong and he's a gutty guy. I hope he makes it."

Fishel called up Dean Vogelaar, the Royals' public relations director, to offer some counsel on this chase that was becoming larger than life. He volunteered that he had himself messed up, big-time, when he was in charge of public relations for the Yankees in 1961 and Roger Maris was eaten alive by the fuss. Fishel told Maris back then, in a rather matter-of-fact fashion, to ask for help if he needed it. Maris required it, badly, but never asked because he was too proud, as are most ballplayers. Maris also didn't help himself in these situations, occasionally leaving for reporters at his locker a small statue of a hand with an extended middle finger. Fishel advised Vogelaar not to ask Brett if he wished intervention. Just do it, Fishel said. Go ahead and become the aggressive, overly protective gatekeeper. Vogelaar took that advice and deflected many of the interview and commercial requests, giving Brett some breathing space—though Brett later would complain anyway he had been sabotaged by the media that season. "I honestly believe George appreciated what we did for him as a club," Vogelaar said. "We managed that pretty darned well. God bless Bob Fishel, because I think it set a template for the future. When Fernando Valenzuela was such a sensation with the Dodgers, I got a call from Steve Brener, their public relations guy, and they did something similar."

Fishel had become a big believer in hands-on crisis management. He and MacPhail learned some lessons the hard way, first with Maris and then by badly botching the Mike Kekich–Fritz Peterson wife-swapping affair in 1973 that embarrassed the ballclub—just as Steinbrenner was taking over the franchise. Now, with the pine tar case before them, MacPhail and Fishel were about to become proactive again. There were only half-precedents available, really. Munson had been called out once for a tarred bat, had his RBI single nullified, but that ruling hadn't been appealed to the league office. Mayberry's homers had been allowed to stand, but in that instance MacPhail merely backed up the umpires on the scene. In this protest, MacPhail was being asked to overrule an entire umpire crew, which is hardly a stance that any league president wishes to take. One of the chief duties of the American League office was to support the men in blue on the front lines. The umpires had enough problems from players and managers without worrying about whether MacPhail had their backs. Besides, protests were almost never upheld. There had been only a dozen such examples before 1983 in the history of baseball. Only two protests have been upheld since: a 1986 Cardinals-Pirates game, because not enough time was allotted for rain to stop before the game was postponed; and a Giants-Cubs game in August 2014, because the Wrigley Field grounds crew failed to adequately protect the field from flooding.

Nonetheless, MacPhail owned a strong, innate sense of righteousness when it came to the game of baseball, and clearly Brett was wronged in this instance. MacPhail and Fishel discussed the matter at some length, and then upheld the protest. Fishel was quite excited, energized by the whole thing. On July 27, while the

Yanks were on the road at decrepit Arlington Stadium, he warned reporters to be ready the next day for a ruling. Fishel was a man of considerable restraint, yet there was a sense of real anticipation when he told one reporter, "You might be surprised a little." Thursday, July 28, was an off day for the Yankees, traveling from Texas to Chicago for a series against the White Sox. The news hit the team like a 34-ounce bat, with or without pine tar.

"Protest is allowed," MacPhail's statement read. "It is the league's position that the meaning and intent [of the rules] is to declare out batters using bats that have been tampered with to increase distance potential, but not to treat pine-tar excessives [sic] in the same manner. The use of bats with pine tar beyond 18 inches should simply be prohibited. The opposing team has the right to ask that the bat be changed or cleaned up."

MacPhail explained that the umpires' ruling on the field was "technically defensible," but, "it is not in accord with the intent or spirit of the rules and the rules do not provide that a hitter be called out for excessive use of pine tar."

It was a shocker, for sure, and the league president said he fully understood that the Yankees would be frustrated by his ruling. MacPhail attempted to salve all wounds with praise for the overruled parties.

"I don't blame the Yankees for doing what they did and I admire them for being so diligent in their pursuit of the rules," he said. "I also have informed the umpires that this decision is not meant to be a repudiation of their decision. If anything, the lack of precise, clear playing rules and the lack of proper administration from our part may have been the prime source of the problem. We've discussed a million things during the course of the season with our umpires and I don't think we ever discussed this. I am advising the clubs and the umpires that any future incidents like this should be decided before the batter hits or else whatever the batter does will be allowed to stand."

The umpires involved were not pleased at the time of the overruling, or ever since. "We don't umpire on the spirit of the rules," McClelland said, twenty years later. "We umpire on the letter of the law and the rules said that we needed to call him out. I'll be the first one to admit that it wasn't a good rule, but we can't rule on the good ones and not rule on the bad ones."

The decision, MacPhail announced, could not be appealed. MacPhail and Fishel looked at the schedules of the Yankees and Royals, then came up with the suggestion that the game be resumed on August 18, when both clubs had an off day and the Royals would be on the East Coast preparing for a series against the Orioles in Baltimore. The Royals would resume the game at bat, leading 5–4 in the top of the ninth with two outs. The Yankees' front office, needless to say, bristled at the notion. "We don't intend to play the game on August 18, and we don't think we should be forced to," said Murray Cook, the general manager. "Hopefully we won't have to play the game at all."

Fishel pointed out almost immediately that the club did not have the power to decline the date, but conceded the players might have the option to veto the scheduled resumption under the terms of their union's Basic Agreement with management. According to that agreement, games could not be scheduled for more than 20 consecutive dates during the regular season. If the suspended game were counted as a playing date on August 18, the Yankees would have a stretch of 31 consecutive "on" dates. More ifs . . . If the August 18 resumption were successfully averted, then the Yanks and Royals would only be able to complete the game on October 3, one day after the regular season ended. And it might never need to be completed, if it did not affect any pennant race. This, clearly, was the Yankees' preferred course of action. If they could just keep this likely defeat out of the American League East standings, out of the minds and hearts of their players, the season would continue on its merry path without a demoralizing setback.

# 19

## The Boss Is Burning

As might be expected, MacPhail's ruling created wildly different reactions from these two polar-opposite franchises. While reason and cautious optimism prevailed in the Royals' offices, wheels were flying off the number-4 subway tracks in the Bronx. The standings had been jiggered, just for starters. The ruling dropped the Yankees' record in the American League East from 56-40, tied for first place with Baltimore, to 55-40, a half-game behind the Orioles. The Yanks were now only a half-game ahead of the Tigers and one game up on Toronto in the ridiculously claustrophobic American League East race.

Martin felt burglarized, and was placed in the extremely unfamiliar position of defending the integrity of umpires. "If they don't honor [the umpires' decision], then everything in the rule book means nothing," he said. "The umpires made the decision, they should stand on it. They stand on everything else the umpires do. Why should this be an exception? What's the old saying—it's all right to cheat as long as you don't get caught? The way baseball has been going on for a hundred years, the umpires have always been upheld and I can't see why that should be changed now. The bat was illegal or else why would the Royals players grab it like they did and run away with it?"

Steinbrenner hadn't been at the scene of the crime, but denounced MacPhail's decision by phone from his American Shipbuilding office in Tampa. This was his hot line to reporters, whenever outrage at an umpire or disappointment with a manager required

175

expressing. There was a small matter of hypocrisy to address at first. Like Martin, Steinbrenner had never before been known to crusade on behalf of an umpire's ruling. "I know in the past I've been a pretty harsh critic of the umpires," he told the *Daily News*, "but here is a situation where I really feel for them . . . I notice in Lee's statement where he makes a futile effort to praise the umpires' actions, while at the same time he overruled them. That's like giving a little kid a cookie with one hand and belting him in the head with the other. This is going to play havoc with our game now. In the future the umpires are not going to bother to make calls on critical rules for fear they won't get the backing from the league office." Steinbrenner further questioned MacPhail's credentials regarding the physics of pine tar, and the substance's impact on a batted ball. "He's not a scientist or a chemist," the Boss said.

This was not an easy or pleasant matter for Steinbrenner, who already possessed mixed feelings about MacPhail. When the two worked together on the Yankees, Steinbrenner viewed MacPhail as a respectful employee. Since MacPhail had joined the American League office, however, Steinbrenner wasn't pleased with the president's reactions to umpire rulings that went against the ballclub. "I don't question his integrity here," Steinbrenner said. "What Lee does is done with honesty and integrity. I just think it was a dumb, ridiculous decision. He's opened a Pandora's box where no rules mean anything anymore and all rules are subject to a new terminology, 'in the spirit of the sport.'"

Nobody could muster indignation like Steinbrenner, and his heat was definitely coming down on the American League president. "It's not uncomfortable," MacPhail insisted at the time. "I don't mind it when I know I'm doing my job. But it's not something I look for." After blowing his stack, Steinbrenner lay low and seemed to take the decision in stride—for a while. He wasn't thrilled, obviously, but the club even made tentative plans to open Yankee Stadium to kids, to all-day summer campers, for the replay of the ninth inning. Then something happened, a synapse suddenly snapped. "Nobody really knew why," said Tom Consentino, the public relations intern. "The thinking became, 'We don't want to play this game.'"

The Boss grew more furious by the day, determined to fight this resumption to the bitter end. His statements about MacPhail grew more pointed. There was talk about whether MacPhail had been influenced by his close friendship with Ewing Kauffman's wife, Muriel, who was also a friend of Steinbrenner's. During one fateful comment that would come back to haunt him, Steinbrenner, intentionally or not, appeared to issue some sort of threat toward MacPhail. The Yanks' owner knew well that MacPhail lived in Manhattan, and walked the 14 blocks from his apartment to the American League office every day. "If the Yankees should lose the Eastern Division race on the ruling of American League president Lee MacPhail, I would not want to be poor Lee living in New York City," Steinbrenner said. "He had better start house-hunting in Missouri, close to Kansas City."

Once things got crazy with Steinbrenner, there was no turning back. Orders were barked. Aggressively paranoid actions were decreed. The public relations director, Ken Nigro, informed Consentino that it was now his job to collect information on every bad trade that MacPhail had made as general manager of the Yankees and deliver that data to Steinbrenner's desk. There was no explanation of how this stuff would be used, but Consentino, a learned fan of the game, went about documenting MacPhail's more blatant failures. Maybe Steinbrenner just wanted some ammo so he could say, "What does MacPhail know about baseball? He once traded Stan Bahnsen (who won 21 games for the White Sox in 1972) for Rich McKinney (who batted .215 for the Yankees that season, and once asked public relations man Marty Appel where he could score some weed)." There was Clete Boyer for Bill Robinson and there was Roger Maris for Charley Smith, all MacPhail's handiwork. In the interest of fairness, Consentino also included in his research MacPhail's deal that sent Danny Cater to Boston for Sparky Lyle, though the intern doubted whether Steinbrenner would ever use that one.

The United Press International ticker in the Yankees' office was now cranking out pine tar stories like crazy. There were dueling, daily press releases from the offices of Fishel and Steinbrenner. On one occasion, Nigro made the mistake of allowing Fishel to use his own typewriter at the Stadium to write an American League press release, which created a furor and further alienated Steinbrenner from his public relations director. After Fishel's death in 1988, the Yankees would post a plaque in the press box for him that still hangs on a wall at the new stadium. "With compassion, integrity and dignity, he elevated his profession," it states. Back in 1983, however, Fishel was very much persona non grata. Nigro, meanwhile, was walking the tightrope every day and knew it, yet he couldn't resist. This was just too much fun. He ordered cans of pine tar delivered from Maryland. He ordered T-shirts for the press that said, "I covered the Pine Tar Game." He took calls from a man who had written a song about the game (not to be confused with C. W. McCall's later "Pine Tar Wars," which called Martin "Tar Baby Billy" and "Cry Baby Billy"). This earlier composer wanted to perform his song in the Bronx as part of a pregame ceremony before the resumption. At one point, Gene McHale, president of the club, came storming into the public relations office holding a can of pine tar. "Who ordered this?" McHale demanded. Nigro was hiding out someplace, nowhere to be found. "They're going to fire me over this stuff," Nigro told Consentino. "But they're going to replay this game, and this is history."

There were still many matters to settle, however, before the game could be resumed. Dave Winfield polled the Yankees' players, as the team's union representative, and said the majority preferred not to participate. A resumption, even if it were to last just four outs, could in theory represent part of a stretch of 31 straight game days for the Yankees, including two twinight doubleheaders, from July 28 through August 29. "We're not pack mules," Winfield said. "We would like the day off. Can they force us to play? Well, we'll have to see."

They could, and they did. Even Donald Fehr, chief counsel to the Players Association, admitted the league could legally overrule the scheduling guidelines in the collective bargaining agreement and the players' veto, if August 18 was the only viable date for the resumption. Steinbrenner, the ultimate workaholic, ironically became an empathetic employer. "I'd like our players to have their day of relaxation," Steinbrenner said. "It's not fair to my team. Look, Kansas City broke the rules. I didn't."

While this circus was going on in and around the Stadium, legal proceedings began just up the hill at the Bronx County Courthouse adjacent to the Grand Concourse. Two cranky Yankee fans, Lawrence Morrison and Madelyn Davis, filed lawsuits seeking an injunction against the resumption of the game. Morrison, 15 years old, was represented in this case by his father, attorney Arthur Morrison. In court papers, the boy demanded free admission to see the replay of the ninth inning, because he held a ticket for the original game. Darrell Fennell, the attorney representing Davis's children, Adam and Gregory, plus other children in a class-action suit, argued that more kids would be able to see the game if it were held after the regular season ended during the afternoon. The sincerity of these lawsuits was questioned in the press, yet the court system somehow considered them at length. The Yanks, thrilled at the chance to sabotage the resumption, piggybacked on these lawsuits in their own way, though they never formally supported the injunctions. Instead, they argued that it was too dangerous to complete the game because angry fans might start a riot. The Yanks, who staged 81 home games per regular season, suddenly could not assure the safety of spectators while staging one inning of baseball against the Royals. An absurd argument was put forth that the ballpark might be overrun by unchecked, frenzied maniacs who could potentially harm each other. The Yanks said that only 25 percent of the usual security force would be on hand due to scheduling conflicts and the union contract. To make this far-fetched plea before a judge, Steinbrenner recruited team attorney John Lang and a very heavy hitter by the name of Roy Cohn.

Roy Cohn was an infamous, commie-hunting lawyer during the red-baiting years of Joe McCarthy, counting among his friends, clients, and associates the likes of J. Edgar Hoover, Richard Nixon, Donald Trump, Rupert Murdoch, Claus von Bülow, Barbara Walters, and George Steinbrenner. Back in 1951, Cohn had been one of the lead prosecutors in the conviction of Julius and

Ethel Rosenberg, who were eventually executed, at Cohn's recommendation, after they were convicted of espionage. This performance earned a strong reference from Hoover to McCarthy. In the following years, Cohn was a right-hand man to McCarthy, chairman of the Government Operations Committee and Permanent Subcommittee on Investigations. The committee subpoenaed hundreds of government workers to testify about alleged involvement with communism, sabotage, and even homosexual relationships. Those hearings unfairly cost many of these workers their jobs. Despite such behavior, Cohn's sphere of influence and friendships was enormous and, to a degree, politically varied. His enemies, including Robert Kennedy, were equally renowned. Cohn was revealed in his final days, as he was dying with AIDS, to be something of a self-loathing homosexual, though his antigay posturing may have derived in part from pure self-preservation. These were not the most tolerant times. His relationship with Walters was particularly noteworthy, and typically complex. Walters's father was attending a family outing in Las Vegas and failed to show up for a court date in New York. As a favor to Walters, Cohn had the court quash a warrant for her father's arrest. Cohn then used this relationship with Walters to make it appear there was a romantic link. "I was his claim to heterosexuality," Walters told the *San Francisco Chronicle*. "He never said that he was gay, he never admitted to me that he had AIDS. He was a very complicated man. He died, alone, up to his ears in debt. He had been disbarred and he was hated. And I might have thought the same way, but he did something when my father was in trouble and I never forgot that. I would not use the word nice. He was very smart. And funny. And, at the time, seemed to know everyone in New York. He was very friendly with the cardinal, he was very friendly with the most famous columnist in New York, Walter Winchell. He had extremely powerful friends."

She might have added Steinbrenner to that list. Cohn was a renowned social butterfly, with several party headquarters around the city. Chief among them, in the late seventies, was the hippest club around, Studio 54. He was the lawyer for co-owner Steve Rubell and may have been a silent partner in the place. It was at this disco palace that he held his most glamorous fetes. Cocaine flowed like champagne, which flowed like water. In Nicholas Von Hoffman's book *Citizen Cohn,* society woman and Cohn's friend Verne O'Hara describes how people unconnected to the famous attorney would line up outside Studio 54 with just the vague hope of getting past the bodyguards.

"It was this masochism that most of the these people would go through being rejected at the door," she said. "It was like—insanity. There was hysteria. If you went to the ladies' room, nobody ever went into the toilet to go to the bathroom. You'd hear all this sniff-sniffing and there would be both boys and girls in there. There would be all the gays and all the girls in there. Studio 54 was like incredible energy. Energy beyond anything you've ever seen in a place."

If you wanted to play in this game, it helped tremendously to know Cohn. He developed an extensive network of friends, trading on favors just like the one with Walters, or on free entrée into Studio 54, until it all fell apart near the end. He became involved with a close Steinbrenner counselor, Bill Fugazy, after purchasing a company called Rosensohn Enterprises that owned the rights to promote a Floyd Patterson–Ingemar Johansson heavyweight title rematch. This was a shaky business, quite volatile in nature. Fugazy soon became involved in a legal battle with his own uncle Humbert, who owned a piece of the action. Cohn defended Bill Fugazy in a series of lengthy courtroom maneuvers, leading his uncle to comment, "Cohn is hoping to delay this trial long enough for me to die."

Cohn's tactics—stall, delay, and then stall some more—were an accurate predictor of what was to come with the pine tar affair. Long before Brett homered to right field off Gossage in 1983, Cohn had established himself inside the Steinbrenner business and social circles as a regular. There were parties, many of them considered clumsy and gauche by New York progressives, where these sorts of movers and shakers would gather. And then there was an auxiliary party space, Suite 332 at Yankee Stadium, also known as the owner's box. This was a sacred region where celebrities of random rank and vocation came together to mingle, drink champagne, and munch on hot dogs. Steinbrenner invited assorted, unrelated heroes and scoundrels to sit, watch a game, and share stories. They generally had a wonderful time. There were six rows of seats, a private chamber with a television set, phones wired for international access, a bar, a bathroom, and a hallway that joined inhabitants with the real world. The owner's box led directly upstairs into Steinbrenner's office, which featured his oversized, intimidating desk, not too dissimilar from the one featured in several *Seinfeld* episodes. Some typically macho, cli-chéd bromides were framed on the wall, sermonizing such sen-timents as, "Lead, follow, or get the hell out of the way." This owner's box was basically the model for what would become a high-end luxury suite in today's stadiums. The *New York Post* columnist Jack Martin was invited there by Cohn and remem-bered his experiences gleefully; how Tom Carvel would be throw-ing ice-cream cakes to the fans and Richard Nixon would chat up everyone about baseball.

"The night I met Richard Nixon I was sitting totally mesmer-ized by something Reggie Jackson was doing," Martin related, in *Citizen Cohn*. "Roy was in the back, ya-ya-ya-ya with Bill Fugazy probably, or George . . . And as soon as Reggie did whatever it was he did, a strikeout or hit a home run, before I could turn my eyes away from the playing field, a hand had been thrust in front of me and I hear a voice saying, 'Hi, I'm Dick Nixon.' It's a jolt to the system, I'm telling you—and then proceeded to engage me for fifteen minutes about baseball, which I know fuck-all. It was little memories like that which endear Roy to me—where else was I going to meet Nixon?"

There was payment to be made by Cohn in this barter-ing arrangement with Steinbrenner. And so when the Yankees decided to fight the Pine Tar Game resumption, Cohn showed up on the morning and afternoon of August 18, in two different courtrooms, on behalf of the club. By this time, he was heavily involved in a messy disbarment case that would eventually claim his right to practice law. He'd borrowed $100,000 back in 1966 from a former client, Iva Schlesinger, and never paid her back. Cohn delayed, delayed, delayed again on the legal front, his habit.

Then he made a mistake, lied in a sworn affidavit about the loan, calling Schlesinger's loan a payment. He had other black marks on his record also and there were many members of the Disciplinary Committee, a panel of lawyers, who did not like Cohn, for good reason. Eventually, before his death in 1986 at the age of 59, he was disbarred.

On August 18, 1983, when he appeared on behalf of the Yankees in the pine tar case, Cohn was likely infected with the HIV virus, though he would not be diagnosed with AIDS until the following year. This was, in any case, a time in New York City when denial was a way of life in the face of a terrible epidemic. Dressed in a maroon, tight-vested, three-piece suit, with his sagging, dark-ringed eyes, Cohn was at this late stage of his life something of a cartoon villain out of *Batman*. His first arguments on the team's behalf that day were heard in Bronx Supreme Court, where Cohn claimed, in a cynical tactic, that a resumption might very well cause an uncontrollable riot in the ballpark. Attorney Arthur Morrison, who had originally brought suit against the Yankees seeking free admission for his son, had abandoned the case and was now on the league's side. But Darrell Fennell, the attorney representing Madelyn and Gregory Davis in a class-action suit, remained persistent in this matter. Fennell argued that more children would be able to see the game if it were held in the afternoon after the season and admission were free to ticketholders from the July 24 game.

As it turned out, Fennell and Cohn were arguing their case to the right judge. Supreme Court Justice Orest Maresca, hardly sounding unbiased in the matter, delivered a seven-page decision at 11:30 a.m. in which he imposed an injunction on a resumption later in the day. Maresca was very clearly a supporter of the team, stating among other things, "Yankee pinstripes are the end-all and be-all of young and sometimes old Yankee fans."

If MacPhail wanted this ninth inning to go off on schedule at 6:00 p.m. that same day, time was now running out on the American League. Hurriedly, the legal scene shifted to Manhattan, to the ornate, 83-year-old courthouse on 25th Street and Madison Avenue. There, league attorney Lou Hoynes asked Appellate

Division Justice Joseph Sullivan to stay the injunction and allow the resumption. Meanwhile, Lang and Cohn continued to argue that the safety risks were simply too imposing. "If just one person gets hurt, the game isn't worth it," Lang argued. "Because of the media hype, people who are not even baseball fans will come to this game."

Sullivan considered the case only briefly, understanding the timetable was now ridiculously tight. The Royals' charter flight already had landed at Newark Airport. He quickly ruled in favor of the American League, lifting the injunction and restoring the ninth-inning resumption. "Let's all try to see that things are conducted in an orderly fashion," Sullivan said. "My ruling can best be summed up in two words: 'Play ball!' "

Cohn, a man of power and access, took the defeat in stride. He'd had many such disappointing moments in his long career, along with the victories. He surely had bigger fish to fry than George Brett's home run. This didn't rank up there in importance for him with the Rosenbergs, or with his disbarment hearings.

"It's out of the hands of the attorneys now," Cohn said with a shrug. "We just have to leave it up to the people at the Stadium."

# 20

## The Resumption

There was no denying it now. All appeals had failed, all legal avenues closed. The Yankees would have to open their Stadium and resume the Pine Tar Game in the early evening of Thursday, August 18. Steinbrenner, Martin, and the Yankee roster were finally united by common outrage, if only for a day. They were convinced the world had conspired to screw the bullies in pinstripes. "I still can't believe they overruled," Goose Gossage said, three decades later. "They just ignored the rule book. We weren't going to get any breaks from the league with George and Billy. Every time the league got a chance to stick it to us, they did." Even sensible Ron Guidry felt the same way. "We always said, if this [pine tar bat ruling by the umpires] had happened to one of our guys, we would have lost the game," he said. "I don't think Lee MacPhail wanted to do something like that to Brett, especially because he hit a home run. Billy was right in making the request. What good are the rules if you don't uphold them? But if MacPhail had done that, ruled against Kansas City, he would have opened another can of worms."

The Royals, meanwhile, were confounded and annoyed by the Yankees' obstructionist tactics. "It's undignified for our industry," John Schuerholz said. They had completed their series in Kansas City against the Tigers on Wednesday with a 10–4 loss, dropping them back to .500. The Royals still weren't certain what to do next. They were scheduled to be in Baltimore to start a three-game set on Friday. Should they go to Baltimore or New York?

While court proceedings lingered, the Royals left Kansas City at 11:00 a.m., local time, arriving in Newark Airport at 2:45 p.m. They sat in the plane for half an hour while officials debated, then finally decided to take a bus to the Bronx, hoping for the best. The Yankees began filtering into their clubhouse at about 3:00, and kept the door securely closed to the press. The Royals arrived at Yankee Stadium at 4:15, less than two hours before the scheduled first pitch. "We didn't know until we walked into the Stadium that we were playing," Dean Vogelaar said. To make matters just a little more complicated, the weather was lousy again. The tarp stayed on the Yankee Stadium infield until resumption time because of thunderstorms in the area.

Brett didn't bother to go on the last leg of the journey, that bus ride from the airport to the Bronx. He wasn't eligible to play anyway, ejected after his epic tantrum. He was lucky, really, that he hadn't been suspended for several games by MacPhail for going after the umps. It helped that Brinkman restrained Brett so quickly, and that no damage was done. "I got kicked out of the game for some reason," Brett said, smiling. "I don't know why I was kicked out, but I was kicked out." He wasn't the only ineligible one. Back on August 5, MacPhail, under advisement from the original umpires, had ejected four of the Royals retroactively for their behavior in the wake of the original pine tar decision. Howser and Colavito were banished and fined for their roles in the melee and Perry was banned for his attempts to confiscate and hide Brett's bat. "Several members of the Kansas City Royals were overaggressive in their reactions to the final out call of umpire Tim McClelland," MacPhail wrote. "George Brett had to be physically restrained by teammates and umpire Joe Brinkman. Pitcher Gaylord Perry wrestled the Brett bat out of umpire McClelland's hands and attempted to carry it off."

Billy Martin had a different solution in mind. He wanted Brett back at Yankee Stadium, playing. Not only playing, but also batting. A do-over would be the perfect compromise, another at-bat against Gossage. "Let him stay in the game and let him hit over again," Martin said. "If he hits another home run, he's got it." That obviously wasn't going to happen. So instead of heading to Yankee Stadium, Brett remained in Newark, dining in a small restaurant near the airport with Larry Ameche, the team's TWA flight representative and the son of actor Don Ameche. Together, the two men watched the last inning on television, gaping at the nonsense on the screen. "From what I saw, I'm glad I didn't go," Brett said.

It was, in fact, hilarious burlesque. Howser was somewhere on-site, but wasn't permitted to manage. Colavito and Perry were already on their way to Baltimore for the next series. Avron Fogelman, the part-owner who had bought 49 percent of the team recently from Kauffman, was on the scene to watch the spectacle and a probable victory for his club. Steinbrenner was in Cleveland with his ailing father, Henry George Steinbrenner, who would die three months later. The Yankees' owner likely wouldn't have bothered to come, in any case. The odds against victory were too steep.

Unbeknownst to most, hours before this game was resumed in comical fashion, there was a real tragedy that sent Yankee officials scrambling for information. Andre Robertson, the team's promising, 25-year-old prospect at shortstop, was involved in a terrible accident on the West Side Highway in Manhattan. Robertson had played the final six innings of the previous game, a 13-inning loss to the White Sox. He'd then met with a casual girlfriend, Shenikwa Nowlin, a ballerina with the Dance Theater of Harlem and former Miss North Texas. According to court documents from a lawsuit filed by Nowlin against both Robertson and the city of New York, Robertson was found to be driving his 1983 Buick Riviera at about 70 miles per hour in a 55-miles-per-hour zone. It was a dangerous part of the highway, and there was no warning sign about the S-curve ahead. Police reported 50 accidents in that area alone in previous years. The car crashed into a concrete median and turned over. Robertson suffered serious neck and shoulder injuries. His spinal cord was very nearly severed, spared by no more than one-eighth of an inch. The woman passenger fared even worse. Nowlin, who later married another man and forgave Robertson, was paralyzed for life from the waist down. Nearly ten years later, she would be awarded $7.5 million in damages by the New York Court of Appeals. Though Robertson would eventually return to baseball the next season, he was never the same player. At game resumption time, however, Yankee officials knew only that Robertson had been in a serious accident and announced only minimal details to the press. Most reporters, engrossed in the pine tar proceedings, made the news of Robertson's accident only a short note at the end of their articles.

The game resumed with the Yankees in the field, down a run, two outs in the ninth. The Bombers' lineup was now unrecognizable. George Frazier was pitching, replacing Gossage. Martin started his ace, Guidry, in center field and moved Don Mattingly from first to second base. Neither move, actually, was as crazy as it seemed. Guidry loved to chase and catch fly balls during practice, much the same way Mariano Rivera would do years later, and demonstrated a remarkable range and talent for the job. "Billy always knew I could play center field, that's the ironic thing," Guidry said. "He'd watch me shag balls in center field and he'd say, 'If we can get a ten-game lead with five games left to play, I'll put you in the outfield with Mickey Rivers and six infielders.' Mickey and I could guard the outfield by ourselves. Billy knew I could play." As for the left-handed Mattingly at second, Guidry said, "Donnie could turn double plays. He was athletic, had great hands. And the primary job of a second baseman anyway is to get the force-out. The double play is the extra stuff." There was an additional twist to Mattingly's appearance. He had come into the original Pine Tar Game with a nine-game hitting streak. After that, he got at least one hit in 15 straight games, through August 10. But on July 24, he had been oh-for-one after replacing Steve Balboni. Now Mattingly had a chance to re-create, from nothing, a 25-game streak, very nearly a rookie record, because a hit would be credited to the July 24 box score.

Martin installed other changes as well: Butch Wynegar was batting third in the order instead of Jerry Mumphrey, while catching in place of Rick Cerone. Cerone had come down with an eye infection and was unavailable. Ken Griffey replaced second baseman Bert Campaneris and played first base. Many of these adjustments were dictated by roster moves since July 24. Mumphrey had been traded eight days earlier to Houston for Omar Moreno while Campaneris was out with an injury. But there was no denying that Martin chose to treat this resumption, spitefully, as something of a joke. "I was there at the Stadium, ready to play," said Willie Randolph, who instead watched Mattingly take his regular position at second base. "That was just Billy sticking it to the league." The Royals, now six full games behind the White Sox and doomed to also-ran status, embraced the informality of the occasion. Several of the players' kids sat in the visitors' dugout, wearing Kansas City uniforms.

There were still some plot twists to come. Standing and pacing on the top step of the dugout, his usual perch, Martin immediately ordered Frazier to step off the rubber and throw to first base, then to second base, to appeal Brett's homer. Martin slyly was appealing on the grounds that Brett hadn't touched first or second base during his home run trot, and that base runner U. L. Washington had missed second. Umpire Tim Welke, however, signaled safe at first base. Dave Phillips signaled safe at second. Since this was a different crew from the one that umpired the game on July 24, Martin figured the group couldn't rule on the appeal and the game would have to be suspended again. He walked onto the field, gesticulating to make his point. But here is where Bob Fishel demonstrated a genius that utterly neutralized Martin's mischief. Maybe because of his past association with the Yankees, perhaps because of his background with Veeck and Steinbrenner, Fishel somehow foresaw such cockeyed events. Phillips, the umpire chief, pulled from his left pocket an affidavit, prepared by Fishel and signed by all four umpires at the July 24 game, stating that Brett and U. L. Washington, who scored before him, both had touched every base. Check, and checkmate.

Martin, flabbergasted, was now fully defeated yet still defiant. He informed umpire George Maloney he was playing this game under protest. Maloney drew the letter P with his fingers to indicate Martin's decision. When the public address announcer, Bob Sheppard, told the small crowd about this, the fans burst into applause. Martin didn't bother to watch the rest of the game, preferring instead to walk into the clubhouse lounge to view a rerun of *Barney Miller* on television. Nonetheless, the game continued. Hal McRae had vowed to aim for the fences when this game resumed, because it wasn't worth going all the way back to New York just to get a single. In fact, he did swing from the heels, but struck out against Frazier to end the top of the ninth.

Dan Quisenberry took the mound. A closer by job description and temperament, Quisenberry had fretted for days about this game, fearing he would feel like a starter instead of a reliever. "This is so serious, I think it's funny," he said. He also was to face three left-handed batters at the start, and the Yankees' lefties had collected 14 hits against him in 31 at-bats. He needn't have worried. Mattingly flied out to center, losing his hitting streak for good. Roy Smalley flied out to left field. Oscar Gamble pinch-hit for center-fielder Ron Guidry and grounded out, second to first. "I threw them all sinkers," Quisenberry said, after gaining his 33rd save of the year. "I gave them all the chances they desired. I was behind every hitter." No matter. Ballgame over. After 25 days of waiting, after all the fussing and fighting in courtrooms and club offices, the whole thing on this Thursday had taken nine minutes, 41 seconds.

The resolution had been perfectly peaceable. Despite all that whining about security and possible crowd riots, the Yankees sheepishly announced attendance at a very quiet 1,245—even after rainchecks from the July 24 game were honored. Other tickets were sold at either $2.50 for general admission or $1 for the bleachers, a great bargain to watch ten minutes of baseball history. The Yanks grumbled that the resumption of this game had cost them about $25,000, which really wasn't much even in 1983 dollars. Martin wouldn't talk to reporters afterward and instructed his pitching coach, Sammy Ellis, to order the writers out of the clubhouse after a few minutes. Many of the players also declined to speak. "If I wanted to watch a soap opera, I'd stay at home," Don Baylor said. "The word farce has been used too many times already, but it's the only one I can think of."

# 21

# Post-Pine-Tar Depression

*"I don't know what his vendetta is, but my team is suffering. It's hurt my team the last three weeks. Emotional things cause losses."*
—Billy Martin, about the ramifications of Lee MacPhail's ruling

Among baseball writers, there is a popular theorem, or perhaps more accurately an antitheorem, called "the fallacy of the predestined hit." Typically, it is applied when a runner is thrown out stealing second base, or stretching a single, or trying to score, and the next batter delivers a base hit. In this case, an analyst or commentator may hypothesize that the runner has cost his team a run. But there is no guarantee of this ensuing hit, if the runner had not been thrown out. The pitcher perhaps would have been working out of the stretch, delivering an entirely different pitch. The batter might have been protecting the plate, or trying to hit behind the runner. There is simply no way of knowing.

Given such vagaries to the game, it is certainly an exercise in arrogance to project a path of events that would have occurred if Lee MacPhail had not overruled the umpires' pine tar decision and allowed the Yankees to win that July 24 game, 4–3. Still, we can project one of many possible paths for the Yankees, this one far rosier than the actual course of events that followed. Perhaps the Yanks, having won 12 of their last 13 games before the overruling, would have sustained their momentous surge. Maybe Martin would have righted his own ship, pulled himself together, instead of continuing, even accelerating, his self-destructive ways. Maybe the Yankees (55-41 on July 27, just one game behind Baltimore when MacPhail issued his decision) might have hung in this race, even won the division. Maybe a successful finish to the 1983 season would have changed the mind of Goose Gossage, whose defection to San Diego created the need for Dave Righetti to move from starter to closer. Maybe Dave Winfield would have enjoyed an outstanding postseason, defusing the resentment that boiled inside George Steinbrenner about his player's ten-year, $15 million contract. Steinbrenner had been greatly displeased with Winfield's 1-for-22 performance in the 1981 World Series. Maybe a larger sample of postseason at-bats would have proved helpful to Winfield. That, in turn, might have been enough to deter some of the later, outrageous maneuvering against Winfield by Steinbrenner, who was banished from baseball for a second time in 1990 when their feud exploded into something very ugly.

This can all be dismissed as far-reaching conjecture, as "the fallacy of the predestined pennant." But even considering the infinite range of permutations, a strong argument can be made that the Pine Tar Game—or more precisely, the decision to overturn the pine tar ruling—was a critical turning point in Yankees history. Not a good one, either. The team fell into a tailspin that really wouldn't be reversed for another 13 years. And the effect was almost immediate. From the time MacPhail's decision went against them, until they lost the suspended game to Kansas City on August 18, the Yanks dropped 13 of 22 games, skidding to a 64-55 mark while rapidly falling out of the American League East race. Bad omens hovered quite literally above the team. On August 4, while warming up before the fifth inning, Winfield threw a baseball—playfully, or with deadly intent—at a seagull and killed the bird. He was brought to the Ontario Provincial Police station and charged with cruelty to animals. "It's the first time he's hit the cutoff man all season," Martin quipped. But the problems went well beyond such temporal shenanigans, and even beyond the record. The seeds for long-term ruination were planted. A resentful Martin imploded again, worse than ever. Steinbrenner lost patience with his manager, with Winfield, with his team.

Martin fell into a particular snit, immediately resentful of virtually every umpire's call. On July 31 at Comiskey Park in Chicago, three days after MacPhail's ruling, the manager was in a nasty frame of mind. "That's the way Billy is when he feels he's been cheated," Nettles wrote in his book, *Balls*. "Billy is one sore loser. I could see it building in Billy from the first inning. It was a hot day. About a hundred degrees. I said to somebody on the bench, 'Billy is going to get thrown out today.' I could see it right from the opening, because he was upset from the pine tar ruling . . . I could see he was seething inside." Before the game against the White Sox, Martin met with players and gave them his version of a pep talk. "There's no question we were cheated," he told the team. "MacPhail changed the rules against us. But we have to battle back and show we're true Yankees." Martin's idea of battling was evident quickly enough. He became embroiled in a pointed dispute with umpire crew chief Dale Ford in the fifth inning. Catcher Rick Cerone had just been ejected after arguing a close play at the plate and was replaced by Butch Wynegar. When Ford declared that Wynegar had reached his maximum number of five warm-up tosses, Martin confronted Ford and correctly maintained there was no specific rule in the book mandating such a limit. "Billy just wanted to keep arguing over the previous play," Ford later told reporters Moss Klein and Bill Madden. "I told him twice, 'Let's play.' But he was making a farce of the game, so I ran him." Ford ejected Martin, who returned to the manager's office in the visitors' clubhouse. By the time reporters came into that office after the game (a 12–6 win by the Yankees in 11 innings), Martin appeared inebriated and was looking for a more substantial fight. "Ford's a stone liar, a flat-out stone liar," Martin said. "He doesn't know the rules. I'm calling the umpire a liar, and I know the commissioner and MacPhail will call me on it. But I'm telling the truth. He's a crew chief? He couldn't be chief of a one-man Indian tribe. They ought to call the rule book the funny pages. All it's good for is when you go deer hunting and run out of toilet paper."

At the time, Murray Cook, recently named the Yankees' general manager, was traveling with the team and was witness to this tantrum. "Does that happen often?" he asked reporters. He was told that, yes, unfortunately, it does. The Yanks finished in third place, seven games behind the Orioles. On December 16, Steinbrenner fired Martin and hired Yogi Berra for his second stint as manager in the Bronx. This was the 11th managerial change by Steinbrenner in 11 years, involving eight different men. "The first time I considered a change was last month when Billy and I had dinner in Tampa," Steinbrenner said at the time. "I saw a different side of Billy that night. I sensed a fellow who was beginning to look beyond the dugout for the first time." This, of course, was nonsense. Martin had no constructive career outside the clubhouse. Away from the ballpark, he could be even more toxic, and he would eventually die in an alcohol-related car accident involving a friend. Martin lived and breathed pinstripes. He still had four years left on a $2 million contract, so it was just assumed, correctly, he'd be back again in short order to manage the Yankees no matter what Steinbrenner said. For the moment, however, he was named an adviser and the Yanks said he was free to consider other offers.

Several players were thrilled with the change and could hardly contain their relief at ridding themselves of such a tumultuous leader. Many of the veterans who had arrived here from other teams, such as Don Baylor, Ken Griffey, and Steve Kemp, had barely survived the season with Martin. Griffey's relationship with Martin was poisoned in part by the manager's dislike of children in the clubhouse—an odd double standard regarding professionalism. Ken Griffey, Jr., 13 years old during the 1983 season, always had been welcomed in the locker rooms of the Big Red Machine, when his dad played for the Cincinnati Reds. Martin chased him out of Yankee clubhouse, along with the other players' kids. Ken Jr. never forgave Martin or the Yankees, swearing he would never play for the franchise. He never did.

Baylor was the most verbal about his ambivalence toward

Martin. Martin had once ordered players to hand in a list to coach Don Zimmer of "three pitchers you would like to take the day off with." Baylor told Zimmer he hadn't come to New York for that. After the firing, Baylor told the *New York Times* he expected a more positive experience under the next manager. "If you like the guy you're playing for, you'll go that extra step. Instead of playing the ball off the wall, you'll catch the ball and crash into the wall." Steinbrenner said the club might benefit from a change in attitude, a softer approach by the next manager. "I can't criticize Billy's style and personality," Steinbrenner said. "In many ways, it's a lot like mine. But Yogi's style is a factor in this. It may be the right style for 1984."

It wasn't, of course. At least not the right style for Steinbrenner. The following year, 1984, the Yanks finished third again, 17 games behind the Tigers. Berra would be fired after a 6-10 start in 1985, an act that would infuriate the good-natured Hall of Famer and create a 14-year feud between the catcher and Steinbrenner. In 1984, the Yanks were never in the race, doomed by a 45-51 start. Righetti, the team's promising young starter who had thrown a no-hitter the previous season, was now forced to become the team's closer after Gossage signed with San Diego on January 6, 1984. Gossage's search for a new home had been quite a production, enduring months longer than he had suspected. "Nothing was happening," Gossage said. "The first sign of collusion was that no one was knocking at my door. Nobody wanted to get into a bidding war with George. Finally, I had to hold a press conference and declare that under no circumstance would I entertain an offer from the Yankees. I cried the night I made that decision. But baseball was not fun anymore there. You're in the World Series sometimes, you'd think you should be having fun. But he was the Boss. He was George."

Eventually, the San Diego Padres stepped up and signed Gossage to a four-year deal that would pay him around $1.7 million his first season. There, he and Nettles (traded to San Diego for pitcher Dennis Rasmussen) helped bring the Padres to the World Series in 1984. Some things never changed, however. Even though his manager, Dick Williams, ordered an intentional walk,

Gossage insisted on pitching to Kirk Gibson in the eighth inning of Game 5 of the 1984 World Series. The result was a three-run homer that clinched the title for the Detroit Tigers. Goose continued to feud with those above him. Before he was done in San Diego, Gossage was suspended in 1986 for complaining about the fiscal policies of team president Ballard Smith, who wouldn't sign anyone to long-term contracts. Upset that the players weren't allowed to drink beer in the clubhouse, Gossage also complained that owner Joan Kroc, the McDonald's heiress, was "poisoning the world with her cheeseburgers."

Steinbrenner, stripped of his star closer, at first dialed up Ron Guidry as a possible replacement. This put Guidry in a particularly awkward position, because he understood that his own refusal would mean that Righetti necessarily assumed the role.

"Steinbrenner called me to find out whether I would do it," Guidry said. "There was nobody out there they wanted to sign and they had nobody in the farm system. I told the old man, 'I'd just as soon finish what I'm doing. You've got two or three other starters to do the job.' I called David [Righetti] to tell him what I thought. He was one of my students. When he got to the Yanks, they put his locker next to me. I was supposed to tutor him. From the start, you could see in him somebody special. David and I had a great relationship, and now here it was either he or I would go to the bullpen. I figured I had five, six, seven years left, and I wanted to finish as a starter. I'd been stuck in the rotation, and I figured after starting out as a reliever, I figured I'd learned this. If I were a reliever, maybe I'd play longer, but that's not how you look at it. I looked at me being able to throw 250 innings a year, and I didn't think David could handle it. So I told him, 'You can become a much better reliever overall than a starter. But if you don't want to relieve, tell me.'"

Righetti agreed to the move. And while he was a successful closer, the Yanks' starting rotation suffered from his absence. Meanwhile, Steinbrenner had other problems, some of them about to become very large indeed. First, there was the matter of his behavior toward MacPhail during the pine tar incident, and the protests that followed. He was in trouble because of his public comments. He might have been in deeper waters if anyone knew Steinbrenner had ordered his staff to investigate MacPhail's every transaction. On December 23, 1983, not long after two days of hearings, commissioner Bowie Kuhn fined Steinbrenner and the Yankees $250,000, plus legal fees, the largest fine at the time ever leveled against a sports franchise. Kuhn said Steinbrenner's statements had "contravened the best interests of baseball." He no doubt was referring in particular to Steinbrenner's suggestion that MacPhail had better go house-hunting in Kansas City or risk his life in New York. Kuhn also cited Steinbrenner for his collusion in fostering or joining lawsuits by fans, when the Yankees were hoping to prevent the game's resumption.

The owner heaved a sigh of relief at this penalty. There was no suspension, the punishment he'd truly feared. Negotiations had been going on between Steinbrenner's attorneys and Kuhn's office since August, with every effort made to avoid such a ban. The lawyers, fresh off their defeat in the Pine Tar Game resumption case, had even gone back to New York State Supreme Court seeking an injunction to block the hearings on the possible suspension. They argued that Kuhn didn't like Steinbrenner, that the commissioner already had suspended Steinbrenner once before in 1974 for illegal contributions to Richard Nixon's reelection campaign, and that Kuhn would fail to act objectively in this matter. After a couple of sessions before an unmoved Justice Irwin Silbowitz, however, Steinbrenner withdrew his request and direct hearings began with the commissioner.

Steinbrenner already had been suspended one week by MacPhail in June 1983, for unrelated complaints about umpires—not to be confused with the two times that Martin was suspended during the season for similar behavior. So there was a long track record here with the cantankerous Yankees, and a considerable chance that Kuhn would suspend Steinbrenner. A fine felt almost like a reprieve. Still, this truly was an unprecedented monetary wallop. The Padres had been fined $100,000 for tampering with free agents. Steinbrenner himself had been fined $50,000 earlier in the year for grumping about National League umpires in spring training. The owner learned through that relatively minor event that his choice was clear: Pay the money or face banishment. He vastly preferred the former course.

"While we feel the penalty to be excessive, we will abide by the commissioner's decision," Steinbrenner said, in a late-night statement. He couldn't resist one final volley at the commissioner. "We certainly do not wish to cause him any problems in his last few days as commissioner. In some ways it is ironic. We were not the team using the illegal bat in the first place, but seem to come out worst in the whole matter. Nonetheless, we will abide by Bowie's decision."

Soon enough, however, the Boss would get himself involved in even dirtier business that threatened his hold on the franchise. In 1983, Winfield batted .283 with 32 homers and 116 RBI. He won a Gold Glove for his play in the outfield and made the All-Star team for the seventh straight season. Still, this did not result in any playoff games or mollify the owner. Steinbrenner pined openly for Reggie Jackson, often comparing Winfield in uncomplimentary terms to his right-field predecessor. In 1985, after a poor showing by Winfield during a critical September series against the Toronto Blue Jays, Steinbrenner asked Murray Chass of the *New York Times*, "Where is Reggie Jackson? We need a Mr. October or Mr. September. Winfield is Mr. May." It was just part of the Yankees' painful, 15-year drought, from 1981 to 1996, without a World Series appearance. And during that span, as Steinbrenner grew more and more frustrated, the player's charitable Winfield Foundation became Steinbrenner's chief target. The owner hired a Bronx man, Howie Spira, to dig up dirt on Winfield in this regard. When that private investigation came to light, Steinbrenner was banned for life from baseball, though he was reinstated after two years.

Would this sordid span of Yankees history have been altered for the better if MacPhail turned the other cheek and simply allowed the 4–3 result to stand? If we can't project the next pitch, how are we to imagine the next 15 years? One good thing would come of this pine tar legacy, if nothing else. Steinbrenner annually gave money to the Silver Shield Foundation and to the Baseball Assistance Team, a charitable organization affiliated with Major

League Baseball that supported members of the league's extended family—former players in need, Negro League players, umpires, and team personnel. The Yankees' owner would donate all revenues each year from one game in the Bronx. Right through the eighties, when the Yankees-Royals meetings were extremely well attended, Steinbrenner told his staff the money should come from games against Kansas City, not against lesser opponents. In this instance, a long-standing grudge proved bountiful to the most deserving.

# 22

# To the Victors . . .

The precious pine tar bat that Gaylord Perry attempted to commandeer—and that Tim McClelland disqualified—was sent to the league office for inspection on July 25 and eventually returned to George Brett when the Royals arrived in Detroit on July 28 for a four-game series with the Tigers. It already had begun earning Brett considerable extra pocket money. He signed a six-figure endorsement contract to appear in an Emory Air Freight commercial, which poked fun at the bat's shipping process. Brett drew a red line around the handle of the bat, 18 inches from the knob, and scraped the pine tar down to that legal limit. He kept using it for a while, but then Perry told Brett he was crazy, because it was too valuable a piece of paraphernalia. "That bat is worth a lot of money whole," Perry said. "It's not worth much broke in two." Brett heeded the entrepreneurial veteran's advice, dropped the precious cargo into a bat bag, and then sold it to collector Barry Halper for $25,000. This actually proved a costly transaction for Brett, who began to feel guilty about the sale almost immediately. Brett had plenty of money, after all, and this deal soon grated on his sense of baseball history. He approached Halper, who agreed to sell the bat back to Brett for the same $25,000. To seal the bargain, Brett gave Halper the bat he had used to rip those three homers against the Yankees in Game 3 of the 1978 American League Championship Series. That three-homer Louisville Slugger, in today's market, might have netted Brett a small fortune. But Brett felt better about the whole thing and soon sent the pine tar bat to Cooperstown, where it now rests in peace, not pieces.

In the immediate wake of the Pine Tar Game, John Schuerholz became a familiar talking head—an articulate one, too—on the most popular news and morning programs. He was suddenly being interviewed from Baltimore by Bryant Gumbel on the *Today* show. He appeared on *Nightline* with Ted Koppel, through a satellite feed from the Cross Keys Inn in Baltimore, where the Royals were lodged.

The season continued, along with the fallout for Brett—most of it favorable. For a while, Brett feared he had crossed several lines with some umpires, who might never pardon him. He'd maintained a good relationship with these hard-working men in blue, rarely embarrassing them on strike calls. He was relieved to discover that his tantrum was immediately forgiven. After Lee MacPhail overruled the decision, Joe Brinkman sent Brett a telegram (yes, a telegram; there were no texts or emails): "Congratulations," it read, from the man who'd held Brett in a viselike headlock. "A big day for you. Looking forward to seeing you again." Brett saw that as one of the classiest moves ever by an umpire, who after all had just been contradicted by the league office. Brett kept the telegram as another piece of baseball history. He didn't worry as much about his relationship with McClelland, who had been a friend. When Brett unveiled the bat again in Detroit, McClelland just happened to be behind the plate. As Brett stepped into the batter's box, McClelland removed his mask, winked at him, and said, "You wanna have some fun?" He was going to measure the pine tar against the plate again for the benefit of the crowd. Brett wasn't in the mood that day. "Timmy, let's just let this thing ride," Brett told him. "I'm tired of talking about it already."

The world, however, was not yet suffering from pine tar fatigue. It remained a fun talking point in Kansas City, even as the 1983 season devolved into something dreary and forgettable. From August 28 to September 10, the Royals dropped 12 of 14 games and fell to a very disappointing mark of 66-75. Brett's batting average skidded into the low .300s, mere mortals' territory. The team headed into a difficult off-season marked by drug scandals and roster transition. If the Pine Tar Game began a downward narrative arc for the Yankees, it clearly had little or nothing to do with where the Royals were heading.

At first, they were heading into a courtroom. Less than two weeks after the regular season ended, Willie Wilson, Willie Mays Aikens, and Jerry Martin all pleaded guilty to federal misdemeanor charges of attempting to possess cocaine. Martin, a utility outfielder, had been informed by the club that his option would not be picked up. A week later, Vida Blue, no longer on the roster after his release on August 1, pleaded guilty to a federal misdemeanor charge of possessing three grams of cocaine. Aikens's agent, Ron Shapiro, said his client would enter a treatment program.

Schuerholz found himself in the uncustomary, unpleasant role of fending off the media about a very negative story, telling reporters the Royals would step aside and let the commissioner handle any penalties. "The commissioner's office is a greater power than the club," Schuerholz said. "We could be falling over one another in handing out disciplinary action. We believe that when federal authorities finish their case, then the commissioner's office will decide if any further action is called for."

Aikens was dealt to Toronto in December. When Wilson was reinstated in mid-May, he was embraced by the team and by the community. His .301 batting average and 47 stolen bases that year probably didn't hurt.

By this juncture, Ewing Kauffman had sold 49 percent of the team to Avron Fogelman, the Memphis developer, but maintained control of the operations. Within two years, Fogelman would offer Brett, Wilson, Dan Quisenberry, and Frank White lifetime contracts with the team that included substantial investments in Fogelman's real estate business. White, the talented maverick, turned down the pact. He would continue to have a volatile relationship with the club for many seasons to come, long after his playing career ended. Kauffman didn't like all of these open-ended contracts and did his best to renegotiate the one with Wilson. Schuerholz was now established as the general manager, rebuilding the rotation with a group of young pitchers who eventually would lift the Royals to new heights. Bret Saberhagen, 19, Mark Gubicza, 21, and Danny Jackson, 22, were coming into their own.

The Royals, in transition, somehow managed to win the American League West in 1984 with an 84-78 record, then were swept by the Tigers in the championship series. Brett didn't have his best year, beset by injuries. He played in only 104 games and batted .284. Fogelman came to Brett and gave him what Brett would call the best advice in his life. "You've spent 43 days on the disabled list and I'm paying you more money than anybody else on the team," Fogelman said. "What I want you to do next year is go get yourself in the best shape you possibly can, and you come to spring training and go help us win a World Series." As Jack Brett, his dad, might have commented, Brett on occasion required this sort of kick in the pants to get him started. He worked out hard over the winter, shed some weight, and reported for spring training looking like a different man. His teammates told him he appeared too skinny, almost sick. But Brett hit 30 homers with 112 RBI, batting .335 in that magical 1985 season. Kansas City moved ahead of the Angels with a 12-1 stretch in early September, held on for the division title, and then won the American League Championship Series after a plot-twisting, seven-game marathon against the Blue Jays. The team was built around a strong rotation of Saberhagen, Gubicza, and three lefties—Jackson, Black, and Charlie Leibrandt—plus Quisenberry, still coming out of the bullpen. In the World Series, the Royals' win over the more established St. Louis Cardinals in the so-called I-70 Series was particularly surprising, considering Kansas City dropped the first two games at home, trailed three games to two, and needed to win the last two at Royals Stadium. The series spun on Game 6, and debate that followed over two blown umpire calls definitely invoked the aforementioned theorem, the fallacy of the predetermined hit. The first call came in the fourth inning, during a scoreless tie. White was called out trying to steal second, when replays indicated he was safe. Pat Sheridan then singled, which supposedly cost the Royals a run.

In the bottom of the ninth, down a run, the Royals received a big break when Jorge Orta was called safe on his leadoff ground ball to St. Louis first baseman Jack Clark. Clark's toss to pitcher Todd Worrell clearly beat Orta to the bag. Things got complicated after that, and Orta was eventually thrown out at third base. But pinch-hitter Dane Iorg knocked in two runs for the 2–1 victory and the Royals went on to win Game 7 in a celebratory, 11–0 romp before the home fans.

This was, of course, a cathartic moment for the Kansas City franchise, for its fans, for Kauffman, for Schuerholz, and for Howser. The manager's crowning, well-deserved moment unfortunately proved a prelude to tragedy. Midway through the next season, Howser was diagnosed with a brain tumor that would force his retirement and cause his death in 1987, at age 51. Nobody could have predicted such awful developments on October 27, 1985, when Kansas City celebrated its great conquest. Kauffman made a conscious effort not to appear too triumphant immediately afterward—at least in public.

"I distinctly remember his comment," Dean Vogelaar said. "He said, 'We lost with grace. And we're going to win with grace.'" Perhaps, but there was no hiding this man's glee. "He was so excited, the most excited I've seen him in his whole life," Julia Kauffman said. "One of the biggest thrills in my life happened that deciding game. They took him down from his seat to the clubhouse in the seventh inning and he turned around, looked at me, and said, 'Do you want to go with me?' This was the biggest honor. I was the only kid in there during the celebration. Even my mother didn't go."

Julia Kauffman remembers that her father would then take the World Series championship trophy everywhere he went, for weeks, for months. He brought it to his country club. He took it to the local club where he played gin. He took it to speeches. He showcased it in his home. It was the centerpiece to all parties the Kauffmans staged in their home at Mission Hills. Everyone was more or less forced to stand in front of it, admire the new silverware. "It went on and on like this until Joe Burke finally suggested they have replicas made," Julia Kauffman said. "Daddy made three or four replicas." The daughter still has three of them—one in her home, one in her New York City apartment, one in her father's old office at Marion Labs.

Ewing Kauffman did well to appreciate the moment. This would be his last major trophy. Brett won a third and final batting title in 1990, but the Royals were slipping far out of contention. Then came the real blow: Schuerholz left Kansas City for the Braves after the disappointing 1990 season, and after 22 years in the organization. The decision was extremely difficult for Schuerholz, who agonized over his relocation for weeks and had several sit-downs with Kauffman to discuss his departure.

"He was a remarkable man for me, he did a lot of things to make me grow as an executive," Schuerholz said. "When I decided to become a Brave, I spent many hours talking about it with him. I'd signed on to a lifetime contract. I felt I was a partner in that organization and I never thought I'd ever leave the Kansas City area unless it was in a pine box—that's how much I loved it. I put a lot of blood, sweat, and tears into that organization. But Mr. Kauffman had sold part of the team and it was starting to turn. That's not an indictment of Mr. Fogelman, who was young and dynamic. But Mr. Kauffman's health was not good. I just had the sense it wasn't your father's Kansas City Royals anymore. It was changing. Then I had an opportunity that was presented to me."

That opportunity was with the Atlanta Braves, a team that had been mired in or around the cellar of the National League West for the past six seasons. Schuerholz had worked alongside Braves president Stan Kasten on a committee aiming to help former major leaguers get back on their feet. George W. Bush, the future president, was another member.

"We left a meeting in New York, spent a couple of innings at a game in Yankee Stadium," Kauffman said. "Stan started telling me on the ride back that there's a chance Atlanta was going to keep Bobby Cox in the dugout and bring in a new general manager. It was like one of those cartoons, where a light bulb goes on over your head."

Schuerholz's arrival marked a dramatic Braves revival, though

Cox certainly deserved a good deal of credit for already having brought Tom Glavine, David Justice, and Chipper Jones into the organization. Schuerholz cemented that progress, and the Braves went on to qualify for the playoffs 15 straight years, with the exception of the aborted 1994 season. During that entire span, and beyond, the Royals failed to make it to the playoffs even once. Kauffman would die in 1993 of bone cancer, though with typical foresight he had prearranged a succession plan that would keep the Royals in their small-market home, where they still reside— with George Brett as vice president of baseball operations, more an inspirational presence than a day-to-day counselor. "George was such a major part of the good image of the Royals, he was all about winning and positive representation of the club," Schuerholz reflected. "Officially, his role is vice president of baseball operations, but his primary job is to keep being George Brett, which is a most valuable asset for the Royals."

At times, he has been far more than a mere mascot. Brett tried a real run as an interim batting coach in 2013, after the Royals got off to a terrible start. The team improved considerably, whether or not it was due to his instruction. Brett thought some of the guys were overreaching, going for the big home run too often. "They were trying to be heroes rather than soldiers," he said. Brett would walk around the clubhouse, or dugout, or batting cage, asking each player his name. The player, a bit confused, would answer. Brett would tell him to be that player, not Babe Ruth, Mark McGwire, or Barry Bonds. That was Brett's gimmick, and he thought it worked to some degree. Brett didn't enjoy the travel that came with the job, however, and he didn't feel he was reaching the players on a technical level. He soon quit the daily grind, but not before discovering the players of this modern era knew quite a bit about the Pine Tar Game—just like everyone else.

"I played twenty years in the major leagues," Brett said. "I did some good things, and the one at-bat I'm remembered for is an at-bat in July, not an at-bat in October like Reggie Jackson. Only in New York. It would have never been that big a deal if it had happened in Cleveland. This is just supposed to be a little asterisk to go with a career. But everybody knows about it. The guys on the team today still talk about it. Jarrod Dyson told me, 'You mixed up some dust that day.' I don't even know what that means."

Dust and pine tar. Brett's own three boys, right through their teenaged years, would pop in the tape of the Pine Tar Game, fast-forward it to near the very end, watch Dad go berserk. "They sit around and chuckle," Brett said. A good time is had by all.

# 23

## Different Kind
## of Rivalry

The Yankees arrived in Kansas City on June 6, 2014, for a four-game, wraparound weekend series at Kauffman Stadium that was fairly meaningful, by expansion-era standards. The two franchises, which had drifted in different directions over the previous 20 years or so, had at this time wandered back together in the middle of the pack. Both teams were battling the .500 mark at this time, early Wild Card contenders, though they would soon diverge dramatically in a very unfamiliar fashion. The Yankees would struggle with an anemic offense and sink in the East, out of the playoffs for a second straight year. The Royals, meanwhile, were just starting to put together a remarkable run to their first World Series since 1985—keyed by several substantial winning streaks. The first streak, ten straight victories, would start during this series against the Yankees and lift them to the top of the American League Central. Another eight-game streak, ending on August 11, allowed the Royals to climb back into first for the first time this late in any season since 2003, and only the second time since 1985. They were on a 24-6 tear, soon wrapping up a playoff spot for the first time in 29 years. Kansas City then made real history, becoming the first major league team ever to win eight straight playoff games in the same season. That surge began with the Wild Card game, when manager Ned Yost's team knocked off Oakland in a rollicking comeback, a 12-inning victory at the

K. The Royals then swept the Los Angeles Angels in the Division Series and the Baltimore Orioles in the American League Championship Series. "This is the most fun I've had here since I was playing," said George Brett, on hand for the pennant drive. The Royals eventually came within a hair's breadth of a World Series title, losing 3–2 to the San Francisco Giants in Game 7 of the World Series at Kauffman Stadium. Alex Gordon, representing the tying run, was stranded on third base when Salvador Pérez hit a foul popup caught by Pablo Sandoval.

Back in June, there were already strong clues about a Royals revival, which should have been more than enough to sell some tickets. This was also Derek Jeter's last scheduled visit as an active player to Kansas City, part of his farewell tour—though the future Hall of Famer would return once more in late August to make up a rainout. Jeter bristled at that phrase, "farewell tour." "We're still trying to win games," he said. For gravy, on this perfect, cool evening, the Royals threw in Fireworks Night, the sort of promotion more typically reserved for matchups against lesser opponents on weekday nights.

When the gates opened at Kauffman Stadium, however, there was no rush for the turnstiles. The announced attendance was just 23,418, and the number of empty seats suggested a significantly lower gate number. Before the game, Jeter, a student of the sport, looked around from the visitors' dugout and said he knew well the heated history of this rivalry.

"I was a Yankee fan growing up," said Jeter, who came a little late to that table, since he was born in 1974. "So I'm well aware of the fights and brawls they had. There's a lot of history between New York and Kansas City." He was only three years old when George Brett slid into Graig Nettles and started the brawl during Game 5 in 1977, but he'd seen the clips, heard the stories from Don Zimmer. What struck him as oddest of all was that the game had gone on as if nothing happened. "Neither one of them got thrown out," Jeter said, shaking his head. "That's how much times have changed."

By now the meetings between the franchises had cooled so much that Brett, vice president of the Royals, went on a vacation trip and didn't bother to show up for this series. Or maybe he just didn't want to catch sight again of those uniforms, those caps with the interlocking "NY." "I've heard it's still personal," Jeter said. He had himself spoken with Brett on occasion and found him to be engaging enough. It was difficult for Jeter to imagine such levels of hostility from these teams. There were no such feelings anymore in either clubhouse, or owner's box.

The glory days of Royals-Yankees once had offered a compelling personality contrast: George Steinbrenner, the triumphant, rules-busting bully, versus Ewing Kauffman, the humanistic innovator. If these portraits were often drawn too definitively as simple caricatures, there was surely some truth to the depictions. In the much grayer world of 2014, the franchises offered a different pairing: Hal Steinbrenner, bland custodian of the Yankees, versus David Glass, renowned corporate efficiency expert. There was nothing particularly romantic or striking about this matchup between a nearly unquotable heir and the former president and CEO of Wal-Mart, Sam Walton's right-hand man.

George Steinbrenner died at age 80 on July 13, 2010. Just as his purchase of the Yankees back in 1973 had been a serendipitous financial bonanza for the family, so, too, was the date of his passing. He died during the one year when his wife and four children would not have to pay a penny of estate tax on a franchise then valued at about $1.1 billion by Forbes. The tax, which had been set at 45 percent for estates inherited in 2009, might have cost the family as much as $500 million if they retained the Yankees. After considerable political wrangling in Congress—Republicans wanted to kill this so-called death tax—the rate was reset at 35 percent in 2011. But the tax did not exist at all in 2010, after its expiration at the end of December 2009. This break likely allowed the Steinbrenners to keep the Yankees, rather than sell them off in order to pay the tax bill.

For a period when George Steinbrenner was still alive and his faculties were in decline—a sad span of perhaps three to five years, during which his family and Yankees brass loyally protected the macho image of their patriarch—it appeared that his older son, Hank, might succeed George as primary team operator.

This would have been great fun for the New York media, because Hank was every bit as much the loose cannon as his father. But after George officially ceded control of the club, the safer, quieter Hal was elected chairman of the board on September 28, 2007, and became the reluctant public face of the Yankees as managing partner. There was nothing inherently wrong with Hal Steinbrenner, a good-looking, soft-spoken man. He didn't pretend to be a baseball expert, the way his father believed himself to be the world's best evaluator of talent. Hal generally listened to the advice of counselors such as Brian Cashman. He was reliable and levelheaded. His dad once packed him off to military school and, goodness knows, it couldn't have been easy living up to the father's expectations. Considering all that, Hal Steinbrenner deserved some slack, even admiration. He'd done what was necessary to keep the Yankees in contention, spent plenty of money and then some. He and his brother had in particular reacted quickly to two rare, disappointing years, 2008 and 2013, when the Yankees failed to reach the playoffs. Before the 2009 championship season, the Yanks signed C. C. Sabathia, A. J. Burnett, and Mark Teixeira. While the Red Sox screamed for a salary cap, Hank Steinbrenner said that Major League Baseball should be thrilled to death the Yankees had donated $110 million in revenue-sharing and luxury tax money.

"As long as we're doing that and giving all this money to other teams in revenue sharing, a staggering amount, we should be able to spend on salaries what we want to," Hank Steinbrenner said. "Because of revenue sharing and because of the popularity nationwide, the Yankees are critical to baseball." After a disappointing 2013 season marked by injuries and a burgeoning Alex Rodriguez scandal, Hal Steinbrenner gambled a fortune in the off-season, $175 million, on Masahiro Tanaka, even though the team's prior experiences with untested Japanese pitching imports, Hideki Irabu and Kei Igawa, resulted in fiscal fiascos. He also committed $153 million during that off-season in order to steal Jacoby Ellsbury from the Red Sox, plus many millions more on Carlos Beltran, Brian McCann, and Brian Roberts. The Yankees received largely unsatisfactory returns on these investments.

Tanaka appeared to be the gem of the bunch, but then a midseason tear in an elbow ligament threatened to turn the pitcher into yet another free agent disaster. The team's offense sputtered along terribly with an unfamiliar lineup as the Yanks lagged behind Baltimore in the American League East.

Hal Steinbrenner had tried, anyway. He was no bean counter. It was just that his lack of bravado, his businesslike approach to baseball, lacked the blood and bones of his father. Hal wanted to win. George needed to win. George fired managers over mere losing streaks. Hal gave Joe Girardi a four-year, $16 million contract starting after a nonplayoff season. When Hal Steinbrenner finally piped up at an owners' meeting in mid-August 2013 to say the fading Yankees needed to "step it up," he failed to issue accompanying employment threats, as his father surely would have done. After another disappointing year in 2014, Hal Steinbrenner blamed himself and re-signed general manager Brian Cashman to a three-year contract. "I don't make rash decisions," he said. George Steinbrenner needed to be the focus of public debate, 24/7. It filled a desperate void in the Boss that only a psychiatrist might diagnose after decades of analysis. Not Hal.

"I'm sure it's a difference of personalities, but it's also a conscious decision," Hal Steinbrenner said. "I don't believe that the owner needs to be front and center and out there all the time. I don't think that's one of the most important things to the organization or to the team. But it's also my personality. I'm a pretty introverted guy. It's just not something that I've ever wanted, to be out there in the spotlight. That's not me."

The Royals' modern saga had been even less inspiring until their unexpected emergence in 2014. When Kauffman died in August 1993, he donated his beloved franchise to the Greater Kansas City Community Foundation, a five-member group chaired by Glass. According to a mandate in Kauffman's will, the foundation was given six years to sell the club to a local owner who was willing to guarantee the franchise would stay in Kansas City, and willing to pay at least $75 million for the honor. Not long before his death, Kauffman had expressed fears that "no one would want to buy a baseball team that consistently loses millions of dollars and had little prospect of making money because it was in a small city." Kauffman therefore offered a concession, reluctantly. If no such owner could be found by 2002, the club could be sold to the highest bidder, without guarantee of keeping the franchise in Kansas City. A New Yorker, Miles Prentice, first offered $75 million for the Royals in 1999, but Major League Baseball rejected this sale and Glass eventually purchased the club for $96 million—which was considerably less than what Prentice was willing to pay after a brief bidding war. The league-mandated, minimum personal net worth was an issue with Prentice, but it was also evident that Glass very badly wanted this team for himself.

The son of small-town Missouri farmers, Glass's business acumen and cutthroat, cost-cutting instincts eventually earned him a great fortune. He took over the Royals as interim CEO in September 1993 upon the death of Kauffman and immediately made it clear he would run the Royals in a fashion similar to that which he had maintained at Wal-Mart. While he kept the club in Kansas City, Glass at first appeared only to care about the bottom line.

He slashed the team's payroll from $40.5 million in 1994 to a measly $18.5 million by 1996, as Kansas City's outlay dropped from the fourth-highest to the second-lowest in the league. The club's performance also dived precipitously. Glass had been one of the hardest-line owners during the disastrous 1994 major league strike, demanding a salary cap and supporting the use of replacement players at the start of 1995 spring training. By 2000, Glass was fully in charge and there was considerable resentment about the club's deteriorating performance. The Royals were no longer very cuddly. On two occasions, Glass approached Julia Kauffman to ask if she would approve changing the name of Kauffman Stadium, selling the rights to a company. She reluctantly approved the idea of such sales, though they didn't happen. On June 9, 2006, two local radio reporters, Bob Fescoe and Rhonda Moss, were ordered to hand in their season's credentials after aggressively questioning Glass and new general manager Dayton Moore about the firing of ex-GM Allard Baird. Glass, in a fashion so very unlike Kauffman's, argued openly with Moss and told her she was "completely wrong." The Royals put out a statement on the matter, declaring, "The credentials were not revoked because someone asked tough questions—we get those every day—but for reasons of decorum. The tone, the abruptness, and the forcefulness with which their questions and added commentary were presented, offended many at the news conference." There was also a noticeable drop-off in areas of customer service. After the 2014 World Series, ESPN revealed that food stands at the Kansas City ballpark had been guilty of several critical health violations. Somehow, nothing like this had ever happened under Kauffman's watch.

All this affected not only the standings, but the club's image nationwide. The Royals were once a big draw at Yankee Stadium, the second-hottest ticket behind only the Red Sox. Now, when Kansas City arrived in the Bronx, the Yanks often planned a major promotion in order to sell tickets. The Royals drew an average of only 26,872 fans on the road in 2014, dead last in the majors. At home, they attracted an average of 24,154, ahead of only five other teams, all noncontenders. This was what traditionally happened when a team endured decades of mediocrity. It would require several years of contention to reverse the trend. By comparison, the Yanks drew 42,520 at home and 35,512 on the road in 2014, a second down year in terms of performance on the field.

From 1986 through 2014, the Yanks owned a 165-99 head-to-head edge over Kansas City, generally feasting on these minnows to pad their own record in the American League East. In 1998, the Yanks went 10-0 against Kansas City on their way to a 114-win season. But again, there was no longer a buzz, no sense of occasion. Before interleague and intradivisional play came to dominate the schedules, Kansas City and New York would face each other as many as 12 times during each regular season. In 2014, they met only seven times. The Yanks won four. The two teams also stopped playing each other in the postseason, because the Royals weren't getting into the playoffs.

There were many legitimate reasons for that extended failure on the field. The Royals, as much as any franchise in baseball, were squeezed by the insane economics of the sport. In 2013, the Yanks began the season with a payroll of nearly $229 million, which didn't even account for the luxury tax penalties they would pay to the league. Only the Los Angeles Dodgers were in their ballpark. The Royals, by contrast, began that season with a total payroll of just over $80 million, a hefty sum that still ranked them only 21st in the league. They simply didn't have the infrastructure to bid for the same free agents as the Yankees, or even retain their own star players. Gate revenues were only part of the equation. In 2012, News Corporation purchased 49 percent of the Yankees' YES broadcast network while it was at a valuation of $3 billion. News Corp. had the option of acquiring 80 percent at a valuation of $3.8 billion. As part of the deal, the team's rights fee from YES increased on an upward, sliding scale from $85 million in 2012 to $350 million in 2042. This obviously was an enormous resource for the Yankees, who could bankroll nearly half their player payroll on these rights fees alone. In March 2013, Forbes put the Yankees' value at $2.3 billion, with revenues close to $500 million. That estimated franchise worth was nearly $700 million more than the second-place Dodgers. Meanwhile, Forbes estimated the Royals' franchise value at just $457 million. Kauffman Stadium was worth $80 million of that, with gate receipts of $38 million and total revenue of $169 million. Nielsen ratings rose significantly for Kansas City in 2013, when the Royals remained competitive with a winning team in a weak division. But their television contract with Fox Sports earned them a mere $20 million per year, the fourth-lowest rate in the league, and extended through 2019.

The Royals were trapped. Again, by way of comparison, the Dodgers' contract with Time Warner Cable was worth $250 million per year—though by 2014 that package became rife with distribution problems. Ten teams in the league were getting at least $50 million. The Royals surely were suffering such ignominies in part because of their relatively tiny market, about 2.2 million people. Kansas City was the second-smallest market in Major League Baseball, ahead of Milwaukee. But that wasn't the only factor. There were anomalies galore in this business of network baseball contracts. The St. Louis Cardinals, traditional winners playing in one of the last true baseball cities in America, owned the worst TV contract of all, at $14 million.

Nobody could feel too sorry for Glass, despite the team's financial limitations. He had purchased the Royals for $96 million. During the next 15 years, the franchise increased in value by nearly 500 percent—quite a profit whenever Glass decided to sell. In addition, any sports franchise presents an owner with an assortment of potential tax breaks, particularly during the first years following the purchase. A new owner can soon depreciate so-called assets such as his player contracts, then apply these "losses" to his income tax return. The inventor of this loophole was none other than Bill Veeck, who in 1946 purchased the Cleveland Indians and declared 90 percent of his team's value to be in "intangible assets." He figured that his players' skills deteriorated over the course of their contracts, and that he could deduct their lost value over time. The Internal Revenue Service somehow agreed. This became known as the roster depreciation allowance. As Veeck wrote in his 1962 memoir, *The Hustler's Handbook*, "Look, we play the Star-Spangled banner before every game—you want us to pay taxes, too?"

Others quickly followed his example, even as the IRS refined its rules. From 1977 to 2004, owners were permitted to write off 50 percent of the sales price over five years. Starting in 2004, owners could write off 100 percent over 15 years, a rule change that at least encouraged less immediate turnover. Still, some turnover remained inevitable, so that the next rich guy could make a killing on both resale and taxes.

In addition to all that, Glass and the Royals often enjoyed the benefits built into the league's revenue-sharing plan. Under this program, every team anted up 31 percent of its net local revenue. The money went into a pool and was equally distributed to every team. So Glass received a piece of that big Yankee broadcast contract and gate money, after all. Major League Baseball also maintained a central fund, fed by national broadcast licensing rights, which was divided evenly among the franchises. The plan was in transition, yet it continued to protect the smaller-market teams such as the Royals. In this regard, Glass was certainly in good shape with his team—not that he needed to make a profit on baseball.

Considering these perks, it wasn't hard to understand why Glass finally relented and began spending a little more money on the Royals. A big symbolic trade occurred in December 2012, when Glass okayed a deal that sent outfield prospect Wil Myers to Tampa Bay for expensive veteran pitcher James Shields, who was set to earn $13.5 million in 2014. The trade gave fresh hope to Royals' fans, who finally saw Glass come through financially the way that Kauffman had been willing to do years earlier. There was an immediate payoff, too, in the standings.

"We're not interested in making money, but we don't want to subsidize it to any great extent," Glass said. "Except I've said that if we have an opportunity to win our division or be competitive, we were certainly willing to step up and do whatever it took to take advantage of the opportunity."

Again, the use of the word "subsidize" was not really accurate here, because Glass would more than get his money back on tax breaks through depreciation and any eventual resale. In fact, he was the one being subsidized by the league. This was a no-harm, no-foul business model followed by many sports owners, who still expected operations to break even or turn a profit on an annual basis. Owners in the National Basketball Association and National Hockey League often pleaded poverty, even locked out their players, in order to establish strict and then stricter payroll salary caps. They did this by arguing many of their smaller-market franchises were losing money—which was true, on a short-view, yearly basis. In the long haul, owners were pocketing a fortune in taxes and increased franchise valuation.

When the 2014 season opened, the numbers weren't much different than those in 2013. The Yanks owned the second-highest payroll behind the Los Angeles Dodgers at $203.8 million, rescued only a bit by shedding the majority of the salary owed the suspended Alex Rodriguez. Their roster players received an average annual salary of $8 million, a figure that was greater than the Dodgers and second in the world only to Manchester City of the Premier League—coincidentally, a marketing and ownership partner with the Yanks in Major League Soccer. The Royals came in at $92 million, which placed them 19th out of 30. The average age of the Yanks' Opening Day roster was the oldest in the major leagues, at 31 years, 225 days, even without the suspended Alex Rodriguez. The Royals were more typical in this category, with an average active roster age of 28 years, 360 days. The Yankees were listed by Vegasinsider.com at 12-to-1 to win the World Series while the Royals were at 50-to-1. These were relatively short odds for the Royals, who had demonstrated considerable promise at long last thanks to a rejuvenated farm system. They were a fast base-to-base team, defensively solid. The backbone of the 2014 Royals team had either been developed within the organization or acquired years ago in long-range trades: reliever Greg Holland, center-fielder Lorenzo Cain, first baseman Eric Hosmer, shortstop Alcides Escobar, left-fielder Alex Gordon, and catcher Salvador Pérez. When the Royals surged into contention in August, ownership gave another significant indication it was all-in for this pennant race by acquiring on waivers the power-hitting Josh Willingham from the Twins as a designated hitter. Glass agreed to shell out the $1.8 million remaining on Willingham's contract.

"If we find players that make sense, Mr. Glass has always been willing to add a piece that we think can help us win," Moore said. Spending on such lineup pieces was a necessity for any ambitious contender. Very few low-payroll clubs had captured a championship since the cost of free agent signings spiraled in the late nineties. The 2003 Florida Marlins were an exception, with an Opening Day payroll of less than $50 million, about one-third the cost of the New York roster they defeated in the World Series. When the Yanks crossed the $200 million mark in 2005, the White Sox won the title with a payroll of about $75 million. Other than those exceptions to the rule, the payrolls of major league champions were consistently among the top ten in the league. Several teams, most notably the Oakland A's of *Moneyball* fame, managed to contend for periods of time. The bottom line, though, generally proved to be the bottom line. Until Glass agreed to open his wallet a smidgen, the Royals had been near that bottom.

# 24

## All Is (Almost)
## Forgiven

Induction weekend at the Hall of Fame in Cooperstown is a fickle affair, largely reliant on the whims of baseball writers who vote in judgment of candidates. The weekend can be a joyous, welcoming party when there are fresh inductees. In the summer of 2013, however, it had been a dreary event, devoid of any new faces. No player received the mandatory 75 percent of ballots for entry into the Hall. The writers who submitted ballots were busy snubbing the steroid guys, while the veterans' committee elected three men who had long ago expired. July 2014 was very different. There were six live bodies to fete in Cooperstown, the largest incoming class in more than 40 years: Frank Thomas, Greg Maddux, Tom Glavine, Joe Torre, Tony La Russa, and Bobby Cox. Forty-six other Hall of Famers were on hand for the Saturday procession. This parade was a relatively fresh tradition. The stars, most of them sitting next to their wives, were placed individually in the back of Ford pickup trucks, then driven from Doubleday Field down Chestnut Street, along Main Street to the Hall of Fame museum—now run by Jeff Idelson, yet another former public relations director for George Steinbrenner.

The weather was perfect, the sun shining, as George Brett, class of 1999, and Goose Gossage, 2008, took their turns in the trucks. Gossage had become one of the staunchest, most vocal opponents of steroid users' gaining entrance into the Hall. This had become something of a crusade for him. He was less vocal about the absence of George Steinbrenner, another notable point of debate. Neither Steinbrenner nor Ewing Kauffman had been elected to the Hall by the veterans' committee, a slight that thoroughly annoyed members of both families. While a good argument might be made that Steinbrenner had not lived up to the character clause in the Hall's guidelines, the same could be said for some of the other scoundrels with plaques in Cooperstown. And after all, Steinbrenner's Yankees had won seven world championships. There was no excuse imaginable for Kauffman's omission. He was the exemplary founder of a model expansion franchise, an innovator of the first order, yet was passed over when nominated for the 2008 class.

In any case, their surrogates were on hand in the 2014 Cooperstown parade. Goose Gossage, Reggie Jackson, Dave Winfield, George Brett, and Whitey Herzog—Yankees and Royals, all in a row—took their rides in the pickup trucks before adoring fans pressed against metal barriers along the sidewalks. When Brett and Gossage reached the museum, they would pick up a long-standing conversation started before the parade, and one that will carry on for some time. They are now good friends, though it surely didn't start out that way.

The two men never spoke a word to each other during their active careers, which were lengthy and overlapped almost from start to finish. Brett played 21 seasons, from 1973 to 1993; Gossage played 22, retiring a year later. They hated each other. They would tell you that then, and remind you of it now. "I didn't like Brett," Gossage said. "I had tremendous respect for him, but I couldn't stand him." Then one day in 1995 that all changed. Brett was retired and was down in Davenport, Florida, at Baseball City with the Royals, during spring training. Gossage was with the Yankees, when they were still headquartered in Fort Lauderdale. The two teams were playing an exhibition in Baseball City when one of the clubhouse boys came over to Brett with a message from Gossage, who had decided to break the ice, through an emissary.

"Goose says he's opening up a restaurant in Colorado Springs and would love a bat from you to put up there," the boy said.

Brett said fine, he'd be happy to do it. The clubhouse kid came back an inning later and said Gossage would prefer if the bat were all tarred up. "I went to the traveling secretary and said, 'Give me a bat,'" Brett said. "I got a pine tar rag and loaded it full of pine tar. For nine innings of an exhibition game against the Yankees, I sat there and every half inning I would just put a ton of that stuff on, put a bunch of dirt over it, rosin over the dirt, let it sit for twenty, thirty minutes, then do it again. Boy, by the end of the day that thing looked like it had been through a war."

Brett gave the bat to Gossage at the end of the game, and the two shook hands. "That's really the first words I'd ever said to him," Brett said.

It was also the first time, really, that Gossage was able to view that whole pine tar incident with any good humor. "I never thought it was very funny," Gossage said. The bat headed to Gossage's restaurant, Burgers-N-Sports, in Parker, Colorado. Then the newfound friendship received a big boost in 2008 when Gossage, finally, was elected by the baseball writers into the Hall. Brett had been a no-brainer candidate, elected easily in his first year of eligibility alongside a class that included Robin Yount and Nolan Ryan. Gossage, however, dangled out there for a decade until he suddenly garnered 85.8 percent from the voters. Basically, writers had run out of other candidates and Gossage entered the Hall alone that summer. Just Goose, and his Fu Manchu mustache.

By then, the name of Gossage's restaurant had been changed to Old School Burgers, with two additional Colorado franchises. They all eventually closed, and in 2011 one restaurant was seized by the Colorado Department of Revenue for unpaid taxes. This was a company problem, not a personal one. Gossage was not in dire need of money. But in late fall of 2013, Gossage, no sentimentalist, decided to empty the closets and basement in his Colorado Springs home in order to sell virtually all his baseball memorabilia. During the course of his career, Gossage had earned more than $10 million from nine different baseball clubs. He and his wife, Corna, had modest aims in life. Gossage mostly liked to hunt. But there were three grown boys to consider, who were going to have their own families. "Selling this stuff, we can do some things," Gossage said. "I've always had to work for what I've got, I'm not a trust fund baby. I worked like a majority of Americans worked."

The autographed baseball that Gossage earned with his first major league victory went for $2,022. His 1976 White Sox jersey was sold for $4,147. His 1977 Pirates jersey went for $5,020. His 2008 National Baseball Hall of Fame induction ring was purchased for $41,372. The biggest prize, his 1978 Yankees World Series championship ring, sold for a whopping $66,734. Altogether, sales of his memorabilia totaled $365,000. The bidding was a great success, even if it couldn't quite match another item auctioned in the same session: Jesse Owens's Olympic gold medal sold for $1,466,574. While this was going on for nearly two weeks, Gossage never went on the SCP Auctions website to see how his stuff was selling. "Baseball taught me if it's out of my control, don't worry about it," Gossage said. "Whatever will be, it will be."

One thing, though: He didn't auction the bat that Brett tarred up for him in Baseball City. Gossage didn't think he could get much for it, because it came without the memories included—and without the friendship. "I love him to death now," Gossage said of Brett.

While Brett had come to feel the same way about Gossage, he did not necessarily extend the same affection or courtesies to other former Yankees. He didn't make it a habit to socialize with Jackson or Winfield at the Hall of Fame ceremonies. Not everyone had broken down Brett's still-competitive barriers. The interlocking "NY" remained a red cape to Brett, and to some of his old teammates.

"It's weird, but when I see an ex–Kansas City player, I usually still get the silent treatment," Willie Randolph said. "And especially George Brett. That brother feels deep. He's cordial, it's not like he's spitting at you. But you sense his disdain. I hated them. They hated us. Frank White, Willie Wilson, there's some warmth there. But Al Cowens, Hal McRae, they'll roll their eyes at me when I walk past. They wouldn't speak to me. Brett always had this arrogance that, 'I'm the best hitter in the world and I kicked your ass and I know it and I did my best to do it.' There was mutual respect, but nobody liked anybody."

Inside the National Baseball Hall of Fame in Cooperstown, there is no doubt which major league franchise is king. The New York Yankees practically own the place with their exhibits, uniforms, plaques, and trinkets from every era since Babe Ruth came aboard. The Royals have only a few secondary references, and one small window display. It is on the second floor, honoring Brett and the Royals of the 1970s and 1980s. Behind the glass, there is Frank White's glove and a World Series baseball signed by the American League champions, the 1980 Royals, donated by the Kauffman family. From that same year, when Brett batted .390, the display features his number-5 uniform, size 42. On the right-hand side of the window, unpretentious and artfully low-lit, Brett's pine tar bat stands vertically in place, "loaned by the Brett family." Fifty-year-old fathers stop to explain to their teen-aged children the significance of the red line sketched by Brett that encircles the Model T-85 Louisville Slugger, 18 inches from the handle. Much of the pine tar was rubbed off by the slugger, when he was still using it. Brett wants someday soon to tar up the bat again to where the sticky stuff reached on July 24, 1983. Then visitors to Cooperstown can see for themselves why Brett's fearsome clout, on that gray Sunday afternoon in the Bronx, was once ruled the ultimate oxymoron: a game-losing home run.

# Acknowledgments

Any book, from its first imaginings, is a leap of faith on the part of many people—including the author. Can it be delivered on time? Will it be a quality work? Will it sell a single copy? For some reason, Brant Rumble, my editor at Scribner, took that risk with this book and for that I am very grateful. My agent, David Black, likely had something to do with Rumble's willingness to give it a go. When Rumble later moved on to a new publishing house, Rick Horgan and David Lamb graciously took on the project and saw it to completion.

The cooperation of former Yankees and Royals officials was essential in reporting out this book. Former public relations directors Marty Appel and Dean Vogelaar were particularly helpful. Dean Taylor, still an executive in the Royals' front office, was extremely generous in sharing stories and sending me a copy of the original Pine Tar Game protest letter, which he wisely retained for posterity. Julia Kauffman took the time out to meet and discuss her father, a man she greatly, understandably admired.

Since this is a book about a specific time and place in my reporting life, I should cite the New York writers who made that crazy era particularly enjoyable, or at least palatable. That would include baseball beat guys such as Moss Klein, Jack O'Connell, Murray Chass, Bill Madden, Norm MacLean, Marty Noble, and the late Joe Durso and Mike McAlary; columnists Phil Pepe, George Vecsey, Dave Anderson, and the late Vic Ziegel; official scorers Bill Shannon and Jordan Sprechman; and my peer support group of Harvey Araton, Kevin Kernan, and Nat Gottlieb. Gottlieb didn't often cover baseball, but I will never forget the time he got under Mel Stottlemyre's skin and the usually mild-mannered pitching coach screamed, "I'm gonna smoke your tits." Not quite sure what that meant.

The coaches and managers of that time who were most cooperative included Bobby Valentine, Yogi Berra, Don Zimmer, and Joe Torre—all very different personalities, yet all very helpful to a young and not-so-young reporter.

This project required considerable research, not all of it done on the internet. There is still a place for libraries and librarians, who helped me greatly in Hackensack and at the *New York Daily News*. I required the support and patience of my workplace at the *News*, from editors Teri Thompson, Bill Price, and Eric Barrow; to copy editor John Gruber and photo sales editor Angela Troisi. I have great appreciation for the hospitality shown me in Cooperstown by good friends Elaine Gardner and Ritch Kepler.

Lastly, I'd like to thank my wife, LynNell, for putting up with me in general. I'm not easy, even when I'm quite certain that I am.

# Bibliography

## BOOKS

Angell, Roger. *A Pitcher's Story: Innings with David Cone.* New York: Warner Books, 2001.

Appel, Marty. *Now Pitching for the Yankees.* Kingston, N.Y.: Total Sports Publishing, 2001.

Belmont and Belcourt Biographies. *Derek Jeter; an unauthorized biography.* Price World Publishing, 2013.

Brett, George, with Steve Cameron. *George Brett, From Here to Cooperstown.* Lenexa, Ks.: Addax Publishing Group, 1999.

Madden, Bill. *Steinbrenner: The Last Lion of Baseball.* New York: Harper, 2010.

Madden, Bill, and Moss Klein. *Damn Yankees.* Chicago, Ill.: Triumph Books, 1990.

McIntosh, Ken, and Rod Drown. *The New Westminster Frasers Baseball Club.* New Westminster, British Columbia: Raised Seams Fanatic Publishing, 2010.

Nettles, Graig, and Peter Golenbock. *Balls.* New York: Putnam Adult, 1984.

Randolph, Willie. *The Yankee Way.* New York: HarperCollins, 2014.

Schuerholz, John, and Larry Guest. *Built to Win: Inside Stories and Leadership Strategies from Baseball's Winningest GM.* New York: Grand Central Publishing, 2008.

Veeck, Bill. *The Hustler's Handbook.* New York: G. P. Putnam's Sons, 1965.

Von Hoffman, Nicholas. *Citizen Cohn: The Life and Times of Roy Cohn.* New York: Doubleday, 1988.

Wilson, Willie, and Kent Pulliam. *Inside the Park: Running the Base Path of Life.* Olathe, Ks.: Ascend Books, 2013.

## MAJOR MAGAZINE, WIRE SERVICE, AND NEWSPAPER ARTICLES

Abel, Allen. "Winning Hit Makes Thurman a Nice Guy." *The (Toronto) Globe and Mail,* October 7, 1978.

# BIBLIOGRAPHY

Anderson, Dave. "Steinbrenner Criticizes His Third-Base Coach." *New York Times*, October 9, 1980.

Araton, Harvey. "Illegal Bat Ruling KOs Homer in 9th." *New York Daily News*, July 25, 1983.

Baker, Liana B. "News Corp To Take 49 Percent Stake in Yankees TV Channel," Reuters, November 20, 2012.

Bondy, Filip. "Pine Tar Judge: Play Ball." *New York Daily News*, August 19, 1983.

Bradley, John Ed. "The Headliner Strikeout King David Cone Hopes the News He Makes as a Kansas City Royal Will Be about Baseball, Not Off-the-Field Shenanigans." *Sports Illustrated*, April 5, 1993.

Chass, Murray. "Lyle Shines in Relief, Stopping Royals on 2 Hits in 5 1/3 Innings." *New York Times*, October 9, 1977.

Chass, Murray. "Yanks Take 2d Straight Pennant; Defeat Royals, 5–3, on 3-Run Ninth." *New York Times*, October 10, 1977.

Chass, Murray. "Royals Defeat Yankees, 3–2, and Lead in Playoff by 2-0." *New York Times*, October 9, 1980.

Chass, Murray. "Resumed Game Ends in 5–4 Yankee Loss to Royals." *New York Times*, August 19, 1983.

Chass, Murray. "The Pine Tar Incident. Ten Years Ago Brett Lost His Grip and a Home Run." *New York Times*, July 25, 1993.

Coleman, Nic. "Griffith Spares Few Targets in Waseca Remarks." *Minneapolis Star-Tribune*, October 1, 1978.

Denlinger, Ken. "Yanks Win on Munson's Shot in 8th." *Washington Post*, October 7, 1978.

Feinsand, Mark. "Hal Steinbrenner Talks about His Late Father." *New York Daily News*, March 6, 2013.

Fox, Gene. "Hey, You Should See What's Down Below." *Kansas City Star*, April 8, 1973.

Garrity, John. "Love and Hate in El Segundo; Jack Brett Didn't Ask Too Much of His Four Sons as They Grew Up—Only That They Were the Best There Was in Everything They Ever Did." *Sports Illustrated*, August 17, 1981.

Jackel, Peter. "The Pine Tar Incident." *Referee Magazine*, May 2003.

Kauffman, Ewing. "What Obligations Do Pro Athletes Have to the Fans?" *New York Times*, December 4, 1983.

Koppett, Leonard. "Jackson Surprised at Benching, but Excuses Martin." *New York Times*, October 10, 1977.

Lamberti, Chris. "The Hustler: Bill Veeck and Roster Depreciation Allowance." ChicagoNow.com, June 6, 2012.

Lamberti, Mike. "McClelland Recalls Pine Tar Game." *Belleville (N.J.) Times*, July 25, 2013.

Libman, Gary. "Tense Batting Race." *Minneapolis Star-Tribune*, October 4, 1976.

Lyons, Richard D. "Pine Tar Popular Because It Grips." *New York Times*, July 29, 1983.

Madden, Bill. "A Royal Pain for Yankees." *New York Daily News*, July 29, 1983.

# BIBLIOGRAPHY

Madden, Bill. "George: Decision Is Absurd." *New York Daily News*, July 29, 1983.

Madden, Bill, and Filip Bondy. "Pine Tar in the Courts." *New York Daily News*, August 18, 1983.

Marcus, Don. "Lee MacPhail Profile." *The Record (Bergen County, N.J.)*, August 19, 1983.

McCarron, Anthony. "By George, Brett Sees Royals Pull Off Stunner." *New York Daily News*, October 2, 2014.

O'Keefe, Michael. "The Dodger Blues." *New York Daily News*, January 14, 2015.

Posnanski, Joe. "When George Brett Chased .400." *Baseball Digest*, October 4, 2005.

Vecsey, George. "Yankees Are Dazed by Premature Finish." *New York Times*, October 10, 1980.

Walker, Chris. "Lee MacPhail, Hall-of-Fame Baseball Executive with Orioles and Others, Dies at 95." *Baltimore Sun,* November 9, 2012.

Wiegand, David. "Barbara Walters; The TV Pioneer Gets Personal." *San Francisco Chronicle*, May 6, 2008.

## BROADCASTS

ESPN, *Baseball Tonight*, Chris Chambliss interview. October 2010. Feature producer, Lisa Fenn.

MLB TV, Brett on 30th Anniversary of Pine Tar Game. July 23, 2013.

MLBFanCave.com, George Brett Pine Tar Prank. March 4, 2013.

New York Yankees Video Library. The Pine Tar Game. Broadcasts of July 24, 1983, and August 18, 1983.

## OTHER ARTICLES

An effort was made to cite and credit within the text substantive interviews or factual material believed to be exclusive. Other articles from the following publications and websites were also used as background material or as sources for quotes from group interviews:

Associated Press
*Baseball Digest*
Baseball-Reference.com
BaseballHall.org
*Detroit News*
*High Times*
*Kansas City Star*
*Kansas City Times*
KCRoyalshistory.com
Lasportshall.com

# BIBLIOGRAPHY

*Lysergic World*
*New York Daily News*
*New York Times*
*The Record (Bergen County, N.J.)*
RushLimbaugh.com
SportsBusinessDaily.com
United Press International

# Index

233